JAMES BOND

IN THE CINEMA

Second Edition

Sean Connery with James Bond's creator Ian Fleming
on the set of **Dr. No**

JAMES BOND

IN THE CINEMA

Second Edition

John Brosnan

A. S. Barnes & Co., Inc.
San Diego
The Tantivy Press, London

James Bond in the Cinema, copyright ©1981
by John Brosnan

Second Edition
Manufactured in the United States of America

For information write to:
A.S. Barnes & Company, Inc.
P.O. Box 3051
La Jolla, California 92038

The Tantivy Press
Magdalen House
136-148 Tooley Street
London, SE1 2TT, England

Library of Congress Cataloging in Publication Data

Brosnan, John.
    James Bond in the cinema.

    Includes index.
    1. James Bond films—History and criticism.
I. Title.
PN1995.9.J3B7 1981   791.43′75   80-26573
ISBN 0-498-02546-2

1 2 3 4 5 6 7 8 9 84 83 82 81

Acknowledgments

The author and publishers wish to thank the following organizations and individuals for their cordial help in the preparation of this volume: Harry Saltzman, Albert R. Broccoli, Derek Meddings, Derek Coyte, United Artists, and John Pearson, Ian Fleming's biographer.

Virtually all the stills reproduced in this volume have been supplied by United Artists, to whom the publishers extend warm acknowledgment.

Contents

Introduction

The screen goes dark . . . a pulsating, staccato beat fills the theatre. A series of white dots march across the screen in rhythm to the music . . . one grows in size and we find ourselves suddenly looking down a telescopic sight. A man walks into range and the sight moves to follow him . . . he spins round . . . drops to one knee and fires directly at us. A red veil slowly descends over the screen and the telescopic sight begins to waver . . . then sags downward, shrinks . . . and is once again a white dot.

For film audiences all over the world, the above scenes have brought a thrill of excitement. They have known they were about to be plunged into a fantasy world of fast action and incredible happenings dominated by that ultimate in wish-fulfillment symbols . . . James Bond.

He is agent 007, the man with a license to kill, Ian Fleming's suave superman who has already gained for himself a place in that exclusive gallery of folk heroes that includes King Arthur, Robin Hood, Sherlock Holmes, and Tarzan. For whether you like him or loathe him, you cannot ignore either him or the impact he has had on so many people.

Through the books and films that dealt with his adventures, James Bond became a Sixties phenomenon of international proportions. Such an important myth figure of our times deserves a close examination, but so far he has not received it. There have been a few books covering the literary side of James Bond, but of them only Kingsley Amis's *The James Bond Dossier* was anything more than a superficial commentary. The films, on the other hand, have been totally ignored, except for the occasional magazine article, despite the vast influence they have had on the commercial cinema as a whole. One day someone will have to produce a scholarly volume on the Bond films that will dissect them in depth and place them in their proper context with the rest of cinema. I look forward to reading such a book, but I haven't attempted to write it. My coverage of the Bond films in this book is strictly in terms of how they succeed as entertainment. To me, the James Bond films are fun, and to take them too seriously would spoil the whole game.

Bond and Domino (Claudine Auger) under water in
Thunderball

1

Putting Bond on the Screen

James Bond's creator, Ian Fleming, had high hopes from the very beginning that the character would be quickly snatched up by the film or television industry and thus produce the inevitable financial rewards. After the publication of *Casino Royale* in 1953, he told his friend Roald Dahl (who was to later script *You Only Live Twice*): "If you get a chance of putting in a word with the TV tycoons for *Casino*, I shall be very grateful. Money is despicable stuff but it buys Renoirs." At first it seemed he wouldn't have to wait long before the "despicable stuff" started flowing. In 1954, a number of feelers were put out by both the film and television industries toward Bond, not the least being a request from the famous Hungarian producer Sir Alexander Korda to see an advance copy of Fleming's second novel, *Live and Let Die*. Three different film companies expressed an interest in the first novel, *Casino Royale*, and the Columbia Broadcasting System offered $1,000 for the rights to do a special one-hour adaptation of the novel.

By the following year, however, Fleming was feeling discouraged about ever getting Bond onto the big screen—Korda returned *Live and Let Die* without taking an option and the other three film inquiries also came to nothing. The CBS production of *Casino Royale* was televised as planned, as a segment of "Climax Mystery Theater," but heavily toned down and with an American actor, Barry Nelson, playing Bond (interestingly, Peter Lorre played the villain,

Le Chiffre). It failed to generate any widespread interest in Bond in America and was quickly forgotten (and, because it was transmitted live, no record remains of the first dramatization of James Bond).

Feeling rather jaded at this point, Fleming recklessly sold the screen rights of *Casino* for a mere $6,000 to Gregory Ratoff, a Russian actor/director who'd been working in Britain and America since the mid-Thirties. (Ratoff failed to set the picture up; when he died in 1960, his widow sold the rights to American producer Charles Feldman who made the film in 1967, a year before *he* died.) It seems that Fleming quickly regretted this move, for shortly afterwards, when the actor Ian Hunter inquired in 1955 about buying a six-month option on *Moonraker,* Fleming said he wanted £1,000 for the option and £10,000 for the film rights, adding: "I have an idea that one of these days the film and television rights of James Bond and his adventures may be worth quite a lot of money and I hope you agree there's no point in throwing them away." (Fleming later sold the film rights of *Moonraker* to the Rank Organization but quickly bought them back again.) He was proved right, of course, but had to wait longer than he expected.

The following year, 1956, Henry Morganthau III, a producer with the NBC network, proposed to Fleming that he write a half-hour adventure series entitled *Commander Jamaica.* In the 28-page pilot script that Fleming wrote, the central character bore a remarkable resemblance to James Bond. Named Commander James Gunn, he was based on a yacht moored in a Jamaican harbor, where he received his orders from an Admiral via a hidden loudspeaker. The television project came to nothing but Fleming used the script, which concerned missiles fired from Cape Canaveral, being deflected by villains using remote control, as the basis of his next novel, *Dr. No.*

In 1958, CBS renewed their interest in Bond by suggesting a James Bond television series. Again Fleming agreed, despite his past experience with television, and wrote six episode outlines. Again nothing came of it, but Fleming retrieved three of the plots and used them in his anthology of short stories, *For Your Eyes Only.* The same year he was introduced by a wealthy friend, Ivor Bryce, to a young filmmaker called Kevin McClory who had been an assistant to both John Huston and Mike Todd. McClory had just made his first film, *The Boy and the Bridge,* for which Bryce had provided the financial backing. The idea was for Fleming and McClory to collaborate on an original screenplay for a James Bond film, tentatively titled *James Bond, Secret Agent,* which would be backed by Bryce. Veteran British scriptwriter Jack Whittingham (*Q Planes, Counterblast,* etc.) was also brought into the project and the three of them began work enthusiastically. However, as time passed and nothing definite was achieved, Fleming began to lose faith in his partners' ability to set the picture up (moreover, McClory's film, *The Boy and the Bridge,* hadn't turned out to be the success everyone had been hoping for). Fleming first suggested that they bring in the famous director Anthony Asquith as co-producer and then, believing that Alfred Hitchcock was interested in filming the Bond books, suggested they do a co-production deal with Hitchcock's company (Fleming had been particularly impressed with *North By Northwest,* released that same year, and thought that Hitchcock would be the perfect filmmaker to handle Bond). When Hitchcock declined the offer, Fleming apparently lost interest in the whole enterprise.

3

In 1960, he made his annual visit to his house in Jamaica to write another Bond novel, which eventually became *Thunderball.* Unfortunately, he used as the basis for this novel the screen treatment that he, McClory, and Whittingham had devised. When the book was published, a legal wrangle ensued that lasted until 1963, when McClory was assigned all the film and television rights to *Thunderball.* McClory was thus free to continue with his plans to put Bond on the screen, but by then the situation had changed drastically due to two gentlemen called Harry Saltzman and Albert R. Broccoli.

Broccoli, born in New York in 1909, is actually related to the man who brought the first broccoli seed over to America. In fact, the family name comes from that very vegetable (the family crest even includes a sprig of broccoli). He grew up on Long Island working for various relatives, one of whom was an undertaker (the reason why Broccoli tries to include a joke about coffins or undertakers in each of the Bond films). He decided at an early age that his fortune lay in Hollywood but it took some time to convince Hollywood of this. At first, he worked selling hairdressing materials and Christmas trees (not at the same time), then managed to become a tea boy at the 20th Century-Fox studio and eventually rose to assistant director. World War Two interrupted his rise up the industry ladder and he joined the Navy for the duration. After the war, he moved to London where he set up a partnership with fellow-American Irving Allen (not to be confused with *Irwin* Allen) and formed Warwick Films, a company that produced a series of slick and moderately successful adventure films during the 1950s. Beginning with *The Red Beret* in 1952, Warwick Films produced *Hell Below Zero, The Black Knight, Cockleshell Heroes, Zarak,* and *The Man Inside.* Two of them, *The Red Beret* and *Zarak,* were directed by former British scriptwriter Terence Young, and several were written by American scriptwriter Richard Maibaum.

Maibaum, like Broccoli, was born in New York in 1909. After studying law, he started writing for the then-new medium of radio. While still at college, his first play, *The Tree,* which had an anti-lynching theme, was produced in New York in 1932. He became a member of the New York Shakespearean Repertory Theater in 1933 and played over twenty roles. His play *Sweet Mystery of Life* was produced on Broadway in 1935, which led to offers of work in Hollywood where he wrote screenplays for M.G.M. and other studios (*They Gave Me a Gun, I Wanted Wings,* etc.) while continuing to write plays. After the war, during which he spent four years as the Director of the Army's Combat Film Division, he went to Paramount as a writer/producer and made *OSS, Now and Forever,* and *The Great Gatsby* (among others). After that, he began his long association with Broccoli when he wrote the script for *Hell Below Zero* in 1954 (chiefly memorable for casting Jill Bennett as the captain of a Russian whaler).

"Broccoli gave me two of the Bond books to read back in 1957," said Maibaum, "because he was thinking about doing them even then. Unfortunately, with all their inherent sex and violence, they just weren't producible at that time."

That same year, Broccoli tried to interest Columbia Pictures in Bond. When a Columbia executive asked their story department for information about Fleming, he was told that: "All he writes is travel books," (Ian Fleming having been confused with his brother Peter).

4

Broccoli, however, didn't give up. A few years later, when James Bond had become more popular, he decided to try again, but when he made inquiries with Fleming's agents he discovered that another filmmaker had taken out an option on all the books, with the exception of *Casino Royale.* That other filmmaker was Harry Saltzman . . . .

Saltzman was born in Quebec in 1915. After a variety of occupations in both Canada and the U.S.A., including working in vaudeville and in a traveling circus, he moved at the end of the Thirties to France where he achieved some success as a theatrical entrepreneur. After World War Two and a spell in the French Army, he returned to France and joined the Ministry of Reconstruction, then worked for U.N.E.S.C.O., specializing in communications. "I had a misguided idea, after six and a half years of war, that my generation had mucked up the world so it was our job to make a better one," said Saltzman, "but after three and a half years, I realized I was wasting my time . . . I went back into show business with both feet, and I wish I hadn't." 5

He returned to the United States and soon was flourishing in the television industry, but it was the success of a British play, *Look Back in Anger,* that subsequently led him into films. During the play's New York run in 1957, he approached its author, John Osborne, with the promise that he would raise the money for a film version. Out of this came Woodfall Films, formed by Saltzman with Osborne and the play's director Tony Richardson. The company later became synonymous with the age of the "new realism" in British films (also known as the "kitchen sink" *genre* of films). However, the film of *Look Back in Anger* (1959) turned out to be a financial disaster, as did Woodfall's second production, *The Entertainer* (1960). Fortunately for everyone concerned, their third film, *Saturday Night and Sunday Morning* (1961) proved to be a box office success. After that, Saltzman left Woodfall because he thought their next project, *A Taste of Honey,* was both too provincial and too English (he wanted the film set in France) to be a commercial success. Besides, he was tired of all that social realism: "All the films were designed to show how the other half lives, but for God's sake we *are* the other half," he said. "I thought it was time to go back to

Ursula Andress and Connery on location in Jamaica for
Dr. No

big entertainment and I saw in the Bonds the bigger than life thing. We live in an age of violence and some of the bad people do very well today.''

Having discovered the Bond novels, he made an approach to their author—Fleming, depressed over the *Thunderball* debacle and recovering from his first heart attack, readily agreed to let him take out an option on all the available books. Amazingly, however, Saltzman couldn't interest any of the major film companies in Bond and the option had only twenty-eight more days to run when Broccoli reappeared on the Bond scene. Broccoli was at first tempted to wait and see if the option ran out before making his move, but decided not to take the risk and suggested to Saltzman that they enter into a partnership. Saltzman agreed and Eon Films was formed, a company that was to make film history. (By then Broccoli had ended his partnership with Irving Allen who later produced one of the more successful series of Bond imitations—the Matt Helm films with Dean Martin.)

Together, Broccoli and Saltzman approached both United Artists and Columbia with their proposed Bond film which was going to be based on either *Thunderball* or *Dr. No.* Columbia balked at their request for a budget of $1,000,000 and insisted that they make it for between $300,000 and $400,000, a relatively small amount even in those days. Fortunately, United Artists decided to take on the project under the producers' terms (though U.A. subsequently lowered the budget to $900,000) and Bond was on his way to the big screen at long last.

Originally, the first Bond film was to have been *Thunderball* but by that time, 1961, the property was in litigation so *Dr. No.* was selected as the alternative. Pre-production arrangements were soon underway and Broccoli persuaded both Saltzman and United Artists to use three of his former Warwick Films colleagues: Terence Young as director, Richard Maibaum as scriptwriter, and German-born Ken Adam as production designer (Adam had designed the sets for Warwick's *The Trials of Oscar Wilde*). The script, incidentally, proved a source of difficulty at first; Maibaum, working with Wolf Mankowitz, produced several drafts that didn't satisfy either producer. ''I couldn't get it into anyone's heads,'' said Broccoli, ''that

7

Bond was an important character to be taken seriously. I believe one version had it that Dr. No turned out to be a monkey! 'This won't do,' I said, 'Do it again.' " (Today such a denouement wouldn't be out of place in a Bond film.)

While the script was being hammered into shape, the other major problem involved finding someone to play James Bond. When Fleming, McClory, and Bryce had been preparing their own Bond film, it was felt they needed to have a big-name actor in the part. Fleming wanted his friend David Niven, and other names put forward were Richard Burton (McClory's choice) and, most strangely, James Stewart ("Uhhhhrr, the name's uh Bond . . . errr, Jaaames Bond"). But *Dr. No's* small budget meant that it would be more economical to have an unknown in the role and, after interviewing a dozen or so possibilities, the producers had a short list of three actors. Second on the list was Roger Moore. Number one was Sean Connery.

Thomas Sean Connery was born in Edinburgh in 1930, the son of a truck driver. His early life has more in common with those described on the dust jackets of novels written by northern English authors than with biographies usually associated with British actors. At various times, Sean Connery worked as a paperboy, a milkman, a footballer, a weightlifter, a bricklayer, a coffin polisher (which must have endeared him to Broccoli), an artist's model, a lorry driver, a cement mixer, and then a merchant seaman before ending up, of all things, in the chorus of the British production of *South Pacific*.

Not that Connery could really be classified as an "unknown" when he was interviewed by Broccoli and Saltzman in 1961. After all, not only had he been working in the film industry since 1955, but he'd had starring roles in at least three movies—*Another Time, Another Place* (1958) was the first and represented an attempt by Paramount Pictures to launch him as a big star. But the film, which starred Lana Turner, flopped at the box office and Paramount let his contract lapse, even though its failure could hardly be blamed on Connery—the script and direction were the real culprits. (Connery makes an in-joke reference to this film in *Thunderball* in the scene where he's saying goodbye to Molly Peters at the health farm.) Connery then found himself frolicking with leprechauns in Disney's

Darby O'Gill and the Little People (1959), which was a moderate success but didn't really further his career at the time. Then, after playing a minor villain in a Tarzan movie, *Tarzan's Greatest Adventure* (1959), he had another starring role in a low-budget thriller called *Frightened City* (1960), playing a working-class boxer who takes revenge on a group of gangsters after they kill his manager, but again it didn't seem to affect his career in any favorable way.

Ironically, it was his performance in *Darby O'Gill* that first attracted Broccoli and Saltzman and led them to look at his other films. "He was dreadful in most of them, we thought," said Saltzman. "He had suffered a small but fatal miscasting all the way down the line." But, astutely, both producers decided that he would make a perfect James Bond, despite the Scottish accent. "As he left the office," said a United Artists executive, "we all went to the window and watched him cross the street." "What impressed me," said Saltzman, "was that a man of his size and frame could move in such a supple way." Or as Broccoli put it: "He looked like he had balls."

It's open to debate, perhaps, on how *Dr. No* would have fared if they'd cast Roger Moore or someone else in the role. With hindsight, it seems obvious that the decision to cast Sean Connery as James Bond was one of the main factors that assured its success and created the beginning of the James Bond phenomenon.

The team: Lois Maxwell as Miss Moneypenny, Bernard
Lee as M, and Sean Connery as Bond

2

Why So Popular?

There is no doubt that the James Bond series of films represent a remarkable phenomenon in the commercial cinema. The first one, *Dr. No,* was released in 1962 and now, eleven films later, James Bond is more popular than ever. Other fictional characters have had long-running popularity in the cinema, such as Tarzan and Sherlock Holmes, but never with the same consistency or on such a wide scale as Bond. Why is this? Why, during all the ups and downs in the film industry during the past two decades, were the Bonds alone untouched by the vagaries of the box office, remaining as popular and profitable as ever? What is the secret of their success?

Well, the most obvious answer is that they are *pure* cinema in the sense that they are highly visual films depending on lots of fast-paced action and sheer spectacle. This assures them of a large international audience because they are able to bypass language and cultural barriers and appeal directly to people of various nationalities and age groups, in the same way as did the slapstick comedies of the silent era and the cartoon films of Disney (two film genres that the Bonds have grown increasingly to resemble of late).

Dr. No was really one of the first films to utilize the techniques of television commercials. It wasn't just in the use of lavishly photo-graphed locations and the fast cutting—in reality, the *whole* film was a series of "commercials" strung together, a collection of miniature films each with its own beginning, middle, and end. These "set-pieces" followed each other so rapidly that the eye was dazzled and the mind kept reeling—one didn't have time to think about the overall story. This idea of turning the film into a series of separate set-pieces (or "bumps" as Broccoli calls them) became the classic formula for all the subsequent Bonds. As the series progressed, the set-pieces became increasingly self-contained and related to each other less and less—in recent Bond films there is hardly even a token effort to link up the set-pieces into a cohesive whole.

Another facet of the appeal of the Bonds is the simplicity of their themes—Good and Evil are easy to identify, the black hat of the early Western villain being mirrored by the Chairman Mao jacket of the chief Bond villain and the blatant grotesqueness of his underlings. Bond himself is the contemporary equivalent of the Western hero, someone who can solve all his problems with his fists and a gun. The film series can also be considered as modern folk tales with Bond representing a latter-day St. George fighting evil incarnate, which is invariably personified by some form of technology. Bond may utilize technology in the form of his gadgets, but in almost all the Bond films the threat to mankind is always technology writ-large: Dr. No's atomic reactor and missile-toppling beams; Goldfinger's laser and atomic "device"; Largo's underwater vehicles and stolen atomic bombs in *Thunderball;* Blofeld's rocket-swallowing spaceship in *You Only Live Twice;* Blofeld's mountaintop laboratory with its deadly virus in *On Her Majesty's Secret Service;* his space laser in *Diamonds Are Forever;* Scaramanga's solar complex in *The Man with the Golden Gun;* Stromberg's submarine-swallowing super tanker and the stolen nuclear missiles in *The Spy Who Loved Me;* and Drax's space shuttles and orbiting platform of death in *Moonraker.* In an increasingly complex technological world, the Bonds offer a kind of reassurance by showing that, no matter how big and threatening technology may become, one man can always triumph over it simply by blowing it all up, which Bond does with monotonous regularity.

The Bonds then are basically fantasies. Fantasies about a superman who can overcome all the odds and is never afflicted by self-doubt, anxiety, or feelings of insecurity. In this day and age, when the individual feels increasingly powerless and in the grip of forces beyond his control, the attraction of such fantasies is obvious.

Another important factor in the reason for the success of the Bond films has been their ability to change and adapt to suit their audience's wishes. As Bond scriptwriter Richard Maibaum put it: "*Dr. No* told us what the audience liked, what they sparked to. By *Goldfinger,* we were getting wilder. The whole business was becoming larger than life. Then in *Thunderball,* it became even more so. The production became enormous, more fantastical, almost comic strip. Since then there's no way of bringing them down." But the biggest change occurred with the character of James Bond. While the action and spectacle were important ingredients in *Dr. No,* it was James Bond himself who attracted the most attention. At the time, he was something new and different in screen heroes—he wasn't the typical "good guy" personified by such actors as Errol Flynn, John Wayne, James Stewart, etc., and he was certainly nothing like any previous *British* screen hero. For one thing, he lacked a sense of fair play—he disposed of his enemies ruthlessly and in cold blood (the early screen Bond was much more ruthless than the literary one) and was less than chivalrous towards women.

He was also one of the first manifestations of the so-called "permissive age" in the commercial cinema, and in this area he was ruthless too, using his lovemaking not only as a means of casual gratification but also as a means of achieving some exterior purpose—in *Dr. No,* his dalliance with Miss Taro was merely to keep her occupied until the police could arrive and arrest her; in *From Russia With Love,* he makes love to Tatiana in order to obtain the Russian decoding machine; and in *Goldfinger,* he seduces Jill Masterson just to annoy her boss, Goldfinger, with fatal results for her.

As the films got bigger and more spectacular, the character of James Bond, smoothed down considerably after *Dr. No,* became submerged under all the gadgetry and special effects. By *You Only Live Twice,* Bond had become a kind of wind-up superman doll, a parody of his former self. There was some attempt to breathe life back into his character in *On Her Majesty's Secret Service,* but it was doomed to failure thanks to the amazing miscasting of George

Lazenby as Bond. Then, with the arrival of Roger Moore, the process was complete—James Bond had become James Bland.

Along with Bond himself, the treatment of sex and violence in the Bond films has also changed radically over the years. In fact, much of the change took place during the first three films—*Dr. No* is really alone among the Bonds in that it can be labelled sadistic. For example, there is the scene where the girl photographer (Margaret Le Wars) slashes Quarrel (John Kitzmiller) across the face with a broken flash-bulb; the sequence where Bond shoots Professor Dent in cold blood and then, when Dent is lying on the floor, shoots him again in the lower back to produce a final dying twitch (cut out of some versions); there is Bond's own tortuous climb through the ventilation system; and even the graphic shooting of Strangway's secretary at the start of the picture.

14   While none of the Bonds have ever been given anything but an "A" certificate in Britain (about the equivalent of the American "PG"), it took a fair amount of haggling with the then-censor, John Trevelyan, before both *Dr. No* and *From Russia With Love* were classified "A." Cuts had to be made in both films. For instance, the sequence in *Dr. No* where Bond receives a beating from No's guards was trimmed, and the entire sequence where Honey is staked out for the giant crabs was removed completely. (Interestingly, Trevelyan told me recently that director Terence Young slipped some of the excised material from *From Russia With Love* back into the picture shortly before its release.) But by *Goldfinger* the violence had become much more stylized and in fact during the whole of that picture there is not one glimpse of blood despite the large number of fatalities (we get a close-up of Tilly Masterson's head after she has been hit by Oddjob's steel hat, and there's not a mark on her).

The sadism had also become stylized, with perhaps the exception of the scene where Bond throws the electric heater into his assailant's bathwater. Jill Masterson's death by gold-paint suffocation takes place discreetly off-screen, and the sequence where Bond's manhood is threatened by Goldfinger's laser is, if anything, a parody of a classic sadistic situation. *Goldfinger* was also the last Bond film where there was any attempt at genuine eroticism—

Bond's seduction of Jill Masterson and his fight in the hay with Pussy Galore. Thereafter, the makers steered carefully away from that touchy area and have stuck to safe and simple titillation. (There hasn't been anything like the fight between the two gypsy girls in *From Russia With Love* in any Bond film since then.) "I avoid porn," said Saltzman, confusing pornography with eroticism in an interview shortly after the release of *Diamonds Are Forever*. "That's for home movies. Bond is sadism for the family. You'd have to be kinky to find our films erotic. I mean you don't go to bed with Plenty O'Toole. She's strictly for laughs."

Ian Fleming, Harry Saltzman and Albert R. Broccoli on set

It's extremely unlikely that the early Bond films would have gotten away with so much under the protection of a profitable "A" certificate if it wasn't obvious to most people, including the censor, that from the very beginning the Bond films were "strictly for laughs." The humorous element has always played an important part in the success of the Bonds, yet there remains some mystery over just who decided that the films should be funny. John Pearson, Fleming's biographer, wrote: "As the filmmakers discovered when they first tried turning James Bond into a screen property, there is no joke. The one quality the books lack entirely is humor. Each is written in deadly seriousness...." This is perhaps not entirely fair on Fleming who insisted that the books *were* meant to be funny—and, while none of the books are *obviously* humorous, it does seem that many of them, the later ones at least, are intended as Very Tall Tales told with as straight a face as possible. But, as for putting the humor into the films, it seems that everyone connected with the series has claimed the credit. Richard Maibaum, one of the original scriptwriters, remarked: "Ian Fleming once said to me, 'It's amazing how much funnier your pictures are than my novels.' He didn't understand that we were trying to make them funnier. They were a spoof in the first place, although always in a supposedly deadpan way . . . in *Dr. No,* when Bond edges a hearse off a cliff and, when asked what happened, replies: 'I don't know. I think they were on their way to a funeral,' well now, you know that was *meant* to be funny."

However, according to Guy Hamilton, it wasn't quite like that: "Broccoli had asked me to direct *Dr. No* and for reasons I can't remember I couldn't do it, but he told me not to worry about the script because it had a lot of nonsequiturs in it that they were going to fix. And I said, 'For goodness sakes, Cubby, whatever you do, don't try and justify Fleming—it is fantasy and you must go with it.' And eventually I made *Goldfinger* because Terence Young wasn't available and Cubby had remembered what I'd said. There's no question that *Dr. No* was shot rather straight and lots of people laughed in the wrong places, but I think that one of the best Bonds is *From Russia With Love,* because in that it's obvious that Terence and the producers and the screenplay writer Richard Maibaum had all pulled themselves together very quickly and realized that it should be played for fun."

Sean Connery tells a different story: "The first director, Terence Young, and I worked hard on the character to get in some humor; it certainly isn't in the books I've read." (At one time, the story circulated that Connery's then-wife, Diane Cilento, was responsible: after seeing the script when he was still being considered for the part, she insisted that he refuse the role unless the producers agreed to add humor to the story.) But whoever was responsible, there's no denying that the humor in *Dr. No* gave the film an added dimension that critic Alexander Walker has described as a "submerged complicity with the audience. Most thrillers worked with the screen; Bond was the first film series at that time to work *with an audience.* In a way, it was a return to those Saturday afternoon serials. People who went to see the Bond films henceforth knew the game and anticipated playing it and even working at it as the filmmakers fed them the clues."

It's this aspect of the Bond films that has been concentrated upon and emphasized over the years to the detriment of other ingredients such as plot and characterization. In the first three films, most of the humor emanated from Bond himself, his dead-pan jokes and laconic asides to the audience. As the series progressed, the humor became broader and more visual, at the same time becoming less black. The humor in *Moonraker,* for instance, consists of juvenile double entendres, parodies of other films, and a great deal of old-fashioned slapstick comedy. The once-submerged "complicity" with the audience is now well and truly out in the open—a hard nudge in the ribs as opposed to the earlier knowing wink.

"Basically, we are very conscious that we run a family show," said William Cartlidge, associate producer on *Moonraker.* "You can take your seven-year-old son and your seventy-five-year-old grandmother. We've just got to amaze both of them somehow . . . ." And apparently the Bonds do just *that*—the wilder and funnier the films get, the bigger the audience grows and, as I say elsewhere in this volume, you can't argue with that kind of success.

The two men mainly responsible for this success are Albert R. Broccoli and Harry Saltzman, the original two producers (now, of course, there is only one, Saltzman having sold his share of Bond in 1975). Whoever was originally responsible for deciding to inject the laughs into Bond, *they* were the ones who instantly realized that this was a key element—a gimmick that could be exploited and developed to turn the Bonds into something out of the ordinary. And, despite the many other people who have been involved with the series over the years, the Bonds remained *their* films; in the case of the Bonds, unlike most films, the auteur theory doesn't apply to the directors but to the producers—their stamp is on every film. From the very beginning, it was the two producers who shaped the original material and made the final decision as to what would go into each film, although they incorporated other ideas from all concerned. The producers had a sometimes uneasy partnership of two strong-willed entrepreneurs ("We fight with the distributors, we fight with the agents, and we fight with each other. We're real professionals"—Saltzman in 1972). Together, they created the unique phenomenon within the film industry known as James Bond.

Connery's first appearance as James Bond in **Dr. No**

3

Dr. No

The titles of *Dr. No* are flashed on the screen amid a brilliant jumble of color and sound as silhouettes of dancing women move in time to a vibrant calypso beat. As the last of the credits appear, the women are replaced by the silhouettes of three men moving in single file and carrying walking sticks. The music has now become a calypso version of "Three Blind Mice."

Gradually the surrealistic colors fade into reality and we see that the silhouettes belong to three, apparently blind, Negroes walking down a street. We see them cross the road and then the scene changes to the veranda of a club. Four men are seated at a table playing cards. Immediately one glances at his watch, excuses himself and leaves. As he walks out of the gates of the club house he passes the three Negroes seen earlier. As he goes by he drops a coin into the cup that the first one is carrying. Reaching his car, he opens the door, but before he can climb in he gives a violent shudder and slumps grotesquely forward. The camera pans to reveal the three "blind" men who have all stopped and turned. Each one is holding a gun fitted with a silencer.

A black hearse roars up and screeches to a halt. The Negroes pick up the man's body and fling it into the back, then jump in. The hearse speeds away down the street.

Next scene. An iron gate and a path leading up through a tropical garden to a bungalow. The gate creaks open, pushed by someone unseen. Inside, a girl sits at a bookcase which contains a radio set. She is agitated and keeps looking behind her at the open door, obviously waiting for someone to arrive.

Suddenly there is the sound of breaking glass. Startled, the girl leaps to her feet. At the door and at two of the windows we see the Negroes. The girl screams and we hear the "phhhttt" sounds from the silenced guns. She is sent spinning by the bullets and falls to the ground. The Negroes enter. While two of them pick up her body, the third goes over to a filing cabinet. He opens it and removes a file titled *Dr. No.*

And so begins the first James Bond film. These scenes, taken directly from the novel, successfully establish a mood of unease and tension in a manner that owes much to Hitchcock, though perhaps the old movie magician might have eschewed the use of such blatant violence in a thriller context. (It's difficult now, two decades later, to appreciate just how violent the film seemed at the time. It was the one aspect of the picture that attracted the most adverse criticism but, in the light of how violence has been treated in the cinema since then, it doesn't seem exceptionally tough when seen today. Compared, however, to the more recent Bonds, the violence in *Dr. No* is definitely treated with a great deal more realism.) These opening sequences also established a cinematic style that was to become the hallmark of the Bonds—the swift setting up of a particular situation and the sudden pull of the rug from under the feet of the audience by revealing that all is not what it appears to be . . . a device which producer Cubby Broccoli refers to as a "bump."

From Jamaica the scene of *Dr. No* shifts to London and here we meet James Bond. We see him for the first time in what is to become one of the series' familiar settings—a casino. For most people who have been introduced to Bond via the early films, Sean Connery *is* Bond (as the publicity men used to stress). But those who first followed his exploits in the books have always had their own personal picture of what he should look like. Fleming, for instance, seemed to consider David Niven as the ideal person for the role.

Others agreed with Fleming that Connery perhaps lacked the necessary aristocratic touch as Bond, including Kingsley Amis who wrote in his book *The James Bond Dossier* that "Mr. Connery could put up a show as a Scottish businessman all right, but a Scottish baronet never." (Writing in 1965, Amis was referring to Connery's potential unsuitability for the part in *On Her Majesty's Secret Service* where Bond impersonates Sir Hilary Bray—but in the event an even *more* unsuitable actor, George Lazenby, had that task three years later when the film was made.)

The Connery/Bond of *Dr. No* lacks a certain sophistication. The Scottish accent is heavy and his bushy eyebrows (trimmed in later films) give him a rather wild appearance. But these quibbles apart, he suitably fits the Bond description. No scar down his left cheek, or comma of black hair above the eyebrow, but with a definitely "rather cruel" mouth and "ruthless" eyes. Darkly handsome, Connery quickly proved to be a success with audiences. His performance in *Dr. No* was certainly a professional one and contained a lot more vitality than was apparent in the later films.

Soon after we have met Bond in the casino, he is recalled to Secret Service headquarters. This gives us an opportunity to meet three characters who have become regular members of every Bond epic. The scenes that followed were to become a ritual that was faithfully re-enacted in all of the later films.

First Bond enters the office of Miss Moneypenny, played by Lois Maxwell, who is the secretary of the head of the Secret Service. Moneypenny is obviously infatuated with Bond and their conversation consists of verbal fencing of a mildly suggestive nature. Then Bond proceeds through the double connecting doors between her office and M's. M, played with suitable crustiness by Bernard Lee, is the chief. His purpose in the film is to explain the mission to Bond (and us). In *Dr. No,* it concerns the disappearance of their Jamaican agent, Strangways, and his secretary. M wants Bond to hop over and sort the matter out. And, while he's doing that, he can check up on another little matter. American rockets are being interfered with by remote control and the Americans seem to think that the source of the trouble lies in the Jamaican area.

But, before Bond can leave, he has to endure the attentions of Q, the Secret Service's weapons expert. He is to pop up in all the films, each time saddling Bond with more and more gadgets. The ultimate in gimmickry is reached in *Thunderball* and *You Only Live Twice* when he supplies Bond with enough weapons to wipe out an army.

Bond has his special way of dealing . . .

. . . with the servant problem.

Bond finally reaches Jamaica and is immediately up to his neck in danger. The ride from Kingston airport involves one car chase, a murder attempt (unsuccessful), and a suicide bid (successful). Bond arrives at Government House with his driver sitting very dead in the back seat. "Make sure he doesn't get away," Bond tells the guard at the door, in one of the first examples of the droll humor for which the Bond films were to become renowned. This was the main reason why they were so hard to parody. It is difficult to spoof something that is self-spoofing as the Bond films most certainly are.

The next major development in the film is Bond's meeting with Quarrel and Felix Leiter. Quarrel (John Kitzmiller) is a local Jamaican who had been ferrying Strangways around the nearby islands so that he could collect mineral samples. The late Strangways' reason for doing this is still a mystery to Quarrel, so Bond discovers. Felix Leiter (played by Jack Lord of *Stoney Burke* and *Hawaii Five-O* TV fame) is a CIA agent and a regular character in the books although he doesn't appear in the *Dr. No* novel. In Fleming's second book, *Live and Let Die,* Leiter falls victim to a hungry shark who deprives him of a couple of limbs. From then on he was to hobble about in the books with an artificial leg and steel hook for a hand, but in the film Jack Lord has a full complement of hands and feet. Perhaps the screenwriter thought that one character in the film with artificial appendages was enough.

During Bond's conversation with Quarrel and Leiter, which takes place in a sea-front bar, Bond notices that a girl nearby with a camera is the same girl who attempted to take his picture on his arrival at Kingston airport. He tells Quarrel to grab her. He does so and, on Bond's orders, tries to make her talk by forcing her arm up behind her back. She refuses and retaliates by breaking a flashbulb and scraping it down the side of Quarrel's face.

Bond learns from Quarrel that Strangways' mineral samples were analyzed by a chemist called Professor Dent. Bond pays him a visit. He doesn't get much information from Dent but has his suspicions aroused, as he should, for Dent is an obviously shifty character. And when Bond has left, we discover just how shifty he is. For he immediately goes down to the sea front and hops into a waiting boat.

The boat takes him to Crab Key island and deposits him at a bauxite processing plant (quite a well-known landmark in Jamaica, in fact, though not situated on any island but on the coast only a few miles from Kingston). Dent is escorted ashore by Chinese guards who are dressed in what suspiciously resembles Red Army uniforms. He is led through the bauxite plant and finally shown, alone, into a room.

At this point, the film stops being simply a far-fetched thriller and changes its direction. For here the first suggestion of the fantastic is introduced. The room that Dent finds himself in is no ordinary one. It is empty and without any furniture except a single chair which is positioned under a huge circular skylight set in the high ceiling. The resulting effect is that the chair, and whoever sits in it, is under the scrutiny of some giant eye. This marks the first appearance of Ken Adam's expressionistic sets which would eventually become the trademark of the Bond films.

Expressionism in Bond films. Here, Dent (Anthony Lawson) is imprisoned in a futuristic room.

As Dent remains standing nervously by the door a strange voice, like a magnified whisper, is heard.

"Sit down," it commands Dent. Dent goes and sits in the chair, looking very unhappy.

"Why have you come here?" the voice asks. Dent replies that he came to warn the speaker.

"To warn . . . me?" The tone of the voice suggests perfectly the amusement the unseen speaker feels at the thought, as if an ant had threatened God. For this too is another characteristic of Fleming's villains—their omnipotence. As Kingsley Amis noted in his book *The James Bond Dossier,* the relationship between the villain and Bond in many of the books is one of an all-pervading father figure versus a little boy. Invariably when they talk to him, it is as if they were addressing a child; they know what it's all about whereas he, Bond, is merely playing games. *Dr. No* is the only one of the films to make full use of this particular device and as a result the good doctor seems to possess an aura of omnipotence that is lacking in the other villains.

The nervous Professor Dent explains that Bond is getting close to the truth about Crab Key. The voice orders that Bond be killed and tells Dent to approach a table on the other side of the room. Dent hasn't noticed this table previously (and neither have we). He goes over to it and we see that there is a small cage on it. The camera moves in for a close-up and reveals that the cage contains a large spider.

"Pick it up," commands the voice. Dent, not unnaturally, hesitates. "Pick it up," repeats the voice, harder this time. Dent manages to conquer his natural revulsion and picks it up. Then he hurries from the room, wisely holding the cage at arm's length.

Of course the spider ends up in Bond's bed. This sequence succeeds in making the flesh crawl but could have been handled much more skillfully. For one thing, the spider first appears as a lump moving under Bond's sheet, but it is moving so fast that it is obviously being pulled along on a string. Then, when it emerges into the open it is clearly separated from Connery's expensive flesh (not that one blames him) by a sheet of glass. One good touch, though, is the way in which Bond reels off into the bathroom to be sick after dispatching the creature. It demonstrates that even super-Bond has his human failings.

The following day, Bond obtains a geiger counter with which he checks out Quarrel's boat. On the spot where Strangways' mineral samples had been lying, there is a sign of radioactivity. And the island where these particular samples had come from? Crab Key, of course. But there's nothing there, Leiter tells Bond, except for a bauxite mine owned by a Chinese gentleman called Dr. No.

But before Bond can go off and slay the dragon in his lair, he must first play at being a sitting duck again. A Chinese girl, working as a secretary at Government House, has invited Bond up to her house for the afternoon. He suspects a trap but is unable to resist the bait.

During the drive up to her place he is attacked by our old friends in their hearse. They attempt, unsuccessfully, to force him off the steep mountain road but end up by plunging to their own doom. Exciting to watch, but spoiled by clumsy back projection.

The girl is, naturally, surprised to see Bond but she recovers quickly and makes the best of a bad situation. Before she is dragged into bed by Bond, whose sexual appetite must increase in ratio to the danger he experiences, she manages to make a phone call. After they have made love, off screen, Bond suggests that they go out for dinner. While she dresses he makes a phone call of his own, with the result that when they leave there is a police car waiting out front. A nice *volte face*, this, and we last see the girl as she is being hauled away by the police. She does manage to spit in Bond's eye but he doesn't seem to mind too much. All of which goes to show why feminists have always been less than enamored with James Bond.

With the girl disposed of, Bond returns inside and sits down to wait. Before long Professor Dent arrives, gun in hand. He tries to kill Bond, but Bond has already taken certain precautions and poor Dent wastes all his bullets by shooting at a pillow. Then follows an incident which is totally out of character for Fleming's Bond. Dent, not realising that his gun is empty, has one last attempt at shooting Bond. Bond waits for him to stop clicking his useless weapon then calmly shoots him dead. Cold-blooded murder. In all the books James Bond never did anything like this, and it was the first and last time that the film-Bond did too. Ever since then, Bond has behaved himself, still killing, of course, but doing it nicely. (There was a lapse in *The Spy Who Loved Me* when Bond first suspends one of the villain's henchmen—played by Milton Reid—over the edge of a rooftop by his tie, then casually lets the helpless man fall to his death. It was an action that seemed very out of character for the Roger Moore version of Bond.)

At this point, Bond decides that he has had enough and finally goes to confront Dr. No on his home ground. With Quarrel, Bond sails to Crab Key island. They arrive in the middle of the night, hide their boat and spend the remaining time till morning asleep in the jungle.

Bond wakes to hear the sound of a singing voice. Just coming out of the sea, he discovers the film's romantic interest (or perhaps the film's sexual interest would be a better description), Honey Rider, played by the awesome Ursula Andress. The Honey that met the Bond of the book was rather different (for one thing she was naked), but it is none too hard to ignore the bikini Miss Andress is wearing. This Honey also lacks the broken nose of the other Honey, which is not surprising. One can imagine that both the producers

Ursula Andress as Honey in **Dr. No**

and Miss Andress didn't take too kindly to the idea of having the make-up man flatten her nose.

No sooner have they met than the forces of evil once more return to the attack. A motor launch roars along the beach and sprays the area with a machine gun. No one is hit but Honey's boat is shot full of holes, which means that she is unable to leave the island. Bond is forced to take her along with him. Poor Bond.

As the three make their way across the island, Honey tells Bond about herself. She is, we learn, the daughter of a naturalist whom Dr. No has had murdered. Though now an orphan she is far from helpless. She tells Bond of how her landlord forced his unwanted attentions upon her, and how she exacted her revenge by dropping a black widow spider on his stomach while he slept. "He took a week to die," she says with relish. Bond is a little alarmed at hearing this, but is willing to overlook it providing Honey promises not to make a habit of doing such things. Somewhat broad-minded of him, considering his own recent experience with a spider in his bed.

As darkness begins to fall, Quarrel discovers the tracks of a "dragon" which is rumored to haunt Crab Key. Until the arrival on the island, the character of Quarrel had been treated sympathetically, but from then on he becomes one of those old-fashioned comic Negro types. Particularly distasteful is the scene on the beach where Bond curtly orders Quarrel to "fetch my shoes!" When the so-called dragon tracks are found Quarrel launches into one of those classic "Massa! Massa! I'm scared!" routines complete with eye-rolling. Bond glances at the tracks and condescendingly tells Quarrel that it's a strange dragon that leaves tire tread marks.

At least Quarrel is allowed to die bravely, incinerated by the false dragon as he and Bond vainly try to stop it with their guns. The scene when the tank-disguised-as-a-dragon is bearing down on them, breathing fire from a concealed flamethrower, is very exciting. Unfortunately some of the suspense of the situation is destroyed by the distinctly cross-eyed expression on the dragon's face. Somehow a cross-eyed dragon, breathing fire or not, lacks the necessary menace.

When Quarrel is killed, Bond realizes his position is hopeless and surrenders. The dragon halts and several men, wearing what look like green fire protection suits, climb out and surround him. For the first time in the film, super-Bond has been defeated. Defeated, but still defiant. When one of the guards pushes Honey, Bond, handcuffs and all, attacks him, but he is clubbed unconscious and dragged away. The screen fades on a depressing scene, with the bushes where Quarrel lies dead still smoldering, and Bond completely helpless in the hands of his enemies . . . .

Bond and Honey attacked by the "dragon"

But rebirth is soon to follow. In the next scene, we see that we have left the depressing sand flats and have been transported to fantasy land (we have also exchanged the real location of Jamaica for the studios of England). Actually Bond and Honey are in Dr. No's special delousing house for they have inadvertently become radioactive. There's a nice moment of one-upmanship here when Bond, though obviously at a serious disadvantage, starts to order his captors about—"Do the girl first . . . and get these handcuffs off . . ." Amusingly, they obey.

Bond and the girl are first sprayed with white foam and then given the merest gesture of a wipe-down by a Chinese extra with a long mop. Then they travel along a conveyor belt through a series of showers. As they pass through each spray, a sign lights up in front of them saying how radioactive they are. This is definitely one of the film's sillier sequences.

When they have been declared free of all signs of contamination, they are ushered through a bank vault-type door set in the rock. On the other side, they are welcomed by two Chinese women dressed in white who, in contrast to the cold technicians, gush over them as if they were long lost relatives. "Come in, you poor, poor dears. You must be tired, you poor things!" This is another suitably eerie touch. The sudden change from a hostile situation to a seemingly friendly one is unsettling and is more definitely sinister than if Bond and Honey had been met by a couple of grim-faced torturers. The scene also serves as another example of Dr. No's omnipotence when one of the hostesses tells Bond that he and the girl were expected and that even the sizes of their clothes are known to them.

They are shown to their rooms which turn out to be luxuriously furnished. "Please ring if there's anything you want. Anything at all," says one of the hostesses. "How about two air tickets to London?" says Bond. The hostess gives a pained smile to show her displeasure at Bond's refusal to maintain the charade. She leaves and the featureless door slides shut behind her.

After drinking the coffee that has been provided, both Bond and Honey pass out. As Bond lies asleep on his bed we see the door of his room slide open. The camera shows us a pair of white shoes and the lower part of a pair of immaculately pressed white trousers. The owner steps inside and approaches the bed. Face still hidden to us, he looms over Bond. Then a hand reaches down and pulls back the sheet from under Bond's chin. There is a visual *frisson* here, for this is no ordinary hand, but one made of black metal.

Bond's drugged sleep continues undisturbed while the strange figure merely gazes at him for several moments before leaving the room as silently as he came. Fade-out.

When Bond and Honey awake, they dress and nervously prepare to meet their ominous host. They are taken by elevator into the depths of the island and then shown into an ornately decorated room. The dominating feature of the room is a large glass section of one wall through which we see fish swimming. As Bond and the girl examine it more closely Bond wonders aloud how much it cost. "One million dollars, Mr. Bond," comes the reply from behind them. They turn and see Dr. No for the first time.

He bears comparatively little resemblance to the Dr. No of the book but that's not surprising. According to Fleming: "Doctor No was at least six inches taller than Bond but the straight immovable poise of his body made him seem taller. The head was also elongated and tapered from a round, completely bald skull down to the sharp chin . . . He seemed to glide rather than take steps. His knees did not dent the matt, gunmetal sheen of his kimono . . . The bizarre, gliding figure looked like a giant venomous worm wrapped in grey tin foil . . . ." It is very difficult to reproduce something like that on the screen and the makers wisely do not attempt to do so. Joseph Wiseman's version is of normal height, has hair, and instead of a kimono wears a plain white suit. Also, Dr. No's pincers have been replaced with metal hands—another wise change as, unless one has a handless actor, such things always look wrong.

Joseph Wiseman may not bear much physical resemblance to the Dr. No of the novel, but on an emotional level his portrayal is flawless. He captures perfectly the inhuman, machine-like quality of Dr. No. Every movement is careful and precise, the face remains blank and the voice as bland as something produced by a computer. The overall effect is one of supreme confidence mingled with total ruthlessness—the "Grand Inquisitor" of the novel.

Wiseman is an American character actor who has worked mainly in the theatre, though he has made a number of screen appearances over the years, the first of which was in *Detective Story* in 1951. Other films include *Viva Zapata* (1952), *The Silver Chalice* (1954), *The Garment Jungle* (1957), *The Unforgiven* (1960), *Stiletto* (1969), and *The Valachi Papers* (1972). His individualistic, even off-beat, acting style has meant that he has usually been cast in villainous roles but he has also, on occasion, demonstrated a flair for comedy, notably in *How to Steal a Million* (1966), *The Night They Raided Minsky's* (1968), and *Bye Bye Braverman* (1968).

Joseph Wiseman as Dr. No

Unfortunately, the script in *Dr. No* fails to make use of the character's potential, whereas in the book No gives a chilling Orwellian speech in which he reveals some of his background and offers an insight into what drives him. The motivations for Dr. No's antisocial activities in the film all seem to stem from his rejections by both Eastern and Western countries when he was offering his services as a scientist. But this hardly seems reason enough to start throwing American rockets all over the place. (Fleming's *Dr. No* owes much to two previous literary villains—Sax Rohmer's Fu Manchu, whose exploits Fleming greatly enjoyed when a boy, and Jules Verne's Captain Nemo. Not only does Dr. No share Nemo's obsession with the underwater kingdom and his desire to distance himself from all mankind, but he also shares his name—Nemo meaning "no" in Latin.)

Another departure from the book is that Dr. No is not a free-lance villain but a member of a certain organization. The organization is SPECTRE . . . The Special Executive for Counter-Intelligence, Terrorism, Revenge and Extortion. SPECTRE was Fleming's replacement for SMERSH, which he introduced when it no longer became convenient to have Russians as villains. As described by Fleming, SPECTRE was a small group of criminals consisting of ex-members of SMERSH, the Mafia, etc. But in the films, it has taken on the dimensions of an industrial giant. SPECTRE played a part in all the early films except *Goldfinger,* growing bigger each time. To date, the financial backers of SPECTRE have lost an island, complete with men and equipment; a fleet of boats; a hydrofoil; an artificial volcano, complete with men and equipment; and an Alpine fortress, complete with men and equipment. Ernst Stavro Blofeld, the managing director, must have a difficult time explaining away the losses after each of his abortive projects. And just imagine his staff recruitment problems.

Dr. No even offers Bond a position in SPECTRE but he replies that he would only join on provision that he could work in the Revenge department and of course the good Doctor would be his first target. Bond further antagonizes his host by accusing him of playing at Napoleon . . . or God. The dinner party degenerates rapidly after this.

"You persist in trying to provoke me, Mr. Bond," intones Dr. No. "Usually when a man gets in my way . . .," and he picks up an ornament from the table with his metal hand and crushes it into a shapeless lump. Then he has Honey dragged from the room saying that he's sure the guards will find some way of amusing themselves with her. Bond tries to go to her rescue but No's men hold him in his chair.

Dr. No remains long enough to tell Bond how childish and silly he's been and then excuses himself to go and prepare for another "rocket toppling" job, promising, as he leaves, to deal with him later. But to prevent Bond from becoming bored in the meantime he orders his guards to "soften" him up.

Looking suitably battered, Bond is later thrown into a small cell. But no sooner has the door closed than our hero is on his feet and looking for a means of escape. He soon spots a small grill at the top of one wall and, with difficulty, climbs up to it. As he grips the wire he is sent flying backwards in a shower of sparks: an electric shock and totally unexpected. Unlike most of us, our hero doesn't give in but climbs up to the grill again and batters it in by using his shoe as a buffer. He then crawls into the ventilation shaft.

Bond escaping from super-heated ventilation shaft

In the book what followed was all part of a special obstacle course that Dr. No had especially prepared, but in the film Bond's experiences inside the ventilation shaft are presumably unplanned. They make exciting viewing but the various dangers that Bond has to endure in the shaft lack a certain menace by not being deliberately imposed. Also Bond has it too easy in the film, a short climb and a crawl, a couple of bad moments when the shaft is flooded followed by having to crawl over a few yards of heated metal and then he's home free. (Another quibble here; all the water that passes through the shaft should, by rights, pour out the same ventilation grid that Bond eventually escapes from.)

In the book, Bond is pushed to the limits of his endurance and by the time he's negotiated the obstacle course, which includes a caged section full of tarantulas, he is in bad shape. Incidentally, in the book the shaft leads into the pen of a giant squid, one of Fleming's most far-fetched excursions into the realm of the fantastic. Giant squids are so rare that even Dr. No would have trouble in capturing and domesticating one.

It is here that the book and the film take entirely different paths. In the book, Bond escapes the squid, naturally, and wreaks his revenge on Dr. No by burying him alive under a pile of Guano bird droppings (which must certainly rank high, in more ways than one, among the various esoteric methods of disposal that have been featured in the thriller *genre* over the years).

The climax to the film is not as novel as this but it permits a greater build-up of tension and excitement. After Bond escapes from the shaft, he throttles one of Dr. No's technicians and enters the control room in the dead man's radiation suit. Here Ken Adam has a field day and we are treated to the most colorful laboratory/control room that any mad scientist has ever had the pleasure to call his own. It even has an atomic reactor, wisely shielded in a pool of water, to provide the power.

Bond manages to conceal his real identity from the watchful eyes of Dr. No and takes his assigned place on a catwalk above the reactor. The count-down has begun and the several TV screens in the control room show a rocket sitting on its launch pad at Cape Canaveral (perhaps Dr. No has an arrangement with one of the big American TV networks).

A furious Dr. No ascends the catwalk to his atomic reactor.

The scene changes to an aerial view of Dr. No's establishment (a well-constructed model) and we see an aerial rise up from the top of a tower. Inside the control room, Bond waits until just before the rocket lifts off, then he strikes. He starts to turn a wheel on the reactor's control panel that sends the radiation up to the danger level. One of the technicians notices and tries to stop him but Bond hurls him off the catwalk. His fall alerts everyone else in the room, including Dr. No, but by then it is too late. The reactor has passed the point of no-return and flashing signs announce that the area must be abandoned. Dr. No's staff flee the control room, but the Doctor himself runs towards Bond (Wiseman even manages to make the way Dr. No runs seem strange and machine-like). He climbs on to the catwalk and starts to flail Bond with his metal hands. Bond somehow avoids a fractured skull and fights back.

A fight to the finish between Bond and Dr. No

The climax is in true Saturday afternoon matinee serial tradition . . . both Bond and Dr. No fall to a platform beneath the catwalk which is slowly sinking towards the pool containing the reactor, the water in which is boiling furiously. Bond manages to climb to safety and kicks Dr. No down again when he tries to follow. The Doctor tries desperately to save himself by clutching at the steel supports of the platform but his artificial hands fail to grip and he continues to sink. We last see him as he sinks beneath the bubbling water, his glass helmet cracking open from the heat. (Actually it was stuntman Bob Simmons who made the journey down into the reactor's boiling pool—simulated by means of compressed air, dry ice, and bright underwater lights. Incidentally, not many people noticed a major technical error in this sequence—that the reactor gets hotter when the control rods are *inserted* into the core instead of vice versa.)

Bond races from the control room and starts to search for Honey. He eventually finds her in an odd room where she is chained to the floor. Water is trickling out of a pipe at the other end. Not as nasty a fate as the one Honey endures in the book—staked out naked on a hill for the giant crabs to play with. (There are stills in existence showing Ms. Andress lying on the ground and surrounded by crabs so presumably such a scene was shot and later cut—unless the photographs were for publicity purposes only.) But we notice in the film that now she is only wearing the top half of her Chinese costume; when we last saw her she was also wearing slacks. All of which suggests that something unpleasant has happened in the meantime but it's left up to the sordid imagination of the viewer to supply the details.

As Bond and Honey fight their way out of the late Dr. No's establishment, we once again see the deserted control room where the TV screens and speakers are announcing the successful launching of the rocket.

They manage to obtain a boat, not without difficulty, and speed out to sea . . . narrowly avoiding the holocaust that occurs when the special effects men blow up some models (Actually this sequence is quite convincing. It was a good idea on the part of effects men Frank George and John Stears to shoot the model of No's establishment from directly overhead as this greatly increases the realism of the set-up. For one thing, the water surrounding the model seems to match the scale of the model much better than if it had been shot horizontally. One is surprised that this technique for shooting model sequences hasn't been used more often.) Soon they are met by Leiter who arrives with a boat-load of marines. They are taken in tow but decide that they don't really want to be rescued just yet. So Bond releases the tow rope and we last see them adrift once again. The end credits roll on . . . The End . . . of *Dr. No* . . . But James Bond Will Be Back . . . in *From Russia With Love.*

Truer words were never spoken, for Bond was just beginning.

Mission accomplished: escape from Dr. No

The phoney James Bond has good reason to look nervous.

4

From Russia with Love

Critical reaction to *Dr. No* was mixed. The Vatican immediately issued a warning about the film, and *Time's* reviewer was distinctly unimpressed. The critics who attended the first press showing were apparently equally divided in their opinions. In the FOR camp were Alexander Walker and Dilys Powell, while the AGAINST camp included Derek Hill, Penelope Gilliatt, and Thomas Wiseman, who noted with disgust in the *Sunday Express* that "Bond's methods and morals were indistinguishable from the villain's." As these were the days before High Camp had become a familiar term, many of the critics were confused by the elements of self-parody in the film. Was one really supposed to take Dr. No and his fairyland establishment seriously? Some even dared to suggest that director Terence Young might have had his tongue in cheek when he made it! (One critic even confused Terence Young with Terence Fisher and proceeded to draw parallels between *Dr. No* and various Hammer films.)

Ian Fleming himself seemed to like it, however. "Those who've read the book will be disappointed," he said at the time, "but those who haven't will find it a wonderful movie."

There were only two things on which all the critics were agreed. One was that the inclusion of the recently stolen Goya portrait of the Duke of Wellington in Dr. No's apartment was a wonderfully clever touch, and the other was that the film would undoubtedly make a lot of money. And it certainly did. The takings from the British release alone were a record £700,000, which more than covered the relatively small production costs (just over £300,000). For while the critics may have been divided, the cinema-going public was unanimous in their support.

When *From Russia with Love* was released in 1963, Bond-mania was approaching its zenith and the film was literally assured of being a success. At this point, the makers could have produced a total bomb and it would have still made a fortune at the box-office. They didn't, of course. *From Russia with Love* fulfilled everyone's expectations. But though the basic ingredients were the same (fast action, exotic settings, violence, and sex), *FRWL* differed greatly from its predecessor. In fact, it stands out from all the other films in the series too, which have since tended to follow the science fiction style of *Dr. No*. Of all of Fleming's Bond novels, *FRWL* least follows the formula that he used so often. Many people, including this writer, consider it his best book. It certainly contains the best plot and some of his most effective writing, and while it lacks a villain of the stature of Dr. No or Sir Hugo Drax, it features two of the most repulsive characters ever to appear in the thriller *genre*: Rosa Klebb and Donavan "Red" Grant. But as cinematic material, it doesn't appear to be as promising as the other books, mainly because the plot is slow-moving and complicated, and also because most of the action takes place in confined spaces that don't provide much opportunity for visual spectacle. However, the makers were to overcome this latter problem by adding two outdoor sequences near the close of the film. Even so, it still remains out of step with the rest of the series and Bond fans usually have strong views concerning it; they either consider it to be the best or the worst, probably because it is the one Bond film constructed on conventional—even traditional—thriller lines (it even makes use of a setting beloved of thriller writers in the Twenties and Thirties—the Istanbul Express). Unlike the other Bonds, the fantastic element is kept to a minimum in *From Russia with Love* (it also lacks the distinctive Ken Adam touch); instead, it has more in common with a Hitchcock thriller, in particular *North By Northwest* (interestingly, that film is regarded by many as the prototype for all the Bond movies). As to why the producers chose to film that novel after *Dr. No*, one should remember that it was *From Russia with Love* that had featured on the late President Kennedy's list of favorite books and, therefore, the best-known Bond title in America at that time.

From Russia with Love begins with a short pre-title sequence which was to become a traditional device in all the following films. We see James Bond being stalked through a maze of hedges by a mysterious figure. Bond appears unusually nervous so we immediately suspect that all is not what it appears to be. This is confirmed when he is surprised by his pursuer and actually strangled before our eyes. His assailant accomplishes this feat with a wire that he extends from his watch. Bond falls dead . . . and suddenly the scene is illuminated by a battery of powerful lights. A mansion (actually the main building at Pinewood Studios) and a watching group of men, all dressed in black, can now be seen in the background. One of them strides forward and says to Bond's killer, "Excellent, only one minute, fifty-two seconds . . .," then bends down, hooks his fingers under Bond's chin and peels off a mask, revealing an entirely different face beneath! The man walks back towards the mansion, James Bond's face dangling casually from his hand.

One can't help being impressed by this sequence. It is a nice blend of eeriness and surprise, but it doesn't bear too close an inspection. For, when we think about it, it is obviously very illogical. What, after all, would be the point of training someone to kill a specific person by having him practice on someone disguised as that person? Especially if the target was someone like James Bond. It would be as relevant as training to be a big game hunter by dressing your dog up in a lion's skin. Still, the sequence certainly succeeds in what it was designed to do, and that's to start the film off with a bang.

After the titles, this time designed by Robert Brownjohn and Trevor Bond, which are displayed on various parts of an undulating belly dancer, the film proper begins. Venice is the location and we find ourselves watching a chess tournament. Each player sits on a dais in the center of a large, ornate room, watched by an audience who follow the movements of the game on an over-sized duplicate board on one of the walls. Above it the names of the players are displayed. One of them is called Kronsteen.

The chess match in **From Russia with Love**

A waiter approaches one of the players and hands him a glass of water. As he lifts it up to drink he sees a note at the bottom of the glass which says: "Come at Once." He puts the glass down, calmly tears the note up and, within a few swift moves, wins the game. Then he gets up, ignores the offered hands of his supporters and silently marches out of the room. This is, of course, Kronsteen . . . master planner of SPECTRE. Of all the films, *From Russia with Love* seems to me to be the best cast. Vladek Sheybal, for instance, who plays Kronsteen, is excellent. Sheybal not only possesses one of the most slyly evil faces in films today, but is also a fine actor (which he proved in such films as *Leo the Last* and *Women in Love*). He captures very well Kronsteen's cold, lizard-like personality.

After the chess game, Kronsteen goes straight to a luxurious yacht anchored somewhere near Venice. On board, he is ushered into the presence of Ernst Stavro Blofeld, head of SPECTRE, although he is only referred to as Number One in this film. We don't see his face, only glimpses of his hands and the back of his head. Blofeld was to remain more or less invisible in all the films up to *You Only Live Twice,* when we saw him for the first time. In this scene, Blofeld's famous white cat is also introduced, an innovation on the part of the filmmakers as Fleming never mentioned this feline fixation.

Also in Blofeld's cabin is Rosa Klebb, ex-member of the Russian espionage organization SMERSH. Klebb is played by Lotte Lenya and, though many critics thought she was a little too glamorous for the role, it's hard to imagine anyone else playing Klebb, so memorable is her performance. Anyway, it would have been impossible to find someone who matched her description in the novel: "The thinning orange hair scraped back to the tight, obscene bun; the shiny yellow-brown eyes . . . the wedge of thickly powdered, large-pored nose; the wet trap of a mouth, that went on opening and shutting as if it was operated by wires under the chin . . . She was short, about five foot four, and squat, and her dumpy arms and short neck, and the calves of her thick legs, were very strong for a woman. The devil knows, thought Kronsteen, what her breasts were like, but the bulge of uniform that rested on the tabletop looked like a badly packed sandbag . . . ."

Kronsteen and Klebb have been summoned to Blofeld's head-quarters to discuss the arrangements for SPECTRE's latest operation. They are going to steal a Russian cipher machine, called a Lektor, but in such a way as to throw the blame onto the British; then SPECTRE will sell the machine back to the Russians and make a big profit. Kronsteen is responsible for the planning and he declares that he has devised a foolproof scheme. A Russian girl working for the Embassy in Istanbul will contact the British Secret Service and declare that she is willing to defect with the Lektor, providing that a certain British agent comes to pick her up. The agent whom the British will undoubtedly send, says Kronsteen, will be none other than James Bond. The man responsible for the death of SPECTRE's other operative—Dr. No.

"Won't they suspect a trap?" asks Blofeld.

"Of course," replies Kronsteen, "but the British can never resist a trap."

Screenwriter Richard Maibaum has made the plot of the film much more complicated than that of the book, mainly by introducing SPECTRE into the proceedings. In the book, the Russians were the chief villains and their sole aim was to discredit the British Secret Service by having one of their top agents, James Bond, killed in embarrassing circumstances. But in 1963, when the film was released, the Cold War was beginning to thaw out so it was considered wise, in the interests of world peace, to pin the blame on someone else (not that this placated the Russians—*Pravda* continued to heap abuse on James Bond, accusing Fleming's creation of being the symbol of all that was wrong with the decadent West (nowadays, of course, the Russians look upon Bond as a harmless joke, confirming what many of us feel about Roger Moore's impersonation).

Which also explains why Rosa Klebb has switched from SMERSH to SPECTRE. One wonders what SPECTRE offered to induce her, a dedicated Soviet agent, to join an organization so devoted to the principle of private enterprise. It certainly couldn't have been security.

Blofeld is pleased with Kronsteen's smooth assurances of success and, as he feeds a fish to his cat, he says, "May his death be a particularly humiliating and unpleasant one." From the tone of his voice (provided, presumably, by Robert Rietty who also dubbed the voices of many of the foreign actors in the Bond series, including Adolfo Celi's in *Thunderball*), we know that Bond is going to be in for a rough ride this time.

After the conference on Blofeld's boat, Klebb, who is in charge of putting Kronsteen's plan into operation, goes to SPECTRE Island to check on the man chosen to be Bond's killer. The island is another innovation of the filmmakers'. It was never mentioned in any of the books and has never appeared in any of the succeeding films. From the short glimpse we get of it in *FRWL*, it appears to be devoted entirely to the training of SPECTRE's employees, with yards full of tough-looking men breaking things with their hands, firing guns, and playing with flame-throwers. Klebb is given a quick tour of the place by the black-garbed Morzeny, whom we first saw in the pre-credits sequence (he is played by Walter Gotell who later turned up as the head of the KGB in *The Spy Who Loved Me* and *Moonraker*). She doesn't really seem impressed by it all and mutters, "Training is no substitute for actual experience." Her guide agrees with her. "We realize that," he says, "that's why we use live targets too." And all this is happening somewhere in the Mediterranean!

Fun and games on SPECTRE Island

A medical check-up, SPECTRE-style (Lotte Lenya,
Robert Shaw)

Klebb is taken to meet Donovan Grant, who is found lying on the grass having a massage in a scene that is drawn directly from the novel. When summoned by the training master he springs to his feet, bounds over, and stands stiffly to attention. Dressed only in a towel he is a magnificent specimen of manhood, but Klebb gives no sign of noticing this. She circles him as if she was inspecting a horse, then, unseen by the others, slips a knuckle-duster onto her hand. Then she spins round and strikes Grant with great force in the stomach. He barely flinches under the impact. "He seems fit enough," comments Klebb as she strides away, "have him report to me in Istanbul in the morning."

Robert Shaw, who plays Grant, is perfect in the part. His hair dyed blonde, his face blank, he haunts the film like some sort of animated Greek statue, never saying a word until the climactic episode aboard the Orient Express. Shaw manages to invest Grant with much of that unsettling menace that Fleming so chillingly described in his novel.

The scene changes to Istanbul, and here we see Klebb recruit her next member, Tatiana Romanova. Tatiana works for the Russian embassy but has received orders to report to a certain address where she finds herself face to face with one of the most feared women in Russia. Tatiana, of course, is still under the impression that Klebb is Head of Operations for SMERSH. Klebb loses no time in browbeating the poor girl into complying with her wishes. Not that she has much choice in the matter; Klebb has told her she won't leave the room alive if she refuses. It's interesting to note that only a slight hint of Klebb's lesbianism has reached the screen. During the interview, Klebb's hand slips casually down on to Tatiana's knee but is hastily removed when she sees her reaction. In the book, her attempt to seduce Tatiana is much less subtle.

Tatiana is played by Italian actress Daniela Bianchi, who is competent but doesn't fit one's image of the character in the novel. Perhaps because Fleming described Tatiana as resembling Greta Garbo, this is hardly surprising.

After this long build-up, James Bond finally makes an appearance in the film. We find him in a typically Bond situation, lying in a punt with a pretty girl, and a bottle of champagne tied to his big toe. In the background, we hear a radio playing Matt Munro's vocal version of *From Russia with Love*.

This idyllic scene doesn't last for long, of course. Bond soon receives a summons, via his car radio, to report back to headquarters. There he finds M waiting to send him on his latest mission. M tells him of this Russian girl who has seen his picture in a file and claims that she has fallen in love with him. She's willing to defect, providing Bond comes to Istanbul to collect her, and, as an extra attraction, she'll help him steal a Lektor.

"It sounds like a trap," says Bond.

"Of course," replies M, "but we can't afford to pass up an opportunity like this. We've been trying to get our hands on a Lektor for ages."

Bond still isn't too enthusiastic about the whole idea until M shows him a photo of Tatiana. Then he abruptly changes his mind. But before he can depart for Istanbul, he is forced to endure another visitation from Major Boothroyd of Q Branch. This time Q has provided a special briefcase containing a folding rifle, concealed throwing knife, gold coins, and a teargas bomb designed to explode if the case isn't opened in a particular way. This is the first example of how the gadgets were to dominate the Bond films. All the weapons mentioned play a crucial part later in the film, saving Bond's life at least three times, whereas in the book he relied on his ingenuity for survival.

After the obligatory interlude with Miss Moneypenny, Bond leaves for Turkey. He passes through customs at Istanbul airport with surprising ease and is met by the son of the local British agent.

The British agent, Kerim Bey, played by the late Pedro Armendariz, welcomes Bond into his headquarters which is disguised as a carpet-selling business located in the Grand Bazaar. He's happy to see Bond, but tells him that he is wasting his time in Istanbul . . . things are too quiet. But even as he's saying this Grant is going into action. While one of the Bulgars has been in the Bazaar following Bond, Grant has slipped into their car and overpowered the driver. Then he drives away leaving the other Bulgar standing puzzled on the footpath. Next we see Grant parking the car in front of the Russian embassy's gate. He gets out, immediately climbs into another car and roars away. The guard at the embassy gate is naturally suspicious. He walks over to the abandoned car and opens one of the doors. The driver, looking very dead, falls out. In the other car, Grant, wearing a sated expression, peels a black glove from his hand. Klebb is seated beside him. "Good," she snarls, "now the cold war in Istanbul will not be so cold!"

Meanwhile Bond has been driven to his hotel. After being shown to his room, he begins his usual ritual of checking it out for listening devices. He finds so many of the things that he rings the front desk and asks for another room. There are no more available, he is told, apart from the bridal suite. Bond takes it. Apparently not even suspicious about the switch, he doesn't bother to check his new rooms for bugs.

Elsewhere the cold war, as Klebb has promised, is heating up. As Kerim Bey is about to relax with a female friend, his room is blown apart by a mine. When Bond arrives later, he finds the place a complete wreck though Kerim Bey is unharmed. The Turk is at a loss to explain the attack and suggests that it's time to investigate the situation at the Russian embassy. To accomplish this, he takes Bond underground to a reservoir which extends under the city all the way to the embassy. Beneath the embassy, Kerim Bey has installed a periscope which actually protrudes into the Russians' conference room. This was one of Fleming's original touches and one just has to be impressed by the sheer audacity of the idea.

A conference is in progress when Bond and Kerim look through the periscope and Kerim points out a man whom he knows to be a special killer often used by the Russians. His name is Krilencu and Kerim is sure that it was he who planted the mine in his room. "You should remember his face, James," he tells Bond. "There is a man who *kills* for pleasure." I wouldn't have thought that Bond would be too disturbed by such a man. After all, he's never been averse to a bit of killing himself. But while Bond is peering into the periscope, he sees a pair of female legs appear. Kerim decides that it must be Tatiana. "Hmmm," says Bond, "I'd like to see her in the flesh sometime."

Kerim, worried that Krilencu will make another attempt on their lives, suggests that they spend the night at the camp of some gypsy friends of his.

Kerim (Pedro Armendariz) and Bond spy on the
Russian embassy.

He and Bond are greeted warmly at the gypsy camp and no
sooner have they sat down then they are treated to the sight of a
belly dancer who writhes sinuously about the camp. This is followed
by a more bizarre entertainment—a girl fight. Even Kingsley Amis,
Bond's most prestigious defender, regarded this episode in Fleming's novel as blatantly sadistic. But the film tones down the fight
considerably. The two girls, played by Aliza Gur and Martine Beswick (who also appears in *Thunderball*), huff and puff a lot, screech
and pull each other's hair, but don't do anything really nasty. And
before the fight has a chance to become serious, an interruption
occurs.

This comes in the form of a truck-load of armed Bulgars who
smash their way in through the front gates (never a dull moment in
your average gypsy camp!). The ensuing fight in the camp is a very
neatly choreographed piece of cinema action. Gunfire, screams,

and falling bodies fill the screen while Bond moves calmly through all the chaos, dispatching Bulgars with casual ease while on the soundtrack John Barry's 007 theme pulsates, adding to the atmosphere of electric excitement. But Bond doesn't have it too easy . . . during the battle he comes close to being killed, except that his would-be assassin is felled by a mysterious shot at the crucial moment. Bond's guardian is none other than Grant who is perched unseen on top of a wall.

The gypsy way of settling disagreements (Aliza Gur and Martine Beswick)

The gypsies win the fight and the Bulgars retreat, leaving behind a couple of wounded men from whom the gypsies extract information. Krilencu is behind the affair, Kerim learns, and vows to kill him as soon as possible. He and Bond then return to the city and trace the killer to his hideout. They wait outside in the street below. Bond begins to assemble his rifle.

On the side of the building is a large billboard advertising a Bob Hope movie called *Call Me Bwana* (also produced by Broccoli). The billboard features a giant picture of Anita Ekberg (Fleming readers will recall that it was Marilyn Monroe in the book). Kerim tells Bond to watch her mouth.

When two of Kerim's sons, disguised as policemen, ring Krilencu's front door bell, Bond sees a square of light suddenly appear behind the mouth. A trapdoor opens and a knotted rope is quickly lowered. Bond prepares to shoot but at the last moment Kerim decides that, despite a wounded arm, it is his personal duty to kill this man. He takes the rifle and, using Bond's shoulder for support, shoots Krilencu in the back as he climbs down the rope. For someone who frowns on people deriving pleasure from murder, Kerim seems to draw a suspiciously large amount of satisfaction from his own work. Bond, of course, makes the obvious comment that, "She should have kept her big mouth closed."

Bond returns exhausted to his hotel but as he prepares for a shower he hears strange noises coming from his bedroom. Investigating, he finds Tatiana Romanova, wearing nothing but a black choker, lying in his bed. Despite his weariness, he makes the most of the situation. "Do I come up to your expectations?" he asks her as he slides into the bed.

"I'll tell you," she replies, "in the . . . morning."

The camera pulls back from their entwined bodies to reveal that the large mirror set behind the bed is in fact one-way glass. Hunched over a whirring camera behind the glass is a man, and standing beside him, with an expression of disinterest on her face, is Rosa Klebb.

Bond and Tatiana next meet on a ferry boat where she gives him details of the cipher machine, recording her voice in a tape recorder disguised as a camera. This leads to an amusing scene back in M's

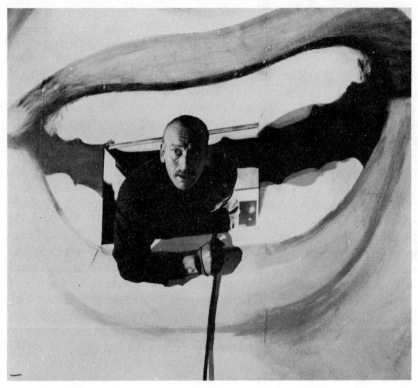

Fred Haggerty as Krilencu tries to escape through Anita Ekberg's mouth.

office where the tape is played to an assembled group of experts and Miss Moneypenny. Tatiana's description of the mechanical details of the Lektor keeps lapsing into passionate murmurings directed at Bond. When she asks him whether he considers Eastern girls to be as exciting as Western ones he begins to recount an experience that he and M supposedly had while in Japan (it must have been a fictional concoction as we all know what M is really like). At this point, M shuts off the recorder and orders Miss Moneypenny from the room.

Bond has asked Tatiana to obtain a plan of the Russian embassy which he intends to compare with an official set that Kerim possesses. The location for this rendezvous is the famous Blue Mosque. The whole sequence is very Hitchcockian in flavor. Bond enters the mosque as a member of a touring party but slips away when he spots Tatiana. Then he sees that Tatiana is being followed by one of the Bulgars, who also notices her leaving the crucial scrap of paper at the base of one of the massive pillars. Bond begins to move in to intercept him but is unaware that Grant is also present in the mosque. When Bond reaches the Bulgar, he finds him already dead, the plan still clutched in his hand. Elsewhere Grant is again peeling off his black glove.... The cathedral-like vastness of the mosque, the tour guide's monotonous voice droning in the background, together with John Barry's music (this time a series of chime-like sounds building toward a climax that never comes) combine to create an atmosphere of mounting tension. The sequence also serves to establish how easily Grant is able to manipulate events, making Bond seem a helpless pawn at the mercy of forces beyond his control.

Bond and Kerim compare the two sets of plans and find that they match perfectly, so the decision is made to go ahead with the raid on the embassy to steal the cipher machine. But as an extra piece of insurance it will take place on the day before the date that Bond has given Tatiana. Bond tells Kerim of the dead Bulgar in the mosque, but though puzzled neither of them seems to appreciate the true significance of the incident.

The actual raid on the embassy is spectacular. Bond enters the building carrying a coat over his arm and approaches a clerk seated at a desk in the foyer. He tells him he wants to inquire about getting a visa and asks if the clock on the wall is correct. The clerk says that it is. Bond waits restlessly in the foyer for a few moments then approaches the clerk again. "Are you sure that clock is correct?" he asks. "Russian clocks are never wrong!" replies the clerk. The next instant there is a loud explosion and the place fills with smoke. The staff immediately panic and begin to stream out of the building, many of them carrying their desk drawers laden with documents. Bond calmly makes his way through the confusion, producing a gas mask from under his coat. Knowing the layout of the building he has no difficulty in finding the room where the Lektor is kept. Arriving there, after disposing of one guard *en route,* he throws a gas mask to the confused Tatiana, snatches up the cipher machine and then makes his way down to the basement where Kerim has blown a convenient hole in the floor. He and Tatiana descend into the underground reservoir and find Kerim waiting for them, plus a horde of nervous rats (the rats were imported especially for the scene and proved to be reluctant actors).

Surfacing in a nearby street, Bond, Kerim and Tatiana leap into a waiting car leaving behind them the chaos which is still raging around the embassy building. Their destination is the railway station and when they arrive they discover that their train, the Orient Express, is just pulling out. Kerim jumps on but Tatiana holds back . . . she has just seen two Russian agents sitting at a nearby table, and they have recognized her. Bond pushes her into the train but they are followed by one of the agents who just manages to scramble on board. Then the camera remains stationary as the rest of the train goes past, until we glimpse Donovan Grant in the last carriage. As the carriage goes by, he slides his window shut with an air of finality.

For a while, the mood on the train is one of relief. The dangers now seem to be behind Bond and his friends and they all relax, unaware that the most terrible menace of all is riding on the train with them. Tatiana is particularly pleased when she discovers that she and Bond are now Mr. and Mrs. Somerset, and even more pleased when Bond shows her the trousseau he has bought for her, which seems to consist entirely of nightgowns. She's more than willing to play the part of the new bride all the way, but Bond manfully resists for the time being. He has other problems on his mind.

Before long, Kerim has spotted the Russian agent and tells Bond. They decide to pay him a visit. Leaving the Russian trussed up and in Kerim's voluble company, Bond returns to Tatiana, who is still trying on nightgowns. At this point Bond's resolve gives way and the scene discreetly fades out . . . (Despite the aura of sex that surrounds the Bond films, the makers have always been careful with their love scenes. No bare breasts, nothing explicit, in fact naught to prevent the films from being awarded an "A" certificate. An "X" would, of course, drastically reduce the size of the potential audience. This also applies to the violence.)

The next scene shows the couple lying almost fully dressed in each other's arms. During a bit of playful banter about what they'll do when they reach England they are interrupted by a knock on the door. The steward has some bad news for Bond. Making sure that Tatiana has locked the door, Bond follows the steward to the compartment where Kerim was guarding the Russian. He finds both men dead.

"They apparently fought and killed each other," says the steward. Bond seemingly agrees, and pays the steward to keep quiet about it until the train reaches Trieste.

Returning to his own compartment, he gives the startled Tatiana a slap across the face and then shakes the truth out of her. She admits to working for Klebb but swears that she didn't know that Kerim would be killed. Bond is now in an awkward position. Without Kerim he is going to have difficulty in getting the Lektor across the Yugoslav border. Now he is going to have to arrange a different escape route.

62

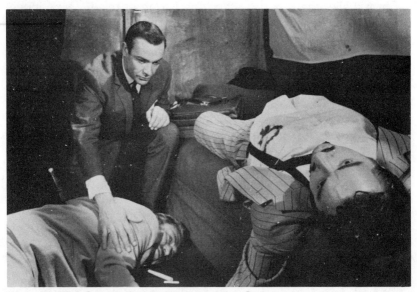

Kerim and the Russian lay dead aboard the Orient Express.

At Belgrade station, Bond alights from the train and walks along the platform, looking for one of Kerim's sons whom he knows will be there to find out why they did not leave the train earlier as planned. Walking parallel to him along the carriages we see the menacing figure of Grant. This scene cleverly reverses the usual method of shadowing someone. Here it is Bond, the prey, who is shrouded in gloom while his follower is illuminated by the lights of the carriage.

Bond finds Kerim's son, explains the situation to him and asks him to contact British headquarters and have them send someone from the Yugoslav branch to meet the train at the next stop. Nearby, Grant overhears every word.

At the next station, Grant leaves the train before Bond and quickly locates the British agent. We see him offer the agent a cigarette, part of the recognition code, then he ushers him into a nearby men's toilet. Before he follows him inside, Grant pauses to pull on his black glove. When he reappears, he is carrying the agent's briefcase and wearing his hat.

By now Bond is also on the station platform looking for the agent. Shaw approaches him hesitantly, then offers him a cigarette. We don't hear what they say but Bond seems satisfied and shakes his hand.

Later, in Bond's compartment, Grant introduces himself.

"My name's Nash. Captain Nash," he says. This is the first time we have heard Grant speak in the film and Shaw does an excellent job in making his voice sound suitably distinctive. It's a kind of pseudo upper-class whine that makes Grant seem even more unpleasant than he looks. He also calls Bond "old man" several times and we can see that it grates on our hero. The real crunch comes in the dining car when Bond, Tatiana, and Grant are having a meal together. Grant commits the ultimate social blunder of ordering red wine with his fish! Bond's nostrils start to flare immediately. Then Grant does something even more suspicious . . . he drops a pill in Tatiana's drink.

After they have carried the doped girl back to her compartment Bond pulls a gun on Grant and demands to know what he was doing. "Easy, old man," replies Grant calmly, "My escape route is only for one, you know. Do you want the Lektor or the girl?" Grant pulls a map out of his pocket and spreads it over one of the seats. "Take a look . . . this is what I've planned . . ." he says. Bond foolishly puts his gun away and bends down to have a closer look, thoroughly deserving the blow on the back of the head that Grant gives him.

As Bond lies stunned on the carriage floor, Grant quickly searches him, removing his gun and cigarette case (a nice touch this, as it was with the latter item that Bond saved his life in the book). When Bond regains consciousness, the obsequious Captain Nash has disappeared . . . in his place is SPECTRE's dread executioner at his most awesome. Shaw gives a stunning performance here, unleashing all the pent-up menace that he has been suggesting throughout the film.

"Red wine with fish," mutters Bond, "I should have known." "You may know the right wines but you're the one on your knees," replies Grant coldly. Grant tells Bond how he's been used and shows him the reel of film taken of him and Tatiana. Bond is disgusted and accuses SMERSH of being a really sick collection of minds to have thought up such a thing. "Not SMERSH," says Grant with a smile. Realization dawns on Bond. "Of course . . . SPECTRE! And what lunatic asylum did they get you out of?" he asks Grant. This question touches one of Grant's sore points and he strikes Bond viciously across the face. He is really angry now. "The first bullet won't kill you," he snarls, "nor the second, nor the third. Not until you crawl across the floor on your stomach and you kiss my *foot!*" Never before or since has the cinematic James Bond been in such a precarious situation. Grant is such a terrifying creation that for once we feel that Bond is in real danger. All the other tight spots of his screen career seem frivolous in comparison.

Grant draws on his black glove and screws a silencer onto his gun. This is it. But Bond stalls for time by asking if he can have a last cigarette. No chance, Grant tells him. Not even if I pay for it, asks Bond. Grant is interested. With what, he asks. There are gold coins in that briefcase, says Bond, indicating the luggage rack. Grant gets up and carefully pulls the case down. He tosses it to Bond. You open it, he says. Bond does so, and withdraws the strip of gold coins. What's going on, we wonder. Has Bond lost his opportunity to use the tear gas bomb? No, because there are two briefcases—Grant has the one he stole from the real Captain Nash. Grant asks whether there are more coins in the other case.

"I would imagine so," replies Bond, "it's a standard kit." "Let me have a look," he says with a display of eagerness. But Grant, instantly suspicious, orders Bond to push the case over to him. "*I'll* open it," he says. He does so, the grenade explodes in his face and all hell breaks loose.

In the book, in one of Fleming's more gruesome pieces of writing, he has Bond dispose of Grant by stabbing him in the crotch with a concealed knife. Not that Grant expires that easily. Despite losing a vast amount of blood as a result of a punctured artery, he still manages to give Bond some bad moments until he is shot several times in the face with a copy of *War and Peace* (the book has a gun in the spine).

The film version is less bloody, but much more violently mobile. It comprises one of the best staged fights ever shown on the screen and lasts for at least two minutes. After the gas bomb explodes, Bond grapples with Grant trying to disarm him. The gun goes off and the compartment is plunged into semi-darkness. During the furious struggle, which takes them into the next compartment, Bond finally manages to disarm Grant but his troubles are far from over. They both go crashing back into the other compartment where Grant succeeds in wrapping the wire from his watch around Bond's neck. The plot has come full circle, for, as we remember, this was how he disposed of the bogus Bond in the beginning of the film. As Bond is slowly choked to death he reaches out frantically for one of his briefcases. His fingers scrabble for the secret catch and—suddenly he has a knife. The gadgets have once more come to his aid.

By plunging the knife into Grant's arm Bond is able to free himself from the deadly wire and manages to wind it round Grant's own neck. A few hefty pulls later Grant is dead, killed by his own insidious device. Those who take up the wristwatch, perish, etc. (If any Australian readers are wondering why they can't remember seeing these scenes, the answer is that the censors cut out practically all of the fight sequence.)

65

This was the real climax of the book and, despite all that follows, is also the real climax of the film. Such was the awesome presence that Grant possessed, that with his death the film loses most of its menace. The remaining dangers in *FRWL* that Bond faces are spectacular but seem to be mere fun and games.

After the fight, Bond drags the still drug-dazed Tatiana out of bed and they both leave the train, which has been forced to stop due to a truck stalled across the rails. The truck is part of SPECTRE's escape route for Grant but Bond has other plans for it. Quickly disabling the driver, by slamming the bonnet on his head, he throws the girl in the back and away they go.

Bond gives "Red" Grant a taste of his own medicine . . .

. . . and strangles him with his own lethal wristwatch device.

The next morning a helicopter appears above the speeding truck. A *black* helicopter so we know what that means. SPECTRE is checking up on things. One of the crew leans out and, through a loudspeaker, orders the truck to stop. When the command is ignored, the helicopter starts dropping grenades until finally Bond is forced to halt the vehicle. Leaving the girl hidden under the truck, he charges off over the hills carrying the Lektor and his folding rifle in an attempt to draw them away. In a series of scenes reminiscent of the famous crop-dusting sequence in *North by Northwest,* Bond is chased by the helicopter, which makes several hair-raising swoops in an attempt to hit him. Eventually Bond reaches two slabs of rock that form a convenient shelter. Quickly he assembles his rifle and, as the helicopter hovers overhead like a large, black insect, he aims upwards. At the precise moment when one of the crew is about to drop another grenade, Bond fires and hits the man in the shoulder. The grenade rolls away inside the helicopter. There is panic among the two crew members, but it's too late. The machine explodes in flames.

68

SPECTRE bombs Bond's escape truck.

Another close shave

On returning to Tatiana and the truck, Bond comments dryly, "I think one of their aircraft is missing...." (One of their aircraft actually *was* "lost" while filming that sequence in Scotland; it fell into a loch.)

Meanwhile, back at the yacht, Blofeld is not amused and has summoned his two erring employees before him. You failed, he tells them. Kronsteen is unperturbed. The plan was perfect, he tells Blofeld, it was Klebb's choice of material that caused the trouble. Blofeld touches a button on his desk and the hulking Morzeny (Walter Gotell again) enters the cabin. You know the price of failure, snarls Blofeld.

Morzeny stops beside Klebb and we get a close-up of the boots he's wearing. He clicks them together and a tiny blade springs out of one of the toes. Klebb looks very nervous. The giant swings back his foot, then abruptly turns and kicks Kronsteen in the shin. Poor Kronsteen dies with a very surprised expression on his face, and as he crumples over Blofeld's desk the head of SPECTRE murmurs, "Someday we must invent a faster-acting poison." (This was to be another popular device of the makers and was used again in the following films, though the actual methods varied each time.) Blofeld tells Klebb, who is wiping her forehead with relief, that it's now up to her to recover the Lektor. Blofeld has promised delivery to the Russians and SPECTRE never fails to honor its commitments.

Bond and Tatiana exchange the truck for a high-speed launch, which is also part of the late Grant's escape machinery. Dumping the truck driver overboard, they speed off into the Gulf of Venice.

Tatiana (Daniela Bianchi) and Bond flee from the
SPECTRE fleet.

The SPECTRE fleet burns.

Again all their troubles seem over, but SPECTRE is still waiting to pounce. This time the danger comes in the form of a flotilla of speed boats (black, of course) full of men armed with machine guns and grenade launchers. The ensuing chase is not only exciting but full of those little touches that make a Bond film distinctive. For example, the men on the SPECTRE boats are acting as if they were on some sort of training exercise. In the lead boat, Morzeny gives them instructions over a loudspeaker, such as "Spectre number three, Spectre number three! You're firing too close! Aim to straddle! Aim to straddle!"

When the spare fuel tanks on Bond's boat are punctured by machine gun fire he lets them fall into the sea and then halts the launch and raises his hands in surrender. The training master orders his fleet to halt also and yells to Bond to prepare for a boarding party. Bond's answer is to snatch up a flare pistol and fire it into the fuel-coated water which results in a series of explosions and a floating inferno. It's a very spectacular sequence and was the work of effects man John Stears and his team. The water around the boats was prepared with plastic bags full of petrol (each bag held about five gallons) that were moored just below the surface. At a given signal all the bags were ignited simultaneously by means of an electrical impulse—the bags exploded out of the water and covered the surface with burning fuel. All the boats were fireproofed but things got a little out of control and two of the boats actually caught fire (the close-ups of the burning boats, and burning men, were shot later in a studio tank at Pinewood).

We next see Bond and Tatiana safely installed in a Venice hotel . . . . But there is more danger yet to come. While Bond is talking on the phone, the door opens and a maid enters. She looks suspiciously like Rosa Klebb (Bond has apparently wiped out all of her underlings so the old girl is forced to step in herself). Tatiana instantly recognizes her boss but Klebb gestures for her to be silent, and Tatiana's former training wins out. She says nothing. Klebb picks up one of the waiting suitcases, then the cipher machine. Bond notices her at this point and tells her to leave the Lektor where it is. Klebb's reply is to whip out a very large revolver. Bond finally realizes who she is.

Motioning the girl out of the room, Klebb slowly backs towards the door, the gun levelled at Bond. Then, as she is about to squeeze the trigger, Tatiana saves the day by knocking the gun out of her hand. Her new loyalties to Bond and Free Enterprise have triumphed over her old ones. But Klebb is not finished yet. Spitting and snarling, she launches herself at Bond, frantically trying to kick him with her spiked shoes. Bond pins her against the wall with a chair but has a rough time until Tatiana obliges him for the second time by shooting her ex-boss with her own revolver. With a choked cry, Klebb sinks to the floor . . . .

"She's had her kicks," says Bond. He can afford to be funny now. In the book, it was very different: Klebb succeeds with her poison shoes and it is Bond who slides, presumably dead, to the floor, although Fleming was obliged to resurrect him for *Dr. No*. (Lotte Lenya recently told an interviewer that ever since she appeared as Klebb, the first thing people do on meeting her is look at her shoes.)

We leave Bond and Tatiana, safe at last, floating down a Venice canal in a gondola and with Bond committing *that* roll of film to the water. What Blofeld's reaction is to it all we never find out.

"She's had her kicks"

Harold Sakata as Oddjob, Goldfinger's fanatical
manservant

5

Goldfinger

Goldfinger represents the peak of the series. It is the most perfectly realized of all the films with hardly a wrong step made throughout its length. It moves at a fast and furious pace, but the plot holds together logically enough (more logically than the book) and is a perfect blend of the real and the fantastic. It is full of sly humor but the humor doesn't detract from the excitement as it does in the more recent Bonds. It is also the most visually attractive of the films; the central theme of gold seems to pervade every scene, giving it a distinctive motif that the other films have lacked.

Goldfinger also has two of the best villains, two of the most attractive women, one of composer John Barry's best scores, and a very witty and clever script by Richard Maibaum and Paul Dehn. The new Bond director Guy Hamilton must also share the credit. His contribution included a smoother and more sophisticated visual style, while at the same time his predilection for juvenile humor was more or less kept under control (it was his idea for Bond to make his first appearance wearing the stuffed seagull on his head), though this was not to be the case when Hamilton returned to the series later on. The only fault with *Goldfinger* is the increasing proliferation of gadgets and a couple of sequences that don't quite work (such as the aerial raid on Fort Knox) and some clumsy special effects.

The problem is that after *Goldfinger* there was nothing new that could be done with James Bond and his world. From then on, it was a case of the makers being forced to repeat the formula again and again, only making it more lavish each time. But I will discuss this aspect of the films more fully in a later chapter.

The excellent pre-title sequence is almost a complete Bond epic in itself. It has no relevance to the actual plot, but that doesn't matter. It is still great fun to watch. It begins with Bond rising out of the murky waters of a little harbor wearing a scuba outfit and the above-mentioned stuffed seagull. Disposing of the seagull, he climbs on to the wharf and, by means of a gun that fires a grappling hook with an attached rope, quickly scales a nearby wall. On the other side is a refinery . . . and a guard. The guard hears a noise, glances up and sees Bond hurtling down towards him. Leaving the guard sprawled on the ground, Bond makes for one of the storage tanks. He kneels at the base of it, fumbles with a hidden switch and a panel suddenly swings open. The next moment we find ourselves in a bizarrely designed room (a typical Ken Adam room, I might add, with the inevitable sloping ceilings, forced perspectives, and the overall influence of German Expressionism). But Bond doesn't seem surprised by his strange surroundings and heads straight for a row of drums marked nitro-glycerine. First, he squeezes a tube of plastic explosive across them, then inserts a detonator with a timing device attached.

We next see him coming back over the harbor, and we laugh as he peels off his wet suit to reveal a white dinner jacket beneath it. And laugh again when he inserts a handy red carnation into his lapel. A nice visual joke that captures perfectly the whole James Bond persona and its appeal.

But the fun is not yet over. Impeccably dressed now, Bond enters a nearby night club. No sooner has he given the scantily dressed dancer an appraising look, than the refinery explodes. As panic breaks out around him, Bond walks unconcernedly to the bar where he has a muffled conversation with a man who tells him he must leave Latin America immediately before the heroin producers, whose establishment he has just blown up, take their revenge. But Bond, as usual, has some unfinished business to attend to.

This particular piece of business is in the bath when he arrives. She soon gets out though and, wrapped in a towel, passionately embraces Bond. Ouch, she says, and complains about Bond's gun which is sticking into her. He obligingly removes his shoulder holster and hangs it by the bath. Why do you wear that thing, she asks. I have a slight inferiority complex, he tells her. They embrace again, but there is another interruption. This time in the form of a man who appears from behind the wardrobe and advances on Bond with an upraised club. Bond, while gazing into the girl's eyes, sees him reflected in her pupils. He swings her round just as the attacker whirls his club and she catches the full impact. An enjoyable fight follows which ends with the man falling into the bathtub. Bond is amused . . . until the man starts to reach for Bond's gun which is hanging nearby. The situation calls for quick thinking and action, so Bond plucks up an electric heater and tosses it into the bath, just as the man is aiming the gun. Some seconds of sizzling and screaming later the man is dead. Bond picks up his gun and replaces his shoulder holster. He looks into the bath. "Shocking," he comments. "Quite shocking."

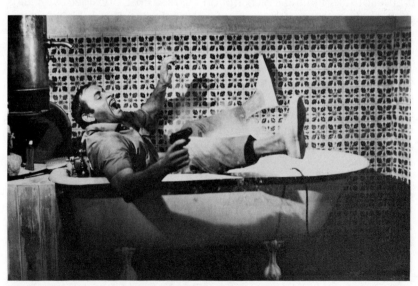

Pre-credit sequence in **Goldfinger:** Bond's assailant dies of electric shock.

The film proper begins with an aerial view of Miami. The camera swings over the city and beach, concentrates on one hotel and zooms in. We see a man, looking incongruous in a business suit amid all the naked flesh lolling around the hotel pool, watching a pair of ice skaters. It turns out to be Felix Leiter, Bond's old friend, this time played by Cec Linder. This is not a very satisfactory piece of casting, and in fact Leiter has never been properly portrayed in any of the films. (Rik Nutter in *Thunderball* came close to capturing some of the boyish charm that Fleming gave him but the script made him out to be a rather insipid character.) Leiter finds Bond lying near the pool and being massaged by, of course, a girl whom Bond introduces as Dink. As it's time for man-talk, Dink is sent scurrying away. Leiter tells Bond of his next assignment which concerns a man called Auric Goldfinger. "Sounds like a French nail

varnish," comments Bond. Conveniently, Goldfinger himself materializes at that moment at the top of some nearby steps. As Goldfinger, Gert Frobe is superb. A huge mass of a man, he fits marvellously Fleming's description of his most outrageous villain, even to the extent of having a football-shaped head. He is somewhat larger than Fleming's version, who was only five feet tall, but one can easily overlook that.

Leiter tells Bond that Goldfinger is suspected of smuggling large quantities of illegal gold about the world but that no one has any idea just how he does it. Bond's job is to find out. Then Leiter indicates the man whom Goldfinger has just joined at a table. Goldfinger, explained Leiter, has been beating this man consistently at cards for several days and won a considerable amount of money in the process.

Suspicious, Bond wanders over to the two men and casually observes them. It doesn't take long before he is looking up at the hotel that looms behind them with a knowing smile on his face. We next see Bond walking along one of the hotel corridors. He stops outside a door, grabs the master key from the waist of a passing maid, and opens it. "You can't go in there," protests the maid, "that's Mr. Goldfinger's suite." "I know," says Bond and gives her a smile that settles all her misgivings. Breaking and entering has never been so easy. . . .

On the balcony of Goldfinger's suite he finds a girl equipped with binoculars, a two-way radio and a very small black bikini.

"The name's Bond . . . James Bond," says Bond as he seats himself beside her and peers through the binoculars. As he suspected, he finds that they're focussed on the card hand of Goldfinger's opponent. All is clear.

The girl is Jill Masterson, played by the extremely beautiful Shirley Eaton, an actress who has been wasted for years by providing decoration in endless mediocre British comedies. Though Jill is an employee of Goldfinger's, she's immediately prepared to switch her allegiance to Bond. It must be the way he smiles.

Goldfinger receives a shock when he hears Bond's voice coming over his receiver, and an ever bigger shock when Bond tells him that now he's going to find out what it feels like to lose. There is a huge close-up of Goldfinger's face as he rages silently. Then Bond breaks the contact and Goldfinger is left on his own. To his opponent's delight he starts to lose almost at once. We have a last view of Goldfinger choked with anger and venting his rage on his ball-point which he breaks in half.

Goldfinger (Gert Frobe) enjoying his favorite hobby—cheating

Bond and the girl have by this time discovered they share a mutual attraction and arrange to meet later in Bond's bedroom for "dinner" (when you lead as hectic a life as Bond does you can't afford to waste time with ceremony). Which is where we next see them, Bond wearing the bottom of a pair of pajamas, Jill the top. But when Bond discovers that the bottle of champagne has lost its chill he manages to tear himself away from the bed and the delightful Miss Masterson to fetch another bottle. "There are some things one just doesn't do, and one of them is drinking Dom Perignon '53 above a temperature of 38 degrees fahrenheit. It's like listening to the Beatles without ear-muffs." (Which gives an interesting insight into Bond's musical tastes.) As he is opening the refrigerator door, he is suddenly felled by a mysterious blow on the back of the neck. When he finally regains consciousness and staggers back into the bedroom he receives a nasty shock.

Bond and Jill Masterson (Shirley Eaton) share pajamas and a quiet moment.

Lying face down across the bed is Jill, covered entirely in gold paint—and dead. (The cause of her death, we learn later, is skin suffocation.) This sequence is both eerie and surreal with the gold of the girl's body reflected by the yellow walls of the dimly lit set.

The location then changes to London, and M's office where Bond is receiving a reprimand from his boss. The usual games with Miss Moneypenny are reserved for a later stage as the mood is still a sombre one. M is critizing 007 for becoming emotionally involved in the case and warns him that 008 will replace him unless he adopts the proper attitude. Bond grudgingly agrees and M tells him of an appointment they have with the President of the Bank of England to discuss Mr. Goldfinger's activities.

The meeting, which takes place over an incredibly long table (Ken Adam decided that the President's real table wasn't impressive enough and enlarged it somewhat for the film) is amusing. Bond upsets M by displaying another facet of his expertise, this time with a bottle of brandy. The sequence also serves to fill us in on Goldfinger's background. He is, we learn, a bona fide gold dealer which permits him to transfer certain amounts of gold between countries. But the Bank of England suspects that he is shifting much more than the permitted amounts, and as this constitutes a danger to the economy, they would like him stopped. The Bank President even has a suggestion as to how Bond might infiltrate into Goldfinger's confidence . . . with a bar of gold recovered from a famous Nazi hoard sunk in a lake in Switzerland. The President hands the bar to Bond who appears eager to fondle it, but M takes it from him saying dryly, "You can pick it up from Q Branch in the morning, with the rest of your equipment." This gives us the opportunity to see the inside of Q Branch for the first time and it bears an uncanny resemblance to the SPECTRE training camp in *From Russia with Love.* Machine guns are being fired to test bulletproof jackets and parking meters are spurting teargas in the background as Major Boothroyd, henceforth known as Q, shows Bond his new bag of tricks (variations on this sequence have been featured in almost every Bond film since). Bond treats the antics with the amused contempt they deserve, especially when Boothroyd shows him his new car, an Aston Martin that has been fitted with everything from twin machine guns to an ejector seat.

"An ejector seat!" exclaims Bond when he learns of the latter modification, "you must be joking!"

"I never joke about my work, 007," replies Boothroyd, deadpan.

Bond next meets Goldfinger at a golf course where he arranges to have a game with him. Here, for the first time, he sees Oddjob, a massively built oriental dressed in morning suit and top hat. Oddjob, Goldfinger's manservant, is played with convincingly bland menace by Harold Sakata, though perhaps the term "played" is inappropriate.

Oddjob demonstrates his hat-throwing ability.

The golf game was a highlight of the book, golf being one of Fleming's chief interests, and occupied an entire chapter. Less attention is devoted to it in the film, but it remains an entertaining metaphor for the struggle between the two men that will be played out in more violent terms later in the film, as well as providing (as it did in the novel) insights into the character of Goldfinger, who looks incredible in his huge pair of plus fours (such a low-key interlude would, of source, be out of the question in one of today's Bond films). There's an amusing scene during the game when Bond displays his gold bar, by dropping it on the green just as Goldfinger is about to putt. Instead of falling in to the hole Goldfinger's ball curves around the bar. The gold has the desired effect of whetting Goldfinger's appetite and he suggests that they raise the stakes to cover the value of the bar. Bond is forced to agree.

But Goldfinger is out-cheated by Bond and loses the game. Handing over a cheque for £5,000 to Bond he also gives him a less than subtle warning. On Goldfinger's command, Oddjob removes his hat and sends it spinning towards a piece of sculpture standing near the clubhouse wall. There is a resounding clunk and the statue's head falls to the ground. Bond asks Goldfinger what the club secretary thinks of such behavior.

"Oh, nothing much, Mr. Bond," Goldfinger replies, "I own the club."

Bond receives another demonstration of just how dangerous these men are when he tosses to Oddjob the golf ball he has used to cheat Goldfinger. "Thought you might like this," he says pleasantly. Oddjob, who is sitting in the driver's seat of Goldfinger's yellow Rolls-Royce, catches the ball then proceeds to crush it with one hand. He wipes off the sticky remains and drives away. Bond appears suitably impressed, but he has also managed to secrete a small transmitting device in the boot of the car, which means he can track it by means of a direction finder installed in his dashboard.

When Goldfinger has his car shipped across to the continent, Bond follows with his Aston Martin. After a very scenic drive across the Swiss Alps, unbroken by any incident apart from Bond being overtaken by a girl in a sports car, Bond halts on the side of a hill to observe Goldfinger and Oddjob, who have stopped further down the road to buy refreshments. A shot rings out and Bond, thinking it was meant for him, returns hurriedly to his car. As he roars down the road he sees ahead of him the girl in the sports car. He gives chase and finally catches up with her on a straight piece of road. At the touch of a switch on his control panel, a spinning set of scythes emerge from his wheels. They rip into the girl's tires and send her car crashing out of control.

Bond is all innocent surprise when he goes to see if she is all right. A double blow-out, he exclaims, I've never seen one of those before. The girl has only suffered a blow on the head. She is not very friendly and seems resistant to the Bond charm. Bond notices that she is carrying a case similar to those used for sporting rifles. But he drops her at a nearby service station before returning to the pursuit of his quarry.

He tracks Goldfinger to a huge factory situated at the base of a tall hill. It is emblazoned with the sign: AURIC ENTERPRISES, so it must be the right place (it pays to advertise, even if you are a master criminal). Night falls and we see Bond creeping down the hill towards the factory. Successfully avoiding the groups of oriental guards dressed in green and yellow uniforms who are patrolling the area (some critics at the time, confused at finding these Koreans in the middle of Switzerland, accused the film of racism), he penetrates the factory perimeter.

Peering through a window, Bond spots Goldfinger giving an important-looking oriental a tour of his establishment, the main point of interest being Goldfinger's Rolls-Royce, which is being dismantled and melted down. The various parts are made of solid gold, you see, which is how Goldfinger was smuggling his stuff in and out of countries. Bond also overhears the words "Operation Grand Slam" mentioned during their conversation, but is forced to retreat soon after that.

Back on the hill, he stumbles across another black-garbed figure, this one lying in the grass with a rifle. Bond struggles with the person, but while doing so the rifle barrel touches an alarm wire, alerting Goldfinger's guards. Then he discovers that the person he's fighting with is none other than the girl he'd just met. He remembers her initials on the rifle case . . . TM: Tilly Masterson, Jill's sister, and she was trying to kill Goldfinger, not him.

But they have no time to talk any further as Goldfinger's guards have arrived on the scene. He and the girl make a dash for his car. Bond disposes of the one hapless guard he encounters by shoving him head-first into the side of the car. Then they roar away. The ensuing chase through the forest gives Bond the opportunity to use all his car's various gadgets. First a smoke screen that diverts one of the pursuing cars into a tree, then an oil slick that sends another car plunging in flames down the side of the hill and into the side of the factory. All very spectacular. But there still seems to be an endless supply of cars following them, and finally they run out of road, which forces Bond to stop. He raises the rear bullet-proof screen, then tells the girl to be ready to run for the trees when he gives the word. During the gun battle he hells, "Now!" and Tilly runs for cover. But another car has arrived, this one containing Oddjob. He sees Tilly, takes off his hat, and the next instant Tilly is lying dead (though without a mark on her).

Seeing this, Bond stops firing, gets to his feet and walks over to her body. In silence, he is surrounded by the beaming Oddjob and his men and led back to his car. What follows is somewhat implausible: despite knowing how dangerous Bond is, they let him drive his own car to the factory, with only one guard accompanying him. Now that's asking for trouble!

With Bond's car wedged in the middle of the convoy, the cars enter the factory grounds, passing through a barrier operated by a sweet-looking old lady who smiles at Bond enticingly as he passes. He doesn't seem too flattered by her attention. Then as the cars approach the complex of buildings, Bond makes his next move. He swerves the car violently around, at the same time engaging the seat ejecting mechanism. His guard, wearing a very startled expression, disappears through the roof.

A really mad car chase follows, resembling at times something out of a Mack Sennett comedy, with cars roaring in and out of the narrow lane ways that intersect Goldfinger's factory (actually the passages between the Pinewood sound stages). Bond tries at one point to burst through the barrier but is forced to retreat when the "sweet old lady" waddles out with a sub-machine gun and sprays his windscreen with bullets.

Eventually, Bond is dazzled by his own lights reflected in a mirror attached to one of the buildings and he crashes into a wall. The Aston Martin, and all the gadgets, are reduced to a pile of wreckage from which Bond falls out limply when Oddjob, wearing a wide grin, opens the car door.

Bond regains consciousness to find himself in a pretty tight situation. He is spread-eagled on a table over which is suspended a strange and menacing device. He is in some kind of laboratory. There are white-coated technicians everywhere and a good deal of electronic equipment. Also present is Goldfinger and the Chinese-looking gentleman that Bond saw him talking to earlier.

86

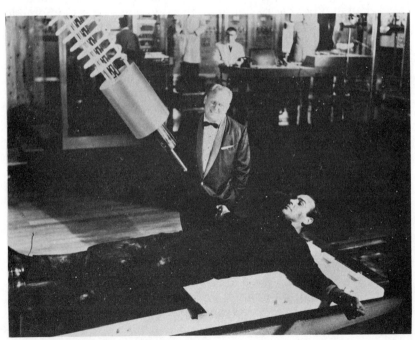

Bond is threatened by a laser.

Goldfinger is amused by Bond's activities and thinks that the car was a really funny piece of equipment. He knows who Bond is, even calls him 007, but doesn't seem worried that the Secret Service are after him. He starts to tell Bond about the device hanging over him. It is, we learn, an industrial laser. A technician activates it and it bursts into glowing life, looking like something out of an old science fiction film. It starts to burn a line along the table between Bond's legs.

This is a very tense sequence, playing as it does on the basic male fear of castration. But I thought the book version was more effective . . . there Bond's manhood was threatened with a circular saw. There is something much more frightening about whirring metal teeth than an insubstantial-looking laser beam. (These scenes are slightly spoiled by lapses in the continuity between the close-ups and the long shots.) Not that Bond doesn't appear just as worried in the film as he did in the book. "If you kill me," he tells Goldfinger, "008 will replace me."

"I trust 008 will have better luck than you," replies Goldfinger.

"You expect me to talk, Goldfinger?"

No, Mr. Bond, I expect you to *die!*" And Goldfinger walks away, leaving Bond to the laser. But Bond has one last, desperate card to play. And, appropriately, it concerns a card-playing term.

"What about Operation Grand Slam?" he yells. This has a definite effect on Goldfinger and, after a nerve-wracking period of mumbled conversation with the Chinese gentleman, he signals for the laser to be stopped. It fades out, a mere inch or so away from the world's most famous crotch. Bond sighs with relief, but is soon faced with another threat. One of the technicians walks up to him, places the muzzle of a gun against the side of his chest, fires, and the scene slowly fades into blackness.

It is scarcely surprising to learn that Bond isn't dead. It was only a tranquilizer gun, and he wakes to find himself in a jet plane, face to face with a beautiful blonde. She tells him her name is Pussy Galore and we can hardly blame him for thinking he's dreaming. Miss Galore is none other than Honor Blackman, who used to play Cathy Gale, Steed's partner in *The Avengers* TV series before Diana Rigg. We learn that she is Goldfinger's pilot and that Bond is on his way to Goldfinger's American establishment. In the book, Pussy Galore had decidedly lesbian tendencies but not much is made of this in the film. There are a few vague hints, but nothing more. Tilly Masterson was of similar leanings; in fact, she became infatuated with Pussy in the written version. Tilly had a much larger role in the book and didn't meet her end, again via Oddjob's hat, until near the finish. (Perhaps it's a good thing that she didn't last very long in the movie as Tania Mallet, who played Tilly, was not the world's greatest actress.)

Maibaum and Dehn make at least two important improvements to Fleming's original plot, one being the reason for Goldfinger's taking Bond with him to America. In the book, he actually hires Bond as a sort of public relations man, believing him to be no more than a free-lance crook. At least in the film Goldfinger is taking no chances, if we can overlook his not doing the proper thing in the first place; that is, torturing Bond until he confessed what he knew about "Grand Slam," and *then* killing him. But a few of these implausible devices are necessary in a Bond film, or book, otherwise there would be no story whatsoever.

On landing in America, Bond is taken directly to Goldfinger's headquarters, in this case a horse-breeding ranch, and thrown into a cell. But friends are nearby. Thanks to a transmitting gadget that Bond has in the heel of his shoe, his location is known to Felix Leiter and his men.

But big things are brewing at Goldfinger's ranch. A meeting is about to take place, between several of America's top gangsters. They have all come to collect money that Goldfinger owes them, as payment for various shady jobs that they have done for him. In this sequence, both Goldfinger and the set designers put on a wonderful show. Practically the whole room is composed of moving parts— billiard tables turn into instrument panels, walls turn into maps, even the floor slides away at one point to reveal a huge diorama . . . of Fort Knox.

And this is what "Operation Grand Slam" is all about. Goldfinger plans to break into the world's richest money deposit. And his meeting with the hoods is to try and convince them that the whole thing is feasible. If they wait until the operation is completed he'll pay them $10 million each in gold, instead of the promised million.

But while Goldfinger's talking, our hero is busy again. He has broken out of his cell and is actually underneath the diorama of Fort Knox. He manages to hear quite a lot of Goldfinger's plan . . . before his feet are snatched from under him and he is sent sprawling. He is surprised to see that his attacker is none other than Pussy. "I didn't know you knew judo," he says, "we must have a few falls together sometime." But Pussy isn't that easily overcome. It looks as if the Bond charm has failed again.

Meanwhile, all the gangsters are willing to wait for their money except for one who wants it immediately. Goldfinger appears to be more than happy to oblige and orders the trunk of Mr. Solo's car to be filled with a million dollars' worth of gold. He takes leave of the other gangsters to see Mr. Solo off. The hoods discuss Goldfinger's plan in his absence and one comments that indeed Goldfinger has no real need of them any more. No sooner has he said this than steel shutters fall down over all the windows and doors, and gas starts to hiss into the room. One by one, the gangsters are overcome.

Bond is returned to his cell, oblivious to the massacre that has occurred just above him, and guarded this time by a whole horde of oriental guards. But when one of Goldfinger's men spots Felix and another CIA man on the edge of the property, Goldfinger has Bond brought outside so that they can get the impression he's being treated like a guest. Goldfinger sends Pussy to pretty herself up while he and Bond discuss his plan to break into Fort Knox. This is the other important way in which Maibaum and Dehn have improved Fleming's original. In the book, Goldfinger's plan is actually to steal *all* the gold, a feat which many have pointed out to be impossible through the sheer volume of bullion involved. But in the film, the plan is much more ingenious. Goldfinger intends planting a nuclear device inside Fort Knox and detonating it. The resulting radiation will contaminate America's gold reserves for ninety-nine years or so, thus wrecking the American economy. But the really clever part of the plot is that Goldfinger's own stocks of gold will increase in value ten-fold. Red China is behind this fiendish scheme, though why they would hire such a blatant capitalist as Goldfinger to do their dirty work for them isn't clear. They have even provided him with an atomic bomb to do the job, referred to euphemistically by Goldfinger as a "device." It's a particularly dirty one too, a mixture of cobalt and iodine, and Goldfinger warns Bond that if anything goes wrong with the operation it's likely the device will end up somewhere like the White House or the Polaris submarine pens instead.

The method of disabling the large military establishment that surrounds Fort Knox has also been altered for the better in the film. Fleming's method was to drug the local water supply but the screen alternative has Pussy Galore's team of women flyers spraying the area with nerve gas. But Bond points out to Goldfinger that the nerve gas is a deadly poison, not harmless as he told the gangsters. Goldfinger will be murdering 60,000 innocent people. To that Goldfinger merely shrugs and says, "So what? American motorists kill that many people every two years."

Meanwhile, the unfortunate Mr. Solo, the gangster who wanted to take his share of the gold and leave, has come to a sticky end. Instead of driving him to the airport, our friend Oddjob has killed him and then ensured that his body and car are completely crushed at a local wrecking yard. Bond isn't too happy when he sees the remains of the car brought back to the ranch for he had hidden one of his transmitting devices, together with a note, in Mr. Solo's pocket. But he manages to disguise his disappointment with a typical piece of 007 drollery by saying to Goldfinger, "As you said, he had a pressing engagement."

Bond and Pussy, still putting on a show for the watching CIA agents, go for a stroll round the ranch . . . and soon find themselves alone in a barn. Bond, of course, makes advances, and soon finds himself lying on his back. Pussy, the judo expert, has put him in his place. But Bond doesn't surrender so easily and, after a brief struggle, it is Pussy who finds herself sprawled in the hay. Bond quickly presses home his advantage. As the scene fades, it seems that Pussy has abandoned her lesbian tendencies for more heterosexual ones. . . .

Perhaps the real star of *Goldfinger* is Fort Knox. The full-scale replica built at Pinewood studies, which cost £250,000 to construct, must rank as Production Designer Ken Adam's most impressive achievement. Adam was allowed to inspect the real Fort Knox with-

Bond and Pussy Galore (Honor Blackman) at odds in
the hay

out being permitted inside, but as he later said, "I'm glad I didn't see
the inside. Probably very dull, concrete doors, dusty tunnels, dim
lights." He wasn't impressed with the exterior either and described it
as "just a stone pimple." But the Fort Knox he designed for the film
is completely the opposite, and the interior is extraordinary: a huge,
glittering vault piled high with stacks of gold that reach almost to the
ceiling (a physical impossibility—the gold at the bottom would soften under the weight). Whether or not it bears any relation to the
inside of the real Fort Knox is unimportant . . . this is what Fort Knox
should look like.

The aerial attack on Fort Knox is rather ludicrous. The platoons of
soldiers persist in collapsing woodenly to the ground before the gas
spraying planes are even overhead. These scenes are unfortunate
as they destroy the accumulation of suspense. By contrast, the
scenes that show Goldfinger's bogus military convoy driving
through the town towards Fort Knox are much more effective.
Bodies litter the streets, cars lie overturned at intersections and there
comes a moment of shock when we see Felix Leiter himself lying

Production designer Ken Adams' interior of Fort Knox

sprawled in his car. When the convoy reaches the gates of Fort Knox the excitement is really mounting. A pause while the gates are dynamited then the convoy is through, accompanied by a triumphant surge of music. The convoy draws up before the main doors. One of the trucks, disguised as an ambulance, backs up; there is a humming sound and the laser rises from the top. Within moments it has cut through the massive door and Goldfinger's men have entered the depository.

A helicopter arrives containing Pussy, as the pilot, Goldfinger and the bomb which disappointingly resembles a metal crate. The bomb is removed and loaded on a trolley while Goldfinger climbs up to the combination control board and opens the huge, circular vault door that leads into the interior of Fort Knox. Mr. Ling, the Red Chinese bomb expert, inserts a device which activates the bomb, and then it is wheeled inside the vault. The scene suddenly changes to Leiter's wrecked car. A geiger counter starts to click and all the seemingly dead occupants spring to life.

"The bomb's arrived," says Leiter to an army official beside him, "order your men in."

Back at the Fort, oblivious to the impending disaster, Goldfinger continues to supervise the installation of the bomb. He spares the dazzling display of gold only one feverish glance, probably conscience-stricken at having to blow it all up. As the bomb, with our hero securely handcuffed to it, is lowered in an elevator to the base of the vault, Goldfinger makes his exit. But then comes the sound of fighting from outside and he realizes that things have gone wrong. Whipping off his greatcoat and scarf, he reveals that he is wearing a U.S. Army Colonel's uniform. Swiftly, he bounds up the steps to the combination control board and sends the vault door swinging shut. On the way down the ladder, he is confronted by Mr. Ling who is understandably confused about the direction that events have taken. At that moment a group of soldiers burst in, and without a moment's hesitation Goldfinger whips out a revolver, gold-plated, and shoots Ling dead.

"They're inside the vault!" he shouts to the soldiers, "I'll try and get the door open." As they run past him he picks up a discarded machine gun and shoots them all in the back.

Trapped inside the vault is not only Bond but Oddjob and a henchman of Goldfinger's called Kisch. Kisch isn't too happy about the situation and announces his intention of defusing the bomb. But Oddjob, who has a stronger sense of loyalty, prevents him from accomplishing his objective by picking him up and throwing him over the railing. He lands, with a crunch, near Bond and Oddjob instantly realizes that he has made a mistake, for the keys to Bond's handcuffs are in Kisch's top pocket. Bond is aware of this also and starts to make his way towards Kisch's body, handicapped somewhat by having to drag the atom bomb after him. What hero in the history of cinema has ever been in such an incredible situation? Handcuffed to an atom bomb about to go off, inside Fort Knox, while a giant Korean karate expert bears down on him. . . .

Realizing, as he pounds down the stairs, that he isn't going to reach Bond, Oddjob pauses on one of the landings, sweeps off his hat and sends it skimming at Bond. Bond ducks and it slices a power cable in two on a nearby wall. Then Bond reaches the keys and frees himself . . . though he soon finds out that his problems are just beginning.

The fight between Bond and Oddjob in Fort Knox must rate as some kind of cinematic landmark. The bizarre surroundings, the incredible situation, the stolid implacability of Oddjob as he throws Bond around the vault like a rag doll, fix it in one's memory. Here Bond has more than met his match, for Oddjob is a real superman, letting gold bars bounce off his chest and merely grinning when Bond hits him across the face with a lump of wood. It's an extremely well-staged fight and the man responsible, Bob Simmons, deserves a lot of praise. But during the filming it became rather too realistic for Connery's taste. In one take, his back was injured and he walked off the set (and who can blame him?).

The climax of the fight comes when Bond picks up Oddjob's discarded bowler. At last, a flicker of apprehension appears on the smug face as Bond prepares to throw it. But when the skimming hat misses Oddjob and wedges itself between two bars set in the row that is protecting a pile of gold, his confidence returns. In Oddjob's opinion, Bond has lost his last chance, and to demonstrate the contempt he feels for his opponent, he actually turns his back on Bond as he goes to retrieve his hat. At which point, Bond dives at the broken power cable . . . scoops up a still spluttering end and jams it into the row of bars—at the precise moment that Oddjob's fingers touch his metal hat. With a scream, Oddjob expires amid a colorful display of fireworks. Sakata's eventual fall to the vault floor is also spectacular . . . straight down on his face without any attempt at breaking his fall in the usual manner. One hopes he was well padded.

But the atom bomb is still ticking away in one corner and now Bond has to try and defuse it, while outside the fight between the army and the remainder of Goldfinger's men continues. The latter are finally forced to retreat into the vault itself and soon the interior of Fort Knox is echoing with gunfire, screams, and the thud of falling bodies. All of which is ignored by Bond as he attempts to break open the bomb casing with a bar of gold. He succeeds in smashing the lock but when he opens the lid he is faced with a bewildering maze of electronic wiring and moving parts. On the side of the bomb a meter counts off the seconds ... 13 ... 12 ... 11 ... 10 ... 9 ... 8 ... Bond comes to a decision and takes hold of a handful of wires—but before he can wrench them out a hand reaches across his, touches a switch, and the bomb falls silent. The meter reads 007. Leiter has arrived just in time.

"Where's your Korean friend?" asks Leiter as the army bomb experts finish defusing the weapon. "Oh, he blew a fuse," replies Bond. Bond ask Lieter how he found out about Goldfinger's plan.

"Pussy Galore informed Washington at the last moment. She was the one who helped us switch the gas canisters. Have you any idea what made her change sides?"

Bond replies innocently, "Perhaps I appealed to her maternal instinct."

Oddjob blows a fuse—with Bond's help.

In the next scene, all is bright and cheerful as Bond boards a plane that is to take him to see the President. Leiter and friends wave farewell, the plane takes off and Bond settles back to enjoy the flight. But later, when he rings for a drink, the curtain separating the galley from the rest of the cabin is torn aside by none other than Goldfinger. Still in army uniform, and still carrying his gold gun, he is far from happy with the way things have turned out and tells Bond so in no uncertain terms. Bond, he's determined, is going to get all that's coming to him . . . right now. He takes aim but Bond diverts his attention by asking where Pussy is.

"In the cockpit, where she belongs. I shall deal with her later," he says, foolishly gesturing with his gun. Bond lunges at it and there is a fierce struggle between him and Goldfinger for possession of the gun. It goes off during the fight and the bullet shatters a window. The plane lurches and there's a whoosh of air as the cabin depressurizes violently. Bond manages to cling to a luggage rack but Goldfinger is not so fortunate, and the last we see of him is his bulky body being sucked feet first out through the broken window.

Goldfinger and Bond struggle aboard a hijacked airliner.

Fans of the book will recall that it was Oddjob who met this disturbing fate in a graphically written passage, while Goldfinger was later strangled to death by Bond. But once again I think the scriptwriters have improved on the original. The only fault with this sequence is that it is too hastily done. No explanation is made of how Goldfinger and Pussy manage to commandeer a plane in the middle of an army base. We can only assume that he deceived the authorities with his army uniform, although that hardly seems feasible when we remember that by that time he was being hunted by the whole country. Also, how did Pussy ever persuade the control tower into giving her permission for take-off? Her voice wasn't that deep.

The budget also appears to have run thin near the end of the film. The army plane is obviously the same one used earlier as Goldfinger's private jet, and even the interior looks similar. Also when the plane crashes into the sea at the climax the wires supporting the model are plainly visible. (With the exception of *Dr. No,* the model and optical effects in the early Bonds often left a lot to be desired.) Even trifling lapses like this tend to spoil one's enjoyment of the whole, and I'm surprised that the production team, usually so meticulous with such details, allowed it to occur.

Bond and Pussy, of course, escape from the plane by parachute before it crashes. The film ends with them successfully evading Leiter and friends who are searching for them in a helicopter. As Bond says while he drags Pussy into the folds of the parachute, "This is no time to be rescued."

Adolfo Celi as Largo in **Thunderball**

6
Thunderball

As I mentioned in the previous chapter, *Goldfinger* marked a turning point in the series of Bond films. Between them, the first three movies had more or less covered all the variations that were possible; after *Goldfinger*, the producers were faced with the problem of what direction to take. Money was no problem, for United Artists by this time were well and truly aware that they were linked to a superb investment and allotted a budget of £2½ million for the making of *Thunderball,* which was twice as much as the amount spent on *Goldfinger* and seven times that spent on *Dr. No*.

The producers finally decided to concentrate on making the gadgets, mechanical gimmicks, and the sets more lavish and, in doing so, more or less neglected the other special qualities of Fleming's fictional world, in particular the character of James Bond himself.

With *Thunderball,* James Bond tended to become depersonalized, turning into a sort of bland dummy whose only function was to manipulate the various gadgets and act as a catalyst to keep the whole show moving. As he became less and less a real person it became more difficult to remain involved with what happened to him. Despite all the dangers he faces in *Thunderball,* there's a strange lack of suspense in the film. This is not to say that *Thunderball* is unentertaining—in many ways it is an impressive, spectacular

Pre-credit sequence in **Thunderball:** Bond smites the "widow."

film. But in comparison to its predecessors, it suffers from being slow moving, rather disjointed, and undeniably boring in certain parts. This is despite the fact that the original Bond director, Terence Young, is back in control. Incidentally, the plot of *Thunderball,* as you may recall, was based on an original treatment by not only Ian Fleming but also Jack Whittingham and Kevin McClory. Therefore, although Saltzman and Broccoli are also associated with the production, it is McClory who receives credit as the producer.

Thunderball begins, as is the tradition, with a short pre-credit sequence. The locale for this one is a church. A funeral service is in progress and the coffin, we see, bears the initials "JB." It can't be . . . no, it isn't, for the camera pans up to reveal Bond, accompanied by a girl, watching the funeral from a balcony.

The service over, we see a woman dressed in black, presumably the widow of the deceased, enter a limousine which drives away. We follow the car on its journey until it stops in front of a large country mansion. The widow goes inside and we next see her come into a darkened sitting room. To our surprise, Bond is sitting in one of the chairs. He gets up, walks towards the woman saying, "Let me offer my condolences . . .," and then punches her straight in the mouth. Now we know that Bond has a rough way with women but this is ridiculous! All becomes clear when the "widow" pulls off her hat and veil to reveal definitely masculine features beneath. (One of stunt arranger Bob Simmons' more unusual assignments—the most difficult part, he later claimed, was learning to walk in high heels.) A fierce fight develops during which Bond receives some rather nasty punishment, especially when his opponent starts to belabor him with a poker. But Bond eventually gains the upper hand and manages to break his bizarrely dressed opponent's neck with his own poker. Leaving him lying face-down in the fireplace and, pausing only long enough to throw a handful of flowers over his body, Bond makes a hasty exit. Pursued by a horde of angry guards, Bond reaches the roof and escapes in unique fashion . . . by means of a jet pack which whisks him up and away in true Superman style.

He lands in the road where the girl we saw earlier, and his Aston Martin, wait for him. Flinging the jet pack in the trunk, they climb into the car, but, before they can drive away, the guards arrive on the scene, guns firing. Up goes the Aston Martin's rear bullet-proof screen and out of the twin exhaust pipes come two streams of water at such pressure that the gunmen are knocked off their feet. The car roars away and the credits begin to roll. . . .

Well, we can accept most that without too much strain on our credulity, except for the last scene. To be capable of squirting out that much water at such a high pressure, Bond's car would need to contain a storage tank of vast proportions. When we remember all the other infernal devices that it's supposed to contain—machine guns, ejector seats, etc., it's surprising that there is still room for the engine.

After the credits, we see a mysterious man, wearing an eyepatch, arriving at some Paris address. Despite the innocent exterior, the building is actually the headquarters of SPECTRE, who are back in business after their rest in *Goldfinger*. We follow the man through a secret panel and find ourselves in a room of typically weird Ken Adam design (low ceiling, sloping walls). This is SPECTRE's boardroom, and a board meeting is actually in progress as we enter. But, as we might expect with SPECTRE, even such a mundane occasion as this becomes the setting for some very extraordinary goings-on. As we watch, we see that a progress report on all of SPECTRE's

A board meeting at SPECTRE headquarters

recent criminal activities is being given. One by one the various members offer details of how much money their various projects (professional advice on the Great Train Robbery is included) have netted for the SPECTRE coffers. They make their reports to a man who sits partially hidden on a dais at one end of the room. We cannot see his face but as he's stroking a white cat we realize that it must be you-know-who. All goes well until the final two SPECTRE agents make their report. Blofeld, or No. One as they call him, isn't satisfied with their story. One of them has been holding back on the funds. Blofeld suggests that it is agent No. Thirteen who is responsible. "You know the penalty for such treason," says Blofeld as his finger moves towards a switch. No. Thirteen begins to look very worried indeed while, in the chair next to him, his companion appears unconcerned. But it is the latter man who is suddenly enveloped in a shower of sparks as his seat delivers a fatal electric shock. Then, amusingly, his chair slowly sinks into the floor, carrying his body from sight. The whole scene is really a repeat of the one in *From Russia with Love* when Kronsteen instead of Klebb was kicked with the poison shoe.

With the disciplinary matters completed, the meeting goes on to consider more important things. It seems that this flurry of SPECTRE fund raising has a purpose other than merely filling the pockets of the shareholders. SPECTRE is planning a big, BIG, operation and a lot of money is required to finance it. The man in charge of it all is SPECTRE No. Two, Emilio Largo, played with sinister charm by Adolfo Celi, an internationally-known actor and also a former theatre and TV director in Brazil (though his voice was dubbed).

The plan is to hijack a NATO bomber with two nuclear bombs on board and to hold the Western world to ransom. If the required ransom of £100 million-worth of uncut diamonds is not forthcoming, the bombs will be detonated in two unspecified major cities. The method of carrying out this coup is rather complicated. It involves exchanging a NATO pilot, Major François Derval, who is acting as a French observer on a British-based Vulcan bomber, with a SPECTRE duplicate. The duplicate is being hidden in a health clinic outside London called Shrublands and watched over by another SPECTRE agent, Count Lippe (Guy Doleman). But it is to this same health clinic that James Bond arrives to recuperate from the injuries he received during his recent mission in France. And that is when SPECTRE's plans start to go awry. . . .

At the clinic, Bond encounters Lippe and is immediately suspicious of a tattoo mark on the Count's wrist. Lippe isn't too happy at meeting Bond either and tries to kill him by turning up the power of Bond's traction machine. But before Bond can be fatally stretched he's rescued by pretty nurse Patricia Fearing (Molly Peters). Then he gets his revenge on Lippe by shutting him in a steam cabinet. Checking up with London, Bond learns that the mark on Lippe's wrist belongs to a secret criminal organization which prompts him to investigate Lippe's rooms. During the search, he glimpses a man entirely swathed in bandages, which makes him even more suspicious. . . .

Meanwhile Major Derval has become involved with a beautiful girl called Fiona, who in reality is the head of SPECTRE's Execution Branch. While in the middle of a passionate embrace there is a knock on his door. He goes to open it and finds himself face to face

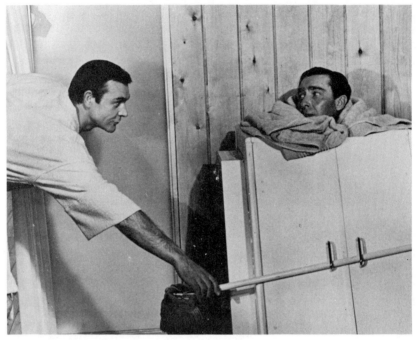

Bond traps Count Lippe in a steam cabinet.

with his own double, who shoots him with poison gas. Derval's body, wrapped in bandages, is taken to the health clinic where the verdict is given that he died of a heart attack. The gas that killed him was cyanide and therefore the symptoms are the same. But before he can be removed from the building, Bond manages to sneak a look at his face, narrowly avoiding being killed by Lippe while doing so. This whole sequence, of course, is too contrived and full of coincidences to be believable, much more so than in the original version, and I cannot understand why the writers, Maibaum and Hopkins, insisted on complicating the plot. For instance, in the book there was no double for Major Derval involved (called Petacchi in the novel) which made everything a good deal simpler. As a result much of the Shrublands sequence is dull and unconvincing, although the scenes concerning the traction machine and steam cabinet, and Bond's picturesque seduction of Patricia in the sauna room, have an undeniable appeal.

By comparison, the scenes showing the hijacking of the Vulcan bomber are very good. They have a realistic, documentary look to them, even when the model-work takes over with the landing of the plane on the sea.

Derval's double takes over the Vulcan by feeding cyanide gas into the crew's oxygen supply. When they are all dead he changes course and flies the plane to the Bahamas, landing it in the sea not far from Largo's waiting yacht, the *Disco Volante*. The *Disco Volante* carries a seemingly inexhaustible supply of frogmen and equipment and soon the sea is alive with all manner of underwater craft. A good proportion of the £2½ million budget is visible in these few scenes. The submerged Vulcan was a full-scale mock-up, fiberglass except for the cockpit which was actually taken from a scrapped V-bomber. The mock-up, which weighed twenty tons, was taken all the way to the Bahamas from England and sunk in sixty-five feet of water. It cost £50,000. The *Disco Volante* cost £100,000 to build and the underwater flying saucer and motorized sleds, designed and built by Ivan Tors Underwater Studios, absorbed almost another £20,000.

The underwater flying saucer (which actually works) is used to carry the two atom bombs away. And while his men are attending to this, Largo sees to Derval's double who has become trapped in his seat. Seeing his plight Largo draws his knife with the apparent intention of cutting him free but instead severs his air hose. The double drowns. . . .

With the bombs safely on board and the plane covered by a camouflage net, Largo sends a radio message to SPECTRE headquarters to say that all is well. Blofeld is pleased but orders the Execution Branch to take care of Count Lippe for his clumsiness in dealing with Bond at Shrublands. The scenes that follow are yet another demonstration of regular Bond special effects man John Stears's impressive skill (he won an Academy Award for his work on *Thunderball*). As Bond drives back towards London, a car, driven by Count Lippe, suddenly appears on his tail. As Lippe starts shooting at Bond, a motorcyclist suddenly looms on *his* tail. The next instant a cluster of rockets hurtle from the cycle and hit the rear of Lippe's car. It explodes and plunges off the road to crash in flames.

This very spectacular sequence was actually as dangerous to shoot as it appeared to be on the screen. Real rockets were fired from the cycle, and the car, driven by stuntman Bob Simmons, had its trunk packed with explosives. But on the first take, things went wrong. The rockets penetrated the armor shielding that had been fixed up inside the car to protect Simmons and he was forced to throw himself from the car just before it somersaulted into the air. Bravely, Simmons repeated his dangerous feat and this time the sequence was successful.

In the film, the mystery cyclist turns out to be the deadly Fiona, as we see when she later disposes of the cycle by sending it into a swamp. But as visually spectacular as the sequence is, I can't help considering it to be rather fatuous. Surely even SPECTRE wouldn't go to such outlandish lengths to kill someone. Besides which, a car being blown to bits on an English country road would tend to attract a certain amount of attention. But Bond doesn't appear to have been even delayed by the incident, nor does he consider it worth mentioning to either M or Miss Moneypenny when he arrives at headquarters.

Bond then attends a special meeting of agents held by the Foreign Secretary (Roland Culver) to discuss SPECTRE's ransom demands. Britain has only two days to decide, and the sign of acceptance is for Big Ben to chime seven times at six p.m. Back in M's office after the meeting, Bond asks to be assigned to Nassau. He has seen a photo of Major Derval and recognizes him as the dead man he saw at Shrublands. The photo of Derval, and also of his attractive sister Domino, was taken at Nassau. M reluctantly agrees and once again Bond is on his way.

When we next see Bond he is underwater, freeing the foot of an attractive girl from between two pieces of coral. They surface and the girl thanks him for saving her life. For a moment or two, it looks as if they will part . . . she climbs into her boat and Bond swims back to his, which is piloted by the lovely Paula (Martine Beswick, first seen in *From Russia with Love*). But Bond's boat has suddenly developed engine trouble, and he calls across to the girl for a lift back to the beach. She agrees and Bond is soon swimming back to her boat, leaving his in the care of Paula.

Luciana Paluzzi as Fiona, head of SPECTRE's execution
branch; below, Martine Beswick as Paula, one of
Bond's helpers in Nassau

At the beach, they are met by a surly looking character called Quist who helps secure the boat. As Bond and the girl walk up the beach, they are watched by at least another two pairs of eyes. Then comes the sound of a ship's siren and we see the graceful *Disco Volante* sliding into the harbor. On seeing the yacht, the girl immediately tells Bond that she must go. Bond asks if he can see her again, inadvertently using her name.

"How did you know my name was Domino?" she asks, suspicious.

"It's on the bracelet you wear round your ankle," he replies.

"What sharp little eyes you've got, Mr. Bond," she says as she walks away.

"Wait until you get to my teeth," mutters Bond.

Bond and Domino meet again that night at the Café Martinique, a luxurious establishment situated on the sea front. Bond also encounters Largo for the first time and becomes involved in a game of *chemin de fer* with him. Recklessly, Bond says that he senses the spectre of defeat at the table which draws a disturbed reaction from Largo. Naturally Bond wins and claims a dance with Largo's apparent possession, Domino. As they dance, it is clear that the old 007 charm is working again, but when Largo appears Domino goes meekly with him.

Next morning, returning to his hotel room from the pool, Bond plays back a small tape recorder that has been hidden in a Bible. He hears the sound of footsteps leading into the bathroom. Preparing to investigate, he is interrupted by a knock at the door. He opens it to admit a friendly looking young man who says, "Hi there, double-0 . . .". He gets no further for Bond punches him in the stomach. Leaving him doubled up, Bond continues his investigation of the bathroom. He reaches round to the hot water tap in the shower stall and turns it on. There's a shriek and a man staggers out to be hit in the face with the bathroom door. Bond then disarms him and shoves him into the bathroom. When he won't say who he works for, Bond tells him to get out.

"Sorry about that, Felix," says Bond when the man has left, "but you were about to say 007, and I didn't want our friend to hear that." The young man is none other than Bond's old C.I.A. friend,

Felix Leiter, looking much more youthful than when we last saw him in *Goldfinger*. This time he's played by Rik Van Nutter.

After leaving Bond's hotel, we see the intruder drive to a palatial house which is guarded by armed men dressed in black. One would think that a private army might attract unwanted attention to Largo's activities, but apparently this isn't so. The sprawling house is Largo's luxurious Nassau residence and his visitor finds him by one of the pools, feeding his sharks . . . (we can hardly expect a member of SPECTRE to have a normal hobby like stamp collecting. Perhaps he's trying to outdo his boss who, of course, has a predilection for collecting unusual fish). Largo is annoyed when he hears how his employee has bungled the job of investigating Bond and admonishes him in the usual SPECTRE manner . . . by having him thrown to the sharks.

Domino (Claudine Auger) with Largo at the "chemin de fer" table

During the day, Bond and Leiter go by launch for a tour of the harbor, their object being to have a look at the *Disco Volante*. But Largo's yacht looks perfectly innocent above the water line and Bond decides that he'll have to take a closer look at night.

On returning to their makeshift base of operations, Bond and Leiter find Major Boothroyd of Q branch waiting. As usual he has a wide assortment of gadgets to dispense to 007. They include a Geiger counter disguised as a camera, a radioactive pill that sends signals when swallowed, a miniature underwater camera, a motorized back-pack that is able to propel its wearer when underwater and that also fires explosive spears and, lastly, a tiny breathing device which is supposed to be an emergency air supply lasting two minutes. If Bond took to the water with that lot, he'd sink straight to the bottom. . . .

That night Bond, in scuba gear, swims out to where the *Disco Volante* is moored in the harbor and proceeds to examine its hull. He soon discovers a pair of double doors but, while he's taking a photograph, he's seen by a patrolling frogman and fired upon. The spear misses Bond but strikes the hull, which immediately sets off an alarm on the bridge. TV screens are switched on which instantly give a picture of Bond fighting with the frogman (none of this fiddling with controls to get a clear picture . . .). But the program isn't to Largo's liking as Bond quickly disposes of the SPECTRE frogman and begins to swim away. Largo orders his men out on deck and they attempt to stop Bond by tossing hand grenades on top of him. Despite being shaken by the concussion, Bond manages to keep going. Having failed with this method, Largo's men then launch a small, high-speed boat, and begin to pursue him. Of course, all Bond needed to do to escape them was to hug the harbor bottom until he was well away from the area (which is what he did in the book), but the scriptwriters allow him to surface so that he can be spotted. This provides everyone with some more exciting moments as Largo's men try to chop him up with their screw. After several near misses, he allows the propeller to hit his air tanks, then he lets them float to the surface along with his mask. This, incredibly, is enough to satisfy the SPECTRE boatmen and they return victoriously to the *Disco Volante*. One hopes Largo has them thrown to the sharks too.

After staggering up the beach, Bond heads for the road and starts thumbing for a lift. A car stops and Bond gets in, not realizing that the beautiful driver is none other than Fiona, SPECTRE's deadly killer. She gives him a fast ride back to his hotel which, by some strange coincidence, is hers also. The following day, Bond and Leiter make a helicopter search for the missing bomber but find nothing. On their way back to Nassau, Bond suggests a brief look at "Palmyra," Largo's residence. Again they see nothing of importance apart from the pool full of sharks. As they hover out at sea, they are unaware that they are being disdainfully observed by Largo and Fiona who are skeet shooting on the beach. Fiona tells Largo that Bond should be killed as soon as possible but he disagrees, considering Bond to be only a harmless snooper.

That afternoon Bond himself visits "Palmyra," having received an invitation from Largo the night before. The first thing he sees 111 after being admitted is Domino swimming in one of the pools (no, not the shark pool) but Largo soon makes an unwelcome appearance and Bond is forced to suffer while he plays the host. The conversation somehow turns to the subject of passions. "I'm not a very passionate man," Bond tells Largo with a glance at Domino. Just then one of Largo's henchmen appears with a tray of refreshments. "Ah, Vargas," says Largo, "tell us what *your* passions are . . ." Vargas, played by Philip Locke, doesn't answer but merely curls his upper lip, thus giving the impression that his passions are very bizarre indeed. This suspicion is emphasized by the clothing he wears, black from head to toe. SPECTRE needs to give lessons to its staff on the art of concealment. Dressed as most of them are, they'd attract attention in the middle of a fancy dress ball. But even the upper echelons of SPECTRE are at fault here; they all insist on wearing rings with grotesque insignia on them (a sort of octopus). Such exhibitionism can prove fatal.

At the skeet shooting range on the beach, a lightly veiled confrontation takes place between Largo and Bond, with Largo demonstrating his skill with a rifle. Though Bond claims that he is unfamiliar with firearms, Largo hands him a rifle saying, "It is not as difficult as it looks." Bond takes the rifle and immediately shoots down a hurtling target. "You're right," says Bond, as he hands the rifle back to Largo, "it *is* easy." (Originally this was followed by Largo showing

Bond over the *Disco Volante,* as happened in the novel, but the sequence was later cut before the film's release.)

That night Bond attends the Junkanoo Parade, the famed native celebration, with Domino. Back at his hotel, Paula is waiting alone in his room when there is a knock at the door. When she opens it, Vargas and Quist, followed by Fiona, burst into the room. Paula is overpowered and drugged with chloroform.

When Bond receives word from Leiter that Paula is missing, he excuses himself from Domino and makes immediate plans to investigate "Palmyra." First, he arranges with the island authorities to cut the power in that area then—dressed in black—he moves. One collapsed guard later, he is inside the grounds. He locates Paula but is too late. She has swallowed poison after being tortured by Vargas.

On the way out, Bond runs into trouble. Largo has his own power supply and Bond finds himself suddenly illuminated. Largo's men spot him but Bond eludes them by climbing over a roof, dropping his gun as he does so. Passing one of the pools he is surprised by a solitary guard. They grapple and both fall into the pool. Attracted by the noise, Largo and his men arrive on the scene but instead of doing the obvious thing, which would be to wait and see who wins the struggle in the water, Largo chooses an indirect method. Throwing a switch by the pool he causes a large metal net to slide across the surface of the water until it completely covers it. Then he opens the doors of the tunnel that connects that pool with the one containing the sharks. By now Bond has killed his opponent, by stabbing him, and the sharks enter the pool, attracted by the blood. But they fail to see Bond (not surprisingly, as they're a very drugged and dopey looking mob of fish) and he escapes up the tunnel into the other pool. Nobody is guarding this one and he is able to climb out and get away.

Arriving, exhausted, at his hotel he discovers Fiona in his bath. Recovering his strength very quickly Bond naturally takes advantage of this subtle seduction ploy. When Fiona asks Bond to hand her something to wear he gives her a pair of bathroom slippers. . . .

Bond makes love to her in an effort to persuade her to change sides; after all, this method has proved successful in the past. But later, as they prepare to leave for the Junkanoo celebrations, Bond receives a nasty surprise . . . the corridor outside is full of SPECTRE thugs. He swiftly slams the door shut, turns round and finds that Fiona is pointing a gun at him. Wisely, he accepts temporary defeat. Fiona greatly enjoys her triumph over Bond. "The great James Bond," she sneers, "outsmarted by a woman!" But Bond is ready with a cutting reply. "Do you think I enjoyed making love to you?" he asks, "I did it for Queen and country."

Bond is bundled into a waiting car and driven away, but as the streets of Nassau are jammed with people enjoying the festival, it is not long before the car is forced to come to a halt. Just then a friendly local thrusts a bottle of wine through one of the windows and offers the occupants a drink. "Tell that idiot to go away," snarls Fiona as she lights a cigarette. Bond seizes the opportunity to lash out with his foot and sends the bottle flying. Ignited by Fiona's lighter it sprays over the driver who falls, screaming, out of the car with his hand on fire. Bond leaps from the car and makes a break for freedom. Shots are fired and one hits him in the calf. But Bond manages to keep running (it was only a flesh wound, as they say).

The following chase through the Junkanoo is one of the highlights of the film. Through the twisting lines of dancing, costumed people Bond and his pursuers, consisting of Fiona, Vargas, Quist, and another heavy (they *do* stand out in a fancy dress ball) zigzag back and forth. At one point, Bond hides on one of the elaborate floats which is covered in beauty queens, but Fiona detects the trail of blood he's leaving and he is forced to move.

The chase terminates in the Kiss-Kiss night club where Bond first bandages his leg in the toilet and then joins the crowd on the dance floor. To camouflage himself he grabs a passing girl and asks her to dance with him. But as they dance there's a tap on the girl's shoulder and a voice says, "May I cut in?" It's Fiona. The girl walks away in a huff saying to Bond, "You should have told me your wife was here."

As Bond dances with Fiona, he glances about anxiously, looking for her men. He spots a couple of them on the edge of the dance floor but he doesn't see the one who has hidden behind a backdrop near the band. As the bongo drummer in the group approaches a climax in his playing, the SPECTRE man prepares to fire. But at the last moment Bond, noticing that Fiona is looking expectantly over his shoulder, spins her round, at the precise instant the gun is fired (shades of the pre-credits sequence in *Goldfinger*). Fiona receives the bullet meant for Bond and dies in his arms. Placing his hand over the bullet hole Bond carries her over to a nearby table and props her up in a chair, saying to the other occupants, "Do you mind if my friend rests here a moment . . . she's just dead." And while the SPECTRE agents retreat, leaderless, in disarray, he makes his escape.

The next day Bond and Leiter make another helicopter search for the bomber. This time they are more fortunate. Spotting a school of sharks that appear to be acting suspiciously they go down for a closer look. Landing on the water, Leiter keeps the sharks busy with a rifle while Bond, in scuba gear, goes beneath to investigate. He discovers the Vulcan under its camouflage net and enters it to see if the bombs are still on board. They are not, and Bond swims along to the cockpit where the bodies of the crew are still sitting. In the book, this scene was a real spine-chiller, Fleming's writing being at its best when describing the underwater world. With the decomposing corpses and all manner of scuttling creatures in the cockpit, Fleming managed to evoke a real atmosphere of claustrophobic horror. But the screen version is much tamer, and the bodies appear to be in better condition than many people one sees walking about the streets. Bond stays long enough to remove the false Major Derval's watch; then he returns to the surface, dodging drowsy sharks on the way (some of which are clearly anchored by lines attached to their tails).

That afternoon he and Domino have an underwater rendezvous and make rather wet love among the coral. "I hope we didn't scare the fish," says Bond as they walk through the shallows towards the beach. Then Domino steps on a sea anemone and gets a spine in her foot. On the beach, Bond obligingly removes it with his teeth. Afterwards he tells her of Largo's criminal activities and asks her help. She is unwilling at first but when he proves to her that Largo was instrumental in having her brother killed she swears that she will help Bond destroy Largo. Bond gives her the Geiger counter disguised as a camera so that she can check if the bombs are on board the *Disco Volante*. As they talk we see that the strange henchman of Largo's, Vargas, is creeping through the trees towards them. He stops at the edge of the beach, screws a silencer on the barrel of his gun and takes aim at Bond. But Bond sees him, snatches up a CO_2-powered speargun and fires. The spear hits Vargas in the chest and pins him to the trunk of a nearby palm tree. "I think he got the point," says Bond dryly.

Domino tells Bond of a secret channel near "Palmyra" where Largo's frogmen gather every night at the same time. That evening Bond joins them, after first disposing of one of the men and stealing his suit and equipment. Their target is the cave where the bombs have been hidden. Tonight they are being moved and Bond watches as they are loaded on the underwater saucer preparatory to being taken back to the yacht. But then Largo recognizes him and signals for one of his frogmen to attack him. While Bond is kept busy, the bonds are removed and Largo and his men make their exit, leaving Bond trapped behind the massive doors.

Vargas (Philip Locke) gets the point

When the bombs are on board the yacht, Domino's Geiger counter starts clicking but, while she's investigating, Largo becomes suspicious of her "camera." Discovering its true purpose, Largo drags Domino to her cabin, ties her up on her bed and proceeds to question her, with the aid of a lighted cigar and a bowl of ice cubes.

"You have given me much pleasure, Domino," he tells her, "but now I must cause you much pain." But the screen-Domino is much more fortunate than her namesake in the book who suffered extensive burns, for no sooner does Largo get down to business than he is interrupted by Professor Kutee, his tame physicist, who informs him that it is time to be moving. As Largo leaves he tells Domino, "Your position is hopeless. There is no one to rescue you."

Largo prepares to extract some information from Domino.

But wait! All is not lost. For back in the cave Bond has discovered an exit in the shape of a pot hole that leads out to a coral reef. It is too high for him to climb so he swallows his radioactive pill and sits down to wait rescue—which is not long in coming. Leiter has picked up his signals and soon arrives on the scene in a Navy helicopter which winches him up to freedom. Once on board, Bond immediately sends a radio message to alert the U.S. authorities that Miami is the first target for SPECTRE's bombs.

Next we see a plane discharging a team of U.S. Navy "Seabees" into the sky just off the Miami coast. Far below, and clearly silhouetted in the bright green water, can be seen Largo's submarine and men, looking like a school of sardines. The "Seabees," wearing red wet suits so that we can tell them apart from the SPECTRE frogmen (who of course wear black), splash down into the sea and the battle begins.

Never before have scenes involving so many people been filmed underwater; Ivan Tors Underwater Studios, veterans of TV shows such as *The Aquanauts* and *Flipper*, were faced with various unforeseen problems. The underwater battle is slow moving at first, but builds up into a breathtaking spectacle. The fight is well under way when Bond arrives on the scene propelled at high speed by his motorized back pack. Actually it makes him appear rather a clown and we can't blame the first SPECTRE frogman who spots him for staring in shocked disbelief. But the next moment Bond is roaring through the underwater battle lines like an underwater Superman, ripping off face-masks as he zooms by and causing general chaos.

The fight drags somewhat after this, while we watch Bond doing silly things with his explosive gadgets, such as severing the ropes holding up a hatch cover on a sunken wreck so that it falls conveniently on a SPECTRE frogman. This kind of thing is getting too near the comic books for my taste. One sequence is amusing though, and that is when Bond tricks two frogmen into following him inside the wreck. He exits rapidly, leaving his back pack behind to fool them, then drops a grenade through the hatch. There's an explosion and a solitary flipper comes floating up in a cloud of bubbles.

From then on, the battle picks up momentum. A drawback to filming underwater is that all movement is automatically slowed down considerably but here the combination of fast editing and Barry's exciting music succeeds in quickening the pace. The fighting, as it increases in ferocity, becomes almost an underwater ballet with the red and black forms flashing all over the screen. There's one beautiful scene when the camera, pointing up toward the surface, shows the grappling and writhing frogmen brilliantly outlined against the sunlight.

At this point, some of the local wild life are introduced to the fray so that the frogmen find themselves having to fight not only each other but also sharks and sting rays. But now the battle is almost over and the surviving paratrooping frogmen mop up the remains of Largo's force. Making his way through a sea of dead frogmen, Bond reaches Largo and his saucer carrying the bomb. But Largo hasn't given up yet. Spearing anyone in his way, he swims toward the *Disco Volante*. Bond, who has lost his face-mask during the fracas, is delayed while he grabs a replacement from a drifting corpse. Bond has also lost his air tanks and is breathing via one of those miniature mouthpieces mentioned earlier. They're only supposed to

The underwater saucer complete with hydrogen bomb

Bond struggles with one of Largo's men during the big underwater battle.

have two minutes' supply of air but this particular one must be a special model as it seems to last indefinitely.

As Bond reaches the *Disco Volante*, the screws start to turn and it begins to move off. But Bond manages to grasp a vane protruding from the hull. Up above, Largo is still having problems. It seems as if the entire U.S. Navy is after him and the shells begin to fall thick and fast around the *Disco Volante*. But Largo still has a couple of tricks up the sleeve of his wet suit. First he lets loose a smoke screen and then he orders his first mate, "Jettison the cocoon!" In a startling shot, the *Disco Volante* then separates into two sections—the cocoon-like after-section, bristling with guns, being left to fight a rearguard action, and the front section becoming a speedy hydro-foil. For this amazing scene alone, it was almost worth all the money they spent on the craft.

The aft section doesn't last very long against the Navy and is soon blown up, but the hydrofoil, with Largo and the remaining bomb on board, swiftly outdistances the pursuit craft. Largo is home free, or so he thinks, and orders champagne. But he is unaware of the familiar figure clinging to one of the hydrofoils (a pretty impressive feat, really, when one considers how difficult it would be to maintain a grip on the vane of a hydrofoil underwater). Bond hauls himself on deck and enters the cabin, much to Largo's horror. An extremely fast and frenzied fistfight takes place with Bond disposing of Largo's crew members with violent effectiveness. Unfortunately, this exciting battle is marred somewhat by the matte work on the windows showing the ocean speeding by outside. That, and a couple of speeded-up exterior shots of the *Disco Volante* skimming along, gave one the impression that the craft is about to achieve escape velocity.

120

Bond and Largo fight to the finish in the ship's wheelhouse.

Only Largo remains now and Bond is gaining the upper hand with him too, when a sudden lurch throws him off balance. When he looks up, it is to find himself staring down the barrel of Largo's revolver. Once again 007 faces certain death . . . but once again he is saved by a woman. Largo suddenly stiffens and drops his gun. He turns slowly and we see the spear sticking out of his back, then he collapses over the control panel. Behind him Domino emerges from a hatchway, followed by Professor Kutee who had set her free.

"I'm glad I killed him," says Domino.

"*You're* glad?" replies a relieved Bond.

But then the physicist announces that Largo has locked the controls as a last dying gesture and the *Disco Volante* is heading straight for a reef. Bond orders everyone to jump overboard, which they do, just before the hydrofoil ploughs straight into the reef and explodes in a colorful mass of flame and smoke. (Another skillful piece of editing here: there's a cut between the boat heading for the reef and the actual explosion.)

121

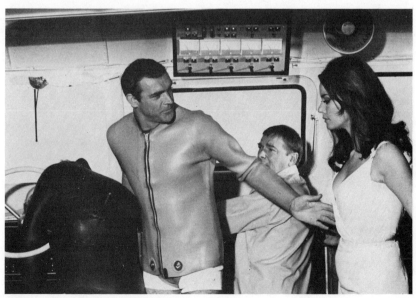

Domino has just speared Largo.

Now usually at this point in a Bond film, Bond has the chance to obtain a little peace and quiet with the leading lady. After all, in *Dr. No* he finds himself alone with Honey in a drifting boat, at the end of *From Russia with Love* he and Tatiana have a romantic gondola ride, and in *Goldfinger* he finishes the film wrapped up in a parachute with Pussy Galore. But in *Thunderball* even this modest privilege has been taken away. A plane appears overhead and dumps an inflatable raft near the couple. They enter it. Then Bond climbs into a kind of harness and releases a miniature blimp which rises rapidly into the sky. Another plane appears, this one with a strange gadget on its nose. As it nears the blimp, Bond takes firm hold of Domino, and the next moment they have been whipped out of the raft and are being winched up into the plane. How undignified!

Back at the Paris headquarters of SPECTRE, one must assume that all is not well. No doubt Blofeld is beating his head and shrieking, "On no! Not again!"

Another safe ending for Bond

Mie Hama as Kissy in **You Only Live Twice**

7

You Only Live Twice

Fleming's novel *You Only Live Twice* is a strange and bizarre book. At the beginning, we find Bond recovering from a breakdown which resulted from his wife being murdered by Blofeld at the end of the preceding novel *On Her Majesty's Secret Service*. Bond has gone to seed and good old M is prepared to throw him out of the Service, but he relents and instead sends him on a minor mission to Japan as a last chance. Here, for most of the book, Bond wanders around soaking up the atmosphere of the place and generally acting like a tourist. Not until the last third of the novel is there any real action.

A certain Dr. Shatterhand, whom the Japanese authorities want suppressed, transpires to be none other than Ernst Stavro Blofeld. But like Bond, Blofeld too has changed. No longer involved with plots to ransom the Western world, he has come to Japan more or less to retire and indulge in his hobbies. But Blofeld being Blofeld, his hobbies are a little out of the ordinary . . . he has bought an island off the Japanese coast, complete with castle, and has constructed a garden of death. The garden is full of poisonous plants, pools of man-eating fish and boiling mud holes. The object is to provide the many suicidally inclined Japanese with a variety of unusual and challenging opportunities for self-destruction. Blofeld's chief pleasure in life now is to wander through the garden dressed in full Samurai armor.

Thirsting for vengeance, Bond breaks into Blofeld's establishment but is captured by his guards. During their final confrontation Blofeld, dressed like Fu Manchu, explains to Bond that he is getting old and bored with life. "I have come to suffer from a certain lassitude of mind which I am determined to combat," he tells Bond. "This comes in part from being a unique genius who is alone in the world, without honor—worse, misunderstood. No doubt much of the root cause of this accidie is physical—liver, kidneys, heart, the usual weak points of the middle-aged. But there has developed in me a certain mental lameness, a disinterest in humanity and its future, an utter boredom with the affairs of mankind . . . ." (Fleming himself was suffering from ill health at this stage and had already had the first of his heart attacks, so it doesn't take much of an imaginative leap to suggest that Blofeld's catalogue of complaints reflected Fleming's own state of mind in 1963 when the book was written.) He then tries to dismember Bond with a Samurai sword, but instead Bond strangles him to death and then blows up his castle. The book closes with Bond, his memory gone, living in a Japanese fishing village and being cared for by a local diving girl, while back in England he's considered as dead and his obituary appears in *The Times.* Bond has symbolically died but has been reborn as a virtual innocent into a new life.

The film, *You Only Live Twice,* combines a great deal of money and impressive talent, including newcomers to the series like director of photography Freddie Young (long associated with David Lean), writer Roald Dahl, and director Lewis Gilbert (*Reach for the Sky, The Greengage Summer*), but it had little to do with either Ian Fleming or James Bond. The name was the same but the plot had been changed to protect the box office.

The budget this time was £3 million (after all, the preceding films grossed, up to 1967, a staggering total of £125 million, so United Artists weren't exactly risking the money). A million of it went on location work in Japan and it seems as if production designer Ken Adam was allocated the remainder—one set alone cost almost £400,000, which was more than the total cost of the first film *Dr. No.* As sheer spectacle, it is unsurpassed, and in many ways it is extremely impressive; but it is simply not a James Bond film. He is seen occasionally on the screen, looking weary, bored, and slightly overweight, but for most of the time the emphasis is on the sets and the machines. The machines are everywhere . . . space capsules, submarines, cars, helicopters (big and small), airplanes, rocket ships . . . they swamp the screen. As one critic remarked at the time, it was like watching an episode of TV's *Thunderbirds*. (Unfortunately this was the film on which most of the subsequent Bonds were to be modelled.)

Gone is Bond as the dark avenging angel, mainly because he has nothing to avenge as the producers have reversed the sequence of the books, making *You Only Live Twice* before *On Her Majesty's Secret Service*. Gone too is the doom-laden atmosphere of the book, gone are the garden of death, the castle, and the bored Blofeld in his Samurai gear. In its place is the plot from *Dr. No* with a mysterious island being run by SPECTRE to interfere with American space vehicles and which is eventually blown up by Bond. *You Only Live Twice* is really only a lavish re-make of *Dr. No* but despite the vast amount of money spent on the later production, *Dr. No* remains the more entertaining film. As *Time* magazine noted somberly when the film was released, "The Bonds are losing their value."

The film opens in outer space. An American space capsule orbits the Earth while one of its crew, attached by a life-line, goes for a "walk" in space. Far below in the Cape Canaveral control room, there is sudden consternation when another blip is sighted on the radar screens. Whatever it is appears to be heading straight towards their capsule. The ground technicans warn the astronauts who at first don't see anything, but then sight a strange object rapidly approaching them from the rear. As the mysterious craft draws nearer its nose opens like a petal of a giant metal flower. When the capsule is completely enclosed the nose shuts, severing the life-line of the astronaut outside the capsule. Then the mystery rocket ship heads back towards Earth. It is followed part of the way by the American radar scanners but they lose it before they can see where it lands.

Despite the mediocrity of the special effects, this sequence succeeds in evoking a mood of eeriness, especially in the scene which shows the hapless astronaut drifting helplessly away into space.

An urgent meeting between the great powers is held to discuss the matter. The U.S.A. accuses the Soviet Union of being responsible and the Soviet Union in turn accuses the U.S.A. of pulling some kind of trick. But the calm voice of the British delegate interposes and suggests that perhaps neither country is responsible. An observer in Singapore thinks he saw something go down in the Sea of Japan, and the delegate announces that their man in Hong Kong is looking into the matter at that very moment. . . .

Their man in Hong Kong turns out to be James Bond, but the only thing he appears to be looking into are the eyes of a Chinese girl with whom he is in bed. The girl, under the pretext of going to prepare some food, gets out of the bed and walks across to the doorway. Here she presses a hidden button and the bed, containing Bond, folds very rapidly into the wall. A moment later two Chinese gentlemen with machine guns burst into the room and fill the bed with bullet holes.

Next we see a police car roaring through the crowded Hong Kong streets. It stops outside the house and a squad of police race into the bedroom. The bed is lowered from the wall to reveal Bond lying in a pool of blood.

"At least he died on the job," one of the police officers comments, "he would have wanted it that way."

Being a Navy man, Bond receives a funeral with full Naval honors and we watch as his body is ceremoniously committed to the sea from the deck of a British destroyer. Wrapped in canvas his body sinks to the bottom of the Hong Kong harbor but no sooner has the mud settled than a group of frogmen appear. They retrieve the body and carry it to a submarine that is waiting nearby. Inside the sub the body is laid out on the deck and the canvas wrappings cut open. Bond, dressed in a Navy officer's uniform, opens his eyes and removes a breathing device from his mouth. "Permission to come aboard, sir?" "Granted. Welcome aboard, Commander Bond," replies the captain. This submarine turns out to be full of surprises, including M and Miss Moneypenny, both also in naval costume.

"That funeral should convince your many enemies that you're dead," says M, "Or at least keep them out of your hair long enough for you to devote your full attention to your next mission. It's a big one, 007."

M gives Bond a briefing on the situation and tells him that he must find out where the interceptor rockets are being launched from, and by whom, before the Americans launch their next capsule, which is in two days' time.

On the way out, Bond pauses to receive the password from Miss Moneypenny, appropriately enough, "I love you." She also gives him a book called *Instant Japanese* but Bond returns it to her. "You forget," he tells her, "I got a First in Oriental languages at Cambridge."

Bond is then sealed in a torpedo tube, wearing nothing but a wet suit and goggles, and fired in the general direction of the Japanese coast.

We next see him walking fully dressed down a street in Tokyo (where he got the clothes from is not explained). His destination is the Sumo wrestling arena and here, in the wrestlers' changing room, he meets his first contact, one of the combatants, who hands him a seat ticket. Bond then enters the vast arena and finds his seat where he is soon joined by an attractive Japanese girl. They exchange passwords and the girl suggests he accompany her. The few scenes that we see here of an actual Sumo wrestling match are among the most remarkable in the whole film. Two great mountains of men first face each other, and then charge head-on with incredible bone-breaking force.

The girl, whose name is Aki (played by Akiko Wakabayashi), takes Bond to see Henderson, an English agent who has lived so long in Japan that he's gone native. In the book, he was called Dikko Henderson and was an Australian but in the film he is unquestionably British, as played by that fine actor Charles Gray (who, incidentally, was to return to the series as Blofeld himself in *Diamonds Are Forever*). Henderson is half-way through telling Bond about his suspicions of a crowd called the Osato Chemicals Corporation when he stops in mid-sentence. Bond discovers that he has been stabbed in the back, the knife having been thrust silently through the paper wall behind him. Bond immediately crashes through the wall and gives chase to a fleeing figure. He catches the man in the garden and kills him, then removes his face mask and shoes. Waiting in the road outside is a car with the engine running. Groaning loudly Bond climbs in and lies down on the back seat.

Bond visits a sumo wrestling arena.

Fooled, the driver takes him straight to the Osato Chemical building and carries him up to an office on the top floor (surely he would have noticed that Bond weighed more than the average Japanese). He places Bond on a couch in the office and removes his mask, at which point Bond lets loose with a powerful punch to the jaw. But the Jap, who is built like a Sumo wrestler, is not even stunned and Bond discovers that he's picked an opponent that outclasses him. This suspicion is confirmed when he is thrown through one of the walls into the next room. There he desperately picks up a couch and uses it as a battering ram but the Jap merely plucks it out of his hands and tosses it to one side. This is definitely the best staged fight of the film and reminds one of the good old Oddjob days. The climax comes when Bond snatches up a handy stone statuette and, as his opponent makes a lethal charge, hits him over the head. The Jap skids across the floor, and when he finally comes to a halt, is obviously dead. Bond glances down at the statuette and sees that it has broken clearly in half.

Shoving the body into a drinks cabinet, Bond then sets about breaking into the safe he has found. He succeeds, but as he opens the door an alarm bell is set off. Scooping out the papers he is about to leave when he hears the sounds of approaching guards. He avoids them and reaches the elevator before they spot him. Outside there are more guards and Bond has to shoot his way to freedom. Luckily, Aki is waiting with her sports car and Bond gratefully accepts a lift.

Aki takes him to a deserted underground train station where she suddenly leaves him. Bond chases her but while doing so falls down a trapdoor beneath which is a long chute. This delivers him, in a very undignified manner, into the office of Tiger Tanaka, head of the Japanese Secret Service (another example of the tendency in this film to sacrifice logic for spectacle . . . why would anyone go to the fantastic lengths of building a gigantic metal chute for the sole reason of embarrassing visiting secret agents?). Tetsuro Tamba, who plays Tanaka, is rather disappointing. For one thing he's much too young for the part. Tanaka fought in the Second World War and is in fact an ex-*kamikaze* pilot (you'll have to read the book to find out how anyone can *be* an ex-*kamikaze* pilot) and therefore someone like Toshiro Mifune would have been more suitable.

131

Bond drops in to see Tiger Tanaka.

Tanaka not only has an office full of elaborate electronic equipment, including revolving TV screens, but also his own private train. He tells Bond that is is too dangerous for him to travel the streets of Tokyo. "But no doubt M has something similar?"

"Oh, yes," replies Bond as if the idea is extremely funny. He must have forgotten that he only recently left M in his own personal submarine.

Tanaka takes Bond back to his home or palace or whatever it is (the Japanese Secret Service obviously pays well) and showers him with hospitality, which includes the services of his servant girls, who bathe Bond with great affection. "I'll wager your English girls wouldn't perform this simple service," says Tanaka.

"Oh, I know one or two who might," replies Bond.

With the aid of Tanaka's equipment a micro-dot is discovered on one of the documents that Bond stole from the Osato office. It is enlarged to reveal a picture of a ship and a fragment of Japanese writing. Tanaka translates the latter as saying that the woman who took the picture, an American tourist, has since been eliminated.

The next day Tanaka arranges for Bond to pay an official visit to the Osato Chemical Corporation disguised as a businessman.

After introductions, Bond and Osato begin their business talk while the secretary, Helga (played by Karin Dor), goes to fetch a bottle of champagne from the drinks cabinet. Bond stiffens, expecting the body to fall out when she opens the door . . . but the cabinet is empty.

As he talks with Osato, Bond doesn't realize that he is being scanned by an X-ray machine in Osato's desk which reveals Bond's gun in his shoulder holster. "You should stop smoking," says Osato (Teru Shimada), "it is bad for your lungs."

Their phoney business completed, Bond makes his departure, but as soon as he has left the office Osato snarls at Helga, "Kill him!" And as Bond walks down the building's driveway, a black car bristling with gun barrels slowly creeps along behind him. But once again Aki saves the day by being in the right place at the right time. Bond leaps into her car just as the gunmen open fire. A rather tame chase through the streets of Tokyo ensues but it becomes more colorful when they reach the outer suburbs. Aki had radioed

Tanaka for help and it comes in the form of a giant helicopter which sweeps the villains' car off the road by means of a giant magnet. Bond watches on a TV screen in Aki's car as the helicopter carries the car high over Tokyo Bay and then dumps it into the water. (One wonders where the TV pictures were coming from, because in the long shots the helicopter was alone in the sky.) "What do you think of Japanese efficiency now?" asks Tanaka via the TV screen.

"A mere drop in the ocean," replies Bond. One is curious to know if this is a common method of disposing of carloads of gangsters. If so, one can imagine the headlines in the Tokyo newspapers—ANOTHER CAR DUMPED IN BAY BY SECRET SERVICE.

Japanese efficiency at work.

Tanaka then informs Bond and Aki that the ship featured on the microdot has been traced to Kobe docks and he suggests that they go there at once. Bond and Aki do so and on arrival at the docks they discover tanks of liquid oxygen, a vital ingredient of rocket fuel, ready for loading on board the Osato ship. But before they can get away to report their find, they are surrounded by a menacing crowd of dock workers, all apparently in the pay of Osato. Bond shoots a few of them (Bond shoots an awful lot of people during this film but the deaths are treated so casually that one hardly notices them; Roald Dahl, the screenwriter, was told the he could have Bond kill as many people as he liked, so long as he didn't do it

Trouble with the dockers at Kobe

sadistically) and they escape up to the roof. They are surrounded again, but Bond draws off the majority of the assailants while Aki slides to freedom down a rope. There's a marvellous aerial shot then of Bond running across the tops of the warehouses chased by a large formation of dockers. As attempts are made to block him off, Bond casually sends the men flying and they are left littering the rooftop like discarded dolls. Finally, when there is nowhere left to run, Bond leaps off the roof and lands in a pile of cartons. (A rather obvious substitution "gag"—the stuntman, presumably Simmons, lands on the boxes, rolls, and drops to the rear and Connery takes his place.) Considering himself home and dry, Bond straightens his tie and walks calmly away, only to be hit on the head from behind by a lone guard. He slumps to the ground.

When he wakes up, he finds himself in the presence of Helga. For once he's in a situation where the girl has the advantage, for Helga has him securely tied up in a chair. What's more, she's also hinting that she's going to start work on him, with an instrument that plastic surgeons use to remove skin. But Bond tells her that he's only an industrial spy and suggests that she join forces with him. Helga appears to believe him and cuts him free. He returns the favor by cutting her free of her dress. Discreet fade-out.

When we next see them, they are both in Helga's plane and heading for Tokyo. Bond is still busy chatting her up from the back seat when she suddenly turns nasty by throwing a smoke bomb on the floor and pressing a switch that sends a wooden board springing across Bond's lap. Then, equipped with parachute, she leaps out of the plane, leaving Bond to his own devices. Offhand, I can't think of a more involved, roundabout, complicated or expensive way of killing someone. Why didn't she use a simple gun or poison, instead of going to all that trouble? Of course Bond breaks loose from that silly little board and manages to pull the plane out of its dive. It crash-lands but he is able to get clear before it explodes.

The next scene shows Bond back at Tanaka's luxurious residence. The Osato ship has been traced to an Ama island off southern Japan and Bond is going to take a look at the area in "Little Nellie," the flying counterpart to Bond's Aston Martin. "Nellie" has been shipped secretly from England in four leather cases and has been assembled in Tanaka's garage. Accompanying "Nellie" is Major Boothroyd, who explains the weapons system to Bond. The flimsy little helicopter comes equipped with machine guns, rockets, flamethrower, aerial land mines, and heat-seeking missiles. As Bond zooms off down Tanaka's driveway, we are very surprised to see that the thing is actually able to take off.

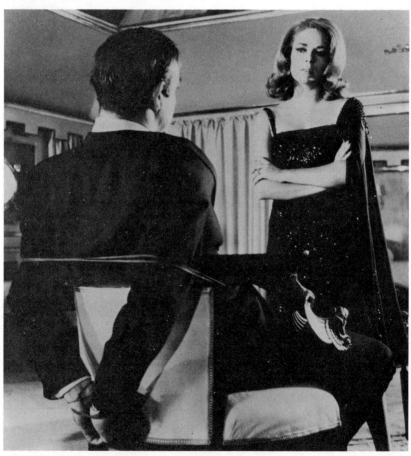

For once, Bond is at a disadvantage with a woman (Karin Dor).

Bond and "Nellie" are soon zooming over the island where the ship had been sighted, but apart from a large volcano there is nothing of interest to be seen. Bond flies into the actual crater of the volcano for a closer look and sees that there is a lake covering the bottom. Circling the island for the last time Bond looks down and observes the shadow cast by his helicopter on the rocks below. But later, when he glances down again, he sees that there are now five shadows—his, and four bigger ones. He looks round and discovers that he is being followed by four black helicopters.

The battle that follows is breathtaking as far as aerial photography is concerned, but lacks suspense because of its predictability. Bond dispatches each of the four enemy helicopters with boring ease, using his various weapons in almost the same sequence that Booth-royd explained them to him. One enemy he destroys with the rockets, the next with aerial mines, and so on. Also, the shots of the helicopters exploding are too obviously those of models. And really, there is no point for the battle to have taken place. Bond hadn't found anything and, if it wasn't for the attack by the helicopters, would have reported that the island was clean. This is the main trouble with *You Only Live Twice:* it has pace and spectacle, but the various episodes just do not blend togehter.

The man responsible for the magnificent aerial photography in these sequences was John Jordan. His technique was to hang from below the copter in a specially designed harness which gave him an unrestricted field of vision. Unfortunately, during the shooting, one of the helicopters he was filming from above moved too close and the rotor blade struck his leg. Jordan kept his cool during the crisis and actually trained the camera on his shattered lower leg in order to assist the surgeons by having a record of the damage. His leg, however, had to be amputated below the knee but he soon re-turned to work and performed a similar function on the next Bond film, *On Her Majesty's Secret Service.* Tragically, he was killed while working on *Catch 22.*

Meanwhile, up above, another international crisis is being precipi-tated, this time involving a Russian vehicle. Again, we see the mys-tery rocket swallow the capsule and then begin the descent back to Earth. But this time we follow it all the way down to its secret base

. . . which turns out to be the same volcano that Bond investigated. As the rocket hurtles down through the atmosphere the lake in the volcano's crater *slides open* to reveal a fully equipped launching pad inside. Down through the crater mouth comes the rocket, spewing flame and smoke in an incredible scene which is spoiled only by the cable supporting the full-scale rocket being plainly visible. The rocket settles on its pad, the lake slides back across the crater, and a booming voice inside the volcano orders that the ventilators be activated. Men in various colored costumes begin to swarm out towards the still hissing spaceship.

This hollow volcano, designed by Ken Adam and built at the Pinewood studios for a staggering cost of £400,000, is a truly awesome set. Not only does it contain a full-scale rocket but also a helicopter pad and its own monorail system which completely encircles it. Much more than James Bond himself or any other human performer, this set is the true star of the film.

And who is responsible for all this? The answer is soon forthcoming for when the scene switches to the interior of the control room that overlooks the launching pad we see a seated man with a white cat on his lap. We don't see his face but we know who he is . . . Ernst Stavro Blofeld. SPECTRE strikes again!

Also present in the control room are Mr. Osato and Helga. Blofeld summons them to accompany him to his apartment which is attached to the rear of the control room. As we expect, it is a sumptuous place and even contains a small pool spanned by a metal bridge. Waiting for Blofeld are two Chinese gentlemen who represent Red China. It is they who are apparently behind it all, providing SPECTRE with the money and the equipment to start a war between the U.S.A. and the Soviet Union. But dealing with SPECTRE has its drawbacks, as these two soon discover, for Blofeld has just put the price up several million dollars.

"But that's extortion!" protests one of them.

"Extortion is my business, gentlemen," murmurs Blofeld as he strokes his cat. "I suggest you take a few moments to discuss it between yourselves." Then Blofeld deals with Osato and Helga. He waves an X-ray plate at them. "Only one man we know carries a Walther PPK 38 . . . James Bond! Why didn't you have him killed?"

Ken Adams' brilliant set under construction (above)
and in the finished film (below)

A frightened Osato replies that he gave orders to Helga to do just that but she failed. Blofeld dismisses him and tells Helga that she must not fail again. But as the redhead follows Osato across the ornamental bridge Blofeld's foot touches a pedal beneath his desk. A section of the bridge suddenly gives way and Helga is sent plunging into the water, which just happens to be full of piranha fish. One long scream later, Helga has gone.

Of course it's the old Blofeld surprise victim trick. He's been pulling this one so long it's a wonder his employees still fall for it. But apparently it still exercises its desired effect.

"Kill James Bond!" yells Blofeld and the shaken Mr. Osato exits speedily to fulfil his request. The demonstration has also impressed the Chinese agents who are now more than willing to agree to Blofeld's demands for a higher fee.

140   Tanaka has decided that Bond should investigate more closely the area he flew over and suggests he infiltrate the local village disguised as a Japanese fisherman. So Tanaka's girls dye Bond's skin, fix his eyes, and give him a new hair-do. The result is not very convincing. . . .

Blofeld dispenses rough justice to his employees; here Helga is dumped into a piranha pool.

Tanaka also decides that Bond should have a crash course in the traditional Japanese martial arts and takes him to his Ninja Commando school located at the magnificent Himeji Castle. The scenes here remind one of the similar scenes of the SPECTRE training camp in *From Russia with Love*: men breaking things with their hands, their heads and their feet, others slicing dummies apart with swords and making those faces that only the Japanese can make.

After an exhausting day at the commando school, Bond is sleeping peacefully beside Aki that night when a shadowy figure appears in the ceiling above them. This is Mr. Osato's promised murder attempt, and a very original one it is, too. The would-be assassin first lowers a string until one end is positioned just above Bond's mouth, then he carefully tips a small bottle of poison on to the end he's holding. Very slowly the drops move down the length of the string towards Bond . . . but he is saved once again by Aki, though this time unwittingly. Aki shifts in her sleep so that it is her head beneath the string instead of Bond's and the poison drips into her mouth.

Seeing his error, the SPECTRE agent makes a hurried retreat but Aki's groans wake Bond in time for him to spot the killer. A shot, and a body thuds to the ground outside. But it is too late to help Aki and she expires demurely while Bond looks on helplessly. (Aki is this film's sacrifical lamb. There's at least one or two in every Bond film: Quarrel in *Dr. No,* Kerim Bey in *From Russia with Love,* the Masterson sisters in *Goldfinger,* and Paula in *Thunderball.*)

The next day, while Bond is completing his Ninja training, there is another murder. His opponent in a mock duel with bamboo poles suddenly turns nasty and tries to run Bond through with a concealed bayonet blade. Bond disarms him and runs *him* through with his own weapon. After this, Tanaka decides it was time they were moving on. The opposition is getting too close.

But first Bond needs one more addition to his disguise as a Japanese fisherman . . . a wife. And Tanaka just happens to have one on hand, the beautiful Kissy Suzuki played by Mie Hama. After a quick marriage ceremony, Bond, Kissy, and Tanaka make their way by boat to Kissy's village which is located on an island not far from the volcanic area. Tanaka also arranges to have a hundred of his Ninja warriors hidden on the island in case of an emergency.

Marriage, Japanese style

At her house, Bond and Kissy spend an unsatisfactory wedding night together, at least from Bond's point of view. Kissy insists that the marriage is for business reasons only and resists Bond's amorous advances. Sighing, Bond pushes away a plate of oysters on the table. "In that case I won't be needing these," he says unhappily. Later as Bond lies on his sleeping mat wistfully gazing at Kissy, Tanaka bursts in to announce that the Americans have brought forward the launch-date of their next rocket. The countdown has already started and the President has issued a final warning to the Russians who they still believe to be behind it all. Bond now has only six hours to find the launching site. Serials at the Saturday afternoon matinees were never like this.

At dawn Bond joins Kissy in her boat and they go to investigate a cave on a nearby island where an Ama girl recently died in mysterious circumstances. No sooner have they entered the cave than Bond detects the smell of gas. At his command, he and Kissy dive overboard and swim out of the cave. Realizing that the cave is in some way connected to the volcano above Bond decides to climb up and look into the crater. On the way up, Kissy complains of exhaustion and Bond allows her to rest. One thing leads to another and it is beginning to appear as if Bond has succeeded in convincing her to change her mind about their "business" arrangement when there is a sudden noise. Looking up they see a black helicopter heading for the volcano. As they watch, it disappears into the crater.

They resume their climb and on reaching the top are surprised to see that there is no sign of the helicopter. Mystified, they proceed down into the crater itself.

When they reach the lake, night has fallen, which helps conceal the fact that the action has switched from the Japanese location on a real volcano to the studio-built one. Up close, the lake looks as though it is made of plastic, which it is, but Bond doesn't realize this until he's tossed a rock to see how deep it is and it bounces off the surface. "That's not water!" he exclaims. He walks out over it to investigate further when the whole thing starts to move. Down below, it is almost time for the SPECTRE rocket to be launched. All at last becomes clear to Bond.

Sending Kissy back up the crater to fetch Tanaka and his men, Bond then strips off his Japanese fishing costume to reveal that he's wearing a full commando outfit, complete with special suction equipment perfect for using inside artificial volcanoes (you never know when you're going to run across one). Before the lake can slide shut again (it had opened only temporarily to permit a helicopter to leave), Bond has slipped inside and is clinging like a fly to the ceiling of Blofeld's incredible establishment. Avoiding detection, Bond climbs down and hides himself in one of the monorail cars. By overhearing the technicians, Bond learns where the captive American and Russian astronauts are being held. He breaks into their prison and helps them overcome their guards. Then, wearing their guards' costumes, Bond leads them into a room where one of the SPECTRE astronauts is being prepared. They overpower the occupants and Bond swiftly climbs into the spacesuit (we won't ask how a suit designed for a Japanese of average build can now fit a man of Bond's size so well). Bond joins the other astronaut, is

143

driven out to the rocket and rides the elevator up the huge gantry without being detected. But as he is about to climb into the spaceship a voice booms out from the control room, "Stop that astronaut! Bring him to me!" As Bond is brought down the launching is postponed and the countdown begun again.

As Bond is brought into the control room, a large blond man, dressed in black, moves from where he had been standing protectively in front of a chair. Seated in the chair, and stroking a white cat, is Ernst Stavro Blofeld—in full view at last! One's first impression, however, is that he has shrunk considerably. While one never received a full view of him in the previous pictures, the suggestion was that, as in the novels, he was a *big* man. After all, in *Thunderball* Fleming described him as weighing *twenty stone* and, though he thinned down for his subsequent appearances, he was still a ". . . big man, perhaps six-foot-three, and powerfully built . . . Bond had to admit there was something larger than life in the looming, imperious figure" *(You Only Live Twice)*. Now Donald Pleasence, who plays Blofeld, is an excellent actor and one who has specialized in creating sinister characters, but the one thing he is not is "larger than life"—in the physical sense at least (apparently Pleasence was not the original choice for the role, but was brought in as a replacement when another actor—possibly Robert Helpmann—had to bow out of the production for various reasons. As a result, Pleasence's scenes were shot after most of the picture had been completed).

The makers themselves, and Pleasence, were aware of this failing to a certain extent and Pleasence tells how, in the make-up room at Pinewood, they tried him first with a hump to make him look more unusual, then with a limp, a beard, and a lame hand. They finally settled on a scar, which certainly succeeded in making him look considerably more bizarre (film critic Alexander Walker described him as resembling "an egg that had cracked on the boil").

Unfortunately, this historic confrontation between Bond and Blofeld is rather an anticlimax. I thought the occasion should warrant something special in the way of dialogue but there's not even a single, "So, we meet at last!" After all that Bond has done in the past to upset Blofeld's elaborate schemes I would have expected a bigger reaction from Blofeld at having Bond in his power. I rather

Donald Pleasence as Blofeld

hoped that he might fling himself at Bond in a terrible rage, yelling things like, "This is for Dr. No . . . (kick) . . . and this is for Largo! . . . (kick) . . . and this for that fleet of launches you blew up in the Gulf of Venice! . . . (kick) . . . and those four helicopters you shot down only yesterday!" But no such luck.

Instead, after a bit of mild sneering, Blofeld invites Bond to watch the take-off of the spaceship. And a very impressive sight it is too. These scenes are even more spectacular than those of the ship landing (the full-scale model, belching almost as much fire and smoke as a real rocket, actually rose fifty feet or so up the gantry during the simulated launching).

Outside, hidden on the slopes of the volcano, the rocket is observed by Tanaka, Kissy, and the Ninja commandos. At Tanaka's signal, the latter rise like grey ghosts from the rocks and charge up

towards the crater. They reach the rim then make their way down towards the lake. But at the bottom of the crater they receive a rude surprise—machine gun barrels protrude suddenly from the artificial rocks and all hell breaks loose. Watching the mayhem via hidden TV cameras, Blofeld gleefully informs Bond that, "Your companions are doomed. My crater guns possess enough firepower to wipe out an entire army. You can watch it all on TV if you like . . . it will be the last program you'll see tonight!"

But Bond has one final trick up his sleeve, or rather, up his cigarette. A miniature rocket, in fact. He aims carefully at the technician who is operating the sliding lake controls . . . fires, and the hapless fellow expires in a blaze of glory. Bond then leaps at the control panel and sends the lake sliding open, enabling Tanaka's men to start entering the volcano. But Bond is swiftly overpowered by the guards, dragged away from the controls, and the lake is closed again. Only a few of the Ninjas have forged inside and they are soon killed as they attempt to slide down on their ropes. Blofeld is naturally furious with Bond and here Pleasence acts up to the hilt—maniacal leers, bulging eyes, the lot—as he threatens him with all manner of nasty fates.

But one of the Ninjas is still alive among the girders under the lake. Unseen, he manages to fix a bomb to the underside which blows a big enough hole in the covering to allow Tanaka and the rest of his men access to the volcano. The scene as the Ninjas descend into the volcano like a horde of spiders on their webs is extraordinary. Then the big battle begins, and it soon becomes apparent that SPECTRE is going to emerge second best.

Blofeld, however, is unworried. He orders the steel shutters of the control room to be closed and tells Bond, "Now we are impregnable." But he hasn't reckoned on the massive firepower that Tanaka's men possess and before long it is obvious that the room is anything but impregnable. Blofeld decides to retreat, leaving his hulking, blond bodyguard behind with instructions to activate the SPECTRE rocket's self-destruct system once it has swallowed the American capsule. Blofeld then herds Bond under gunpoint out of the control room and down the stairs to a waiting monorail car. "Goodbye, Mr. Bond," says Blofeld as he aims his revolver. (Bond seems to find himself in this position at the end of every film.) But 147 there is a sudden flash of metal and a star-shaped Ninja throwing knife thuds into Blofeld's wrist, knocking aside the gun. With a cry, Blofeld falls back into the monorail car and it moves off at high speed.

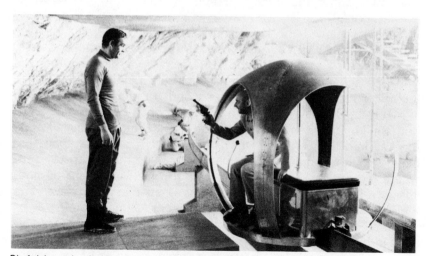

Blofeld on the brink of shooting Bond from his monorail car

It is Tanaka who is responsible for throwing the knife, having arrived just in time on the scene with Kissy. Bond tells him that they must break into the control room before the SPECTRE rocket reaches the capsule. But they discover that the Ninjas are still being held off by the men guarding the control room. They obviously won't last out much longer but long enough to ensure that it will be too late to save the capsule. But then Bond glimpses the technicians from the control room fleeing down some steps in another part of the volcano and he realizes that there must be a second entrance.

With the help of some Ninjas, Bond fights his way up those same stairs and eventually finds himself in Blofeld's apartment. He also finds himself face to face with Blofeld's giant bodyguard who is standing between him and the steps to the control room. In his hand is the key to the rocket's self-destruct system.

The fight that follows between them is well-staged but somehow lacking as a climax to the film, probably because at this point of a Bond adventure we expect a final confrontation between Bond and the chief villain. But as Blofeld must escape so he can appear in the next epic, his bodyguard serves as a substitute, and it is the latter who must suffer the inevitable fate of falling into the piranha-infested pool.

Having retrieved the key, Bond then makes his way into the wrecked control room. He locates the self-destruct control and sees, on a nearby TV screen, that the SPECTRE spaceship, jaws open, is fast approaching the American space capsule. On the control panel, a counter reels off the remaining seconds to interception . . . 012 . . . 011 . . . 010 . . . 009 . . . (a "carbon copy" of the ticking atom bomb in *Goldfinger*'s Fort Knox sequence). Bond frantically inserts the key into the panel and turns it. On the screen the spaceship explodes into fragments only yards away from the capsule (just where were those TV pictures coming from? Was there another space craft up there?). The counter has stopped at 003. Once again a global disaster has been averted, thanks to James Bond.

But it's not all over yet. Blofeld makes an unexpected reappearance in his monorail car, stops beside a section of the volcano wall and throws a concealed switch that begins a series of explosions (there is always one of these switches within easy reach). Soon the whole volcano is falling about everyone's ears and Bond leads Kissy, Tanaka, and the surviving Ninjas down the tunnel towards the sea cave. The shots of the exploding volcano are impressive but they are undercut with several blatantly obvious shots of a model. The scene where a collection of rigid little dummies and a few toy trucks are sent flying into the air by an explosion is ludicrous.

Our hero and company swim hastily out through the sea cave to freedom (the poison gas having been conveniently forgotten). On cue, a plane appears overhead and begins dropping life rafts to the survivors. Bond and Kissy manage to get one to themselves and lie back to watch the display as Blofeld's artificial volcano turns itself into a real one, with even a lava flow in action (the lava flow is a bit shaky due to the matte work).

But, as in *Thunderball*, Bond is not allowed any well-deserved rest alone with the heroine. As they float on a seemingly empty ocean a submarine suddenly rises beneath their raft. M's submarine, no less (MI is painted on the conning tower).

"Have 007 report to me as soon as he comes aboard," orders M.

"A *pleasure*, sir!" replies Miss Moneypenny.

George Lazenby as James Bond

8

On Her Majesty's Secret Service

On Her Majesty's Secret Service is unique among the Bond films for a number of reasons. The most obvious one is that Sean Connery is missing from the cast, his place taken by newcomer George Lazenby. When Connery announced at the completion of You Only Live Twice that he was never going to play James Bond again, no one really took him seriously. "He says that at the end of every film," Saltzman was reported as commenting. But as time went by and Connery gave no sign of relenting, it was realized that this time he meant what he said. A frantic search was then begun for a new James Bond. Names like Lee Marvin, Richard Burton, and Adam West (TV's Batman) were bandied about but nothing definite was announced. As the starting date for filming On Her Majesty's Secret Service (henceforth known as OHMSS) drew nearer, it was rumored that an unknown by the name of George Lazenby, one of twenty applicants screen-tested by the producers, would get the part though there was still no official word. Then, a mere three weeks before filming was due to begin in Switzerland, the two heads of United Artists flew from America to London in a last-ditch attempt to talk Connery into playing Bond again. He refused, and shortly after it was publicly announced that George Lazenby would be the new James Bond.

Lazenby was an Australian with no previous film acting experience though he had appeared in some TV commercials. On first arriving in London, he had worked as a car salesman before starting a successful career as a male model. He was handsome, well built, and, according to *OHMSS* director Peter Hunt, possessed that certain "something," an air of sexual confidence that Connery had. As for his lack of acting experience, Hunt dismissed this, saying that it was possible to get a good performance out of anyone through a combination of good directing and skilled editing.

But when *OHMSS* was released, it was immediately apparent that a serious error in casting had been made. First, Lazenby was simply too young for the part, his face suggesting none of the necessary Bondian world-weariness or ruthlessness. Secondly, his voice, despite the crash elocution course, was totally wrong, particularly when his underlying Australian accent broke through as it frequently did (an Australian James Bond is a contradiction in terms). The only time he sounded right was in the sequences where Bond masquerades as Sir Hilary Bray, and that's because George Baker's voice was used (it's surprising that the producers didn't decide to redub *all* of Lazenby's lines with someone else—it would have made a big difference). Thirdly, and most importantly, it was obvious that Lazenby lacked training as an actor. Putting it bluntly, his performance was both awkward and wooden, and whatever that certain "something" was that Hunt claimed he saw in him, failed to make the transition to the screen (over the years, Lazenby's acting has improved—he was even memorable in *Saint Jack*—and he has stated publicly that he is ready for another shot at Bond, but so far Broccoli has been in no rush to take up his offer). As skilled a director and editor as Hunt undoubtedly is, no amount of cinematic tricks could disguise the fact that Lazenby as Bond was a big mistake. However, Hunt was more successful with the other aspects of the picture.

Hunt had been associated with the Bond series from the very beginning as editor, but this was his first experience at directing a feature film (though he had been second unit director on *You Only Live Twice*). From the start, Hunt had strong ideas on what direction *OHMSS* should take. He wanted to discard the old formula of stupendous sets and far-fetched gadgets and return to the plot of Fleming's original novel. He considered *OHMSS* to be a fine adven-

152

ture story with plenty of human interest, and that's the way he wanted to make the film. Convincing the producers, who had no reason to be dissatisfied with the old formula, was no easy task; but Hunt eventually succeeded. Not since *From Russia with Love* has a Bond film adhered so closely to the novel. (It's interesting to note that, as with *FRWL*, the distinctive designs of Ken Adam are again absent. The former art director of *Dr. No* and *FRWL*, Syd Cain, is production designer this time.) The result is, I believe, the best Bond film since *Goldfinger*. It could have been the best of the series had it not been fatally flawed by Connery's absence.

The pre-title sequence of *OHMSS* begins at good old Universal Export, the cover name for the headquarters of the Secret Service. M is busy examining the latest product from Q Branch. "Radioactive lint," explains Major Boothroyd, "to be secreted in the clothing of an enemy agent and which will enable us to keep track of him." M doesn't seem impressed. "What we need is something to help us keep track of 007," he replies. "Miss Moneypenny, where was he last reported?"

"Portugal, sir," she replies. (Q's blatantly ludicrous radioactive lint is the only gadget from the Branch to feature in this film. An indication, perhaps, of Hunt's general attitude towards the whole gadget business.)

The scene changes to show the familiar Aston Martin speeding along a beach road in Portugal. The driver's face is in the shadows but we know that it is James Bond by the way he lights his cigarette, and by his reaction when he is overtaken by a girl in a sports car. But the girl disappears at high speed and Bond slows down again. Suddenly, as he turns a corner, he sees the same sports car parked, empty, by the side of the road. He pulls in beside it, opens a panel in his dashboard that reveals a rifle laid out in sections and whips a telescopic sight to his eye. Down by the water's edge he sees the car's driver walking into the surf, fully dressed. This is a beautifully photographed scene with the girl, dressed in a flimsy gown that makes her look like a large butterfly, walking into a huge, moonlit sea. A marvelous image of fragile beauty versus the cruel elements.

Bond, always ready to help a lady in distress, immediately sends his car roaring down the slope and on to the beach. Leaping out of the car, he sprints down to the surf and plunges in after her. She resists his rescue attempts at first but then collapses into his arms. He carries her out of the water and lays her carefully on the sand. Her eyes flutter open and she looks up at him. "The name's Bond," he says as we also receive our first full view of him, "James Bond." But before the girl can answer a knife appears at her throat, and at the same time a gun barrel is thrust against the side of Bond's head. A gravelly voice says, "Come with me, Mr. Bond."

As the girl is dragged up the beach by one of the mysterious men, Bond is forced at gunpoint to lie down in a nearby rowboat with his hands behind his head. The man prepares to shoot but at the last moment Bond kicks the gun out of his hand. A very fast and wild fight develops with the editing playing as important a part as the stunt men (editing tends to play a vital role throughout this film). With the help of an oar and various other items of fishing equipment, Bond manages to disable both men, but the girl, abandoned by her guard, seizes her chance to make a dash for Bond's car. She gets in and sends it roaring back up the slope to where her own car waits. There she switches cars and, with screeching tires, disappears into the night. Bond is left with only her shoes. He picks them up and comments wryly, "*This* never happened to the other fellow. . . ." A nice touch.

154

Bond blocks a rather nasty blow.

Then the credits roll, this time a better-than-average combination of visuals and music by Maurice Binder and John Barry, respectively. Binder's title designs, containing brief scenes of the previous films, evoke a definite feeling of nostalgia. No doubt a canny move on the makers' part to make sure audiences realize that, despite the new, unfamiliar James Bond, the film is still part of the grand saga. And for a change, Barry's music isn't hampered by some popular vocalist droning out unlikely lyrics to this theme music. Perhaps the words "On Her Majesty's Secret Service" proved too difficult to set to music.

The film begins with Bond having been recalled to London. M is dissatisfied with the way the hunt for Blofeld has been progressing. After all, Bond has been searching for two years but still seems no nearer to finding his quarry than when he began. "What's the use of having a license to kill if you can't set up your target?" he asks Bond. Bond doesn't agree, of course, but M is adamant and orders him to drop the case. Annoyed, Bond marches out to Miss Moneypenny and dictates his letter of resignation (going one better than Bond in the book, who merely composed his letter of resignation in his head but never went any further). He tells her to pass it on to M and then he goes to his office and starts to empty the drawers of his desk. More nostalgia here as he produces items like Honey's knife belt from *Dr. No* and Grant's deadly wristwatch from *From Russia with Love,* while familiar theme tunes lilt in the background. Misty-eyed, Bond is drinking a toast to the Queen's portrait from a whisky flask when he receives a summons from M. Entering his office, Bond is surprised when all he receives from M is a testy, "Request granted." Rather shattered by this treatment, Bond goes to cry on Miss Moneypenny's shoulder, and discovers that she altered his resignation to a request for two weeks' leave.

"I knew you didn't really mean it," she says.

Bond immediately returns to Portugal. On arriving at Estoril he checks in at a combination hotel and gambling casino. Later that night, while at the *chemin de fer* table, he sees the mystery girl again. She joins in the game by placing a huge bet, loses, and clearly has no money. A very embarrassing situation, but Bond saves the day by announcing that he is the lady's partner and will cover her losses. Afterwards, at the bar, the girl introduces herself and thanks him for saving her the second time although she doesn't seem enthusiastic. She also promises to repay Bond and gives him her hotel room key. Bond takes it and agrees to see her there later.

Tracy, the girl, is played by the beautiful Diana Rigg who is following in the footsteps of Honor Blackman (Pussy Galore) by moving from the Avengers TV series to a starring role in a Bond film. Due to her role in the TV series, she had become typecast as a somewhat cold superwoman but, being an excellent actress, she makes the transition to the more vulnerable and feminine Tracy most successfully.

When Bond arrives in her room, he finds no Tracy waiting for him but instead a very large Negro, who promptly smashes him over the head with a chair. Bond's punches are shrugged off by his opponent, so he is forced to take more violent action and finally triumphs by driving the thug's head through a wall and exits hurriedly, grabbing a handful of caviar (from the "north side of the Caspian . . .") on his way out. In his own room, he finds another surprise, but this time it's Tracy herself, dressed in naught but her underwear and an open bathrobe. She's still playing hard to get, however, and Bond has to grapple with her for his own gun before she'll give in.

The next morning Bond wakes to find the bed empty beside him, except for the robe and a rose. He also discovers that Tracy has repaid in full the money he lent her. Mystified by it all, Bond prepares to have a game of golf but is intercepted in the foyer by the same thugs he fought with on the beach. They take him out to their car and drive him to a heavy equipment construction yard which serves as the cover for Marc Ange Draco, the Head of the Union Corse, which is a kind of Mafia.

Draco, played by the suave Gabriele Ferzetti, turns out to be Tracy's father. This sequence, with Draco telling Bond about Tracy's unhappy life is rather mawkish. It also reveals, yet again, Lazenby's lack of experience. His reaction shots while Ferzetti rambles on are embarrassing to watch.

It seems that Tracy, spoiled as a child and later hurt by a ruinous marriage, is fast heading for disaster. Draco believes that she needs a man like Bond and wants him to marry her. He's even willing to pay a million pounds if Bond will agree to it. But Bond turns him down. "I don't need a million pounds," he says. (Not many people can say that with a straight face.) But then it occurs to him that Draco might have something more valuable, information about Blofeld. Draco has, but he's not giving it to Bond without getting something in return, so Bond agrees to attend Draco's birthday party, a function that Tracy never misses.

Tracy (Diana Rigg) and Bond get acquainted.

The setting for the party is Draco's ranch in Portugal (actually the Da Vinho estate) which even contains its own bull ring. When Tracy arrives she is surprised to see Bond and immediately suspects that her father is up to something. Pumping her father's mistress for information, she learns the truth and orders Draco to tell Bond what he wants to know. Draco is forced to tell Bond that Blofeld has been dealing with a certain lawyer in Berne, Switzerland, by the name of Gumbold.

"Now that Mr. Bond has what he wants," says Tracy, "there's no reason for him to stay any longer." Sobbing, she leaves the party but Bond follows her to her car and assures her that the information wasn't the only reason he came. Love immediately blossoms between them and we are then treated to one of those appallingly romantic sequences that one hoped would never mar a Bond film—a montage containing lyrical, slow-motion scenes of a horse-back ride, lyrical, slow-motion running along a beach and so on—all of it given a vocal blessing by the late Louis Armstrong.

158

With that over, and Bond and Tracy's new relationship firmly established, the film moves on to more important things. First, Bond deals with that lawyer in Berne. With Draco's help he raids his office one lunch hour and breaks into his safe with a combination automatic safe-cracking machine and duplicator. At last the machines are put in their place. While Bond sits reading an issue of *Playboy*, the device works out the combination and then runs off copies of the documents inside.

The location changes to London and for once we receive a brief glimpse of M's home. When Bond arrives, M is busy playing with his butterfly collection. He is annoyed when he learns that Bond has still been working on the search for Blofeld despite his orders to the contrary, but when Bond tells him about the documents found in Gumbold's safe he relents. Blofeld, it seems, is attempting to claim rights to the title of Count de Bleuchamp and, acting through Gumbold, has already been in contact with the College of Arms in London.

Bond visits the College and convinces Sir Hilary Bray (George Baker) to allow him to impersonate him on a visit to Switzerland to investigate Blofeld's claim. We next see Bond, wearing glasses and using Sir Bray's voice (George Baker dubbed his voice for these sequences), arriving at a railway station in Lauterbrunnen, Switzerland. He is met by Irma Bunt, Blofeld's assistant, who is played by Ilse Steppat (the best piece of casting in the whole film). Miss Steppat's playing of Bunt rivals the performance given by Lotte Lenya as Klebb.

Bunt takes Bond by sleigh to a field where a helicopter waits in the snow. Up to this point, they have been followed by another of M's agents but he can only watch helplessly as the helicopter rises rapidly into the sky. There follows a magnificently photographed flight over the snow-covered mountains to Blofeld's headquarters on top of Piz Gloria. The latter is a splendid location and matches perfectly Fleming's description in the novel. In reality the circular structure is a combined cable car terminal and restaurant which sits atop the mountain of Schilthorn, 10,000 feet above sea level. But for the purposes of the film it is Blofeld's Institute of Physiological Research. Bunt tells Bond that the Count is the foremost authority on curing allergies.

One of Blofeld's men draws a bead on approaching helicopter.

Draco's men attack Blofeld's stronghold.

The helicopter dips down with stomach-wrenching suddenness and lands on a circular platform (the terminal lacked a landing pad for helicopters so the film crew hauled several tons of concrete up the mountain and built one). As Bond disembarks, he notices several armed guards standing about. He nervously asks Bunt what they're for and Bunt replies that they're needed to protect the Count's many scientific discoveries. But Sir Hilary Bray isn't reassured. "Guns make me nervous," he tells Bunt.

Bond is first shown to his room and then taken down into the mountain to meet the Count. Our first view of Blofeld in this film is a rather eerie one as he stands bathed in the green glow of a sterilizing cabinet. Then he steps into the room to greet Bond, peeling off his white laboratory coat as he does so. This time Blofeld is played by American actor Telly Savalas and is another unsatisfactory piece of casting (though, unlike Lazenby, not a ruinous one). Savalas, best known for his role in *Kojak,* has been too long associated with brash, uncouth characters. As one of Blofeld's henchmen he'd be fine, but he lacks the necessary style to play Blofeld himself, especially in this film, where Blofeld is trying to convince everyone that he's a Count.

Though Bond and Blofeld have met in the previous film neither seems to recognize the other. This is a major plot flaw, caused by reversing the sequence of the films. In the book, this was the first time the two had ever met and therefore Bond was forced to prove Blofeld's identity by other means. But in the film, as we know they've seen each other before, it all seems rather pointless. Perhaps Blofeld has undergone plastic surgery, for his scar has gone now, and so have his ear lobes. And as for his not recognizing Bond, it's probably due to the glasses.

The lack of ear lobes, Blofeld insists, is a sure sign that he's the real Count de Bleuchamp but Bond asks him to accompany him on a trip to the Bleuchamp family tombs in Austria. Blofeld sidesteps this ruse, which is designed to get him out of Switzerland, and tells Sir Bray that he has all the necessary information on hand.

Bond, frustrated, returns to his room to dress for dinner with Miss Bunt. He emerges later in full Scottish gear, kilt and all, but when he enters the luxurious dining room he receives a pleasant surprise.

Telly Savalas as Blofeld

Instead of dining alone with Bunt as he had expected he finds the room full of beautiful young girls. He learns later that they are all at the Institute for treatment for various allergies.

Seated at dinner, Bond maintains Sir Hilary's rather dull facade by boring the whole company with a long lecture about genealogy. But at least one of the girls, Ruby, played by Angela Scoular, sees through him. When she, without warning, reaches under his kilt and writes her room number on his thigh in lipstick he, not surprisingly, falters in his speech.

"Is anything the matter, Sir Bray?" asks Bunt.

"No Fräulein Bunt," he replies, "I just feel a slight stiffening coming on. . . ."

Despite the strict security precautions, Bond manages to sneak into Ruby's room later during the night. Discarding his kilt he causes Ruby a great deal of amusement, "It's true!" she shrieks. When we rejoin them after the fade-out something strange occurs. The ceiling starts to pulse with colored lights and a humming noise fills the room. "It's part of the cure," says Ruby and promptly goes into a trance. Then we hear Blofeld's voice . . . droning over and over again about how much Ruby loves chickens! It's one of the most hilarious scenes in the film and we cannot blame Bond from retreating from her bedroom looking very mystified by it all.

Bond spends the next couple of days pretending to be working on the proof of Blofeld's claim to the title and keeping up his image as the ineffectual Sir Hilary. But his cover is almost blown when M's other agent is caught trying to climb up Piz Gloria. He sees Bond but they pretend not to recognize each other as he is hustled away by Blofeld's guards.

The real disaster comes when Bond makes his usual visit to Ruby's room. He creeps in without turning on the lights and approaches the bed. "Ruby," he calls softly, "It's me . . . Hillie." But when "Ruby" turns round he finds himself face to face with the awful Fräulein Bunt. Then the roof falls in. . . .

Regaining consciousness, the first thing his eyes focus on is an incongruous toy angel atop a Christmas tree. Then he sees that Blofeld is also present, and looking mean. The polite Count de Bleuchamp has disappeared and in his place is the Head of

SPECTRE. "It will take more than a few props to turn double-0-seven into Sir Hilary Bray," he snarls as he snaps Bond's glasses in half. How did he see through the masquerade? Simple. "Respectable members of the College of Arms don't go around seducing young girls," says Blofeld. (Can he be sure about that?) So once again we've arrived at one of the best parts of a Bond film (or novel)—the big confrontation scene. This is where the villain will explain his dastardly schemes and do some serious gloating. And Blofeld doesn't fail to deliver the goods. His latest plan to hold the Western world to ransom, he tells Bond, involves the destruction of livestock and cereal by means of biological warfare. But it's not just the destruction of one season's crop he's threatening; instead he claims that he's created a virus that can cause permanent sterility in various breeds of animals and strains of plants. And if the United Nations reject his demands, he will unleash it right across the world.

Disguised as Sir Hilary Bray, Bond gets down to some recreation.

"How many millions are you demanding for your services this time, Blofeld?" asks Bond.

"None. This time my fee will be quite different. I assure you that it will amuse you, Mr. Bond." Blofeld is also not saying how he plans to spread his virus about, which is unusually good thinking on his part. Villains tend to give too much away at times like this.

With the gloating and the sneering over, it's time for Bond to start suffering. Blofeld has him taken to his new quarters but on the way they pause beside a window. Hanging upside down outside, frozen solid, is M's other man (this film's "sacrificial lamb"). "Tsk, tsk," says Blofeld, "these amateur climbers are always killing themselves in this manner." Which provokes Bond into an attempt to commit physical mayhem but he is overpowered by the guards and thrust through a nearby door which is bolted behind him. He finds himself in the midst of the machinery that drives the cable cars, a mass of great cogs and gears like the inside of a clockwork toy. I fully realize that an opportunity like this is necessary to enable Bond to escape and thus keep the plot moving . . . but I still find it difficult to accept that a villain of Blofeld's experience (though admittedly his success rate isn't very high) would imprison Bond in such a place.

Bond, of course, is soon climbing hand over hand along the cable towards freedom. Not that he has it too easy. First, he is almost swept back into the giant cog wheels, then, when he reaches the outside, he is almost run down by a fast-approaching cable car. But he avoids an unpleasant fate by jumping down on the roof of the car and riding back up to the Institute. Avoiding the guards, he creeps to a point on the balcony where he can see into the lounge. Inside all the girls have been assembled for a farewell message from the Count before they depart from the Institute. As Blofeld's voice comes over a loudspeaker they all go into a trance and he orders them to open the gift-wrapped package that they have each been given. Inside they find a make-up kit which consists of a compact and atomizer. The compact is a radio receiver with which they can tune into Blofeld's voice anywhere in the world . . . the atomizer they're not allowed to open until they receive instructions. Blofeld's plan to spread his virus is at last clear to Bond. Now the action begins.

After disabling a guard in the foyer Bond breaks into the supply
store and steals a pair of skis. Wishing the trussed up guard a Merry
Christmas, Bond launches himself down the steep slope at high
speed. But he is spotted by another guard who catches him in the
beam of his spotlight. Machine gun bullets spurt into the snow
behind him but he is not hit and keeps on going. "Der Englander
has escaped!" yells the guard and alarm bells start to ring. There's
an amusing scene in Blofeld's room when he hears the news. Leaping to his feet he sends the white cat sprawling to the floor with a
frightened "Meow-w." Unlike the Blofeld of the previous films, or
the books, the Blofeld of this film takes an active part in the dirty
work himself. Swiftly donning his skiing gear, he leads a team of his
men after Bond. (SPECTRE in this film seems much closer to Fleming's original than it has in any of the other films. The organization
appears to consist of only Blofeld and a group of helpers, in direct
contrast to the vast network it was in *Thunderball* and *You Only
Live Twice*. Perhaps Blofeld is having an economy drive.)

The ensuing ski chase down the mountain side is one of the most
exciting pieces of cinema in the Bond series. Much of the credit must
go to Willy Bogner, Jr., the world class champion skier, who photographed some of the most exciting shots of the chase by skiing
backwards with a hand-held camera. The stuntmen, all excellent
skiers, also deserve praise, especially the one who doubled for Bond
and spent most of the chase on only *one* ski. The great success of
the whole sequence was also partly achieved by the fact that the
second-unit director was also the film's editor (John Glen), which
meant he had full control from start to finish.

Some of the stunts performed during the chase were really elec-
trifying. One in particular was when a skier loses control and goes
hurtling off the trail to finish up in the branches of a tree. The chase
also contains the best line of dialogue in the whole film. This is when
Blofeld sights a flare set off by his other team of men as a signal that
they've seen Bond. "Come on," says Blofeld to his men, "we'll
head him off at the precipice!"

The chase comes to an end when Bond is trapped on a cliff top,
the lights of a town far below him (which, due to a jiggling matte
shot, seems to be in the grip of an earthquake). When the first

SPECTRE skier arrives, Bond hits him with his ski while he's still in mid-air which results in the unfortunate fellow's somersaulting over the cliff edge. The camera follows him on his long downward path, and here one must make a complaint: why, oh why, can't film-makers use realistic-looking dummies for scenes like this? Preferably ones that don't look as stiff as boards and bend the wrong way at the knees as this one does.

The next skier to arrive receives the same treatment from Bond, only he doesn't go over the edge and Bond is forced to keep him silent while his companions ski past. But then he breaks free and a fierce struggle takes place before Bond can send him over the edge to follow his friends. As Bond puts on his ski and prepares to move off we can still hear the fellow's scream growing fainter in the background.

When Bond reaches the village he discovers that a Christmas festival is in progress and the place is overflowing with cheerful crowds. He also discovers that Irma Bunt and her men have arrived, too. They soon spot him and the chase is on again as they pursue him through the crowds (this sequence bears striking similarities to the one in *Thunderball* when Bond was chased through the Jun-kanoo celebrations by Fiona and her mob). He manages to elude them for the time being and seeks refuge beside the skating rink where he huddles, a depressed and dejected figure. Suddenly we notice that a pair of very feminine legs belonging to one of the skaters has abruptly changed direction and is approaching Bond. The legs halt before him and the camera follows his gaze as he looks up—and sees Tracy, looking more beautiful than ever. The angel of mercy has arrived!

No time for a fond reunion. Bond immediately asks her if she has her car nearby. She has and they make their way quickly to it. But as they drive out of the village, Bond is seen by the driver of Bunt's car, who alerts the others by blowing the horn. Bond tells Tracy that he must get to a phone as soon as possible so that he can put a call through to London. Tracy drives him to a nearby post office and Bond races into a call box. But before he can make his call Bunt's black limousine slides by and the bullets start flying. Closely fol-lowed by a stream of machine gun fire Bond sprints back to Tracy's car and they roar off. A mildly exciting car chase follows through the snow-covered countryside with both cars skidding into the drifts. But events take a sudden turn for the fantastic when Bond suggests that they make a short cut to throw off their pursuers . . . and find themselves in the middle of a group of cars taking part in a stock car race on a track of ice. This sequence is far-fetched but rather amusing, especially when the SPECTRE car also bursts on to the track with guns blazing. Particularly amusing are the expressions on the various racing drivers' faces when they suddenly find themselves part of a private war.

Though it only runs a few minutes on screen, the whole sequence took several nights to film. The filming was carried out in sub-zero temperatures and there were innumerable problems. For instance, one concerned trying to get a car to roll over at a certain point which the script called for. But though he tried every trick, Austrian professional rally driver Erich Glavitza was unable to make his car roll. Finally, after seven hours of trying, the film men dug a trench in the ice and embedded a tree trunk. Galvitza slammed the car against it and over it went at last. The entire sequence was directed by Anthony Squire.

Bond's and Tracy's troubles are momentarily at an end when the SPECTRE car, while trying to ram them, crashes into the fence. It bursts into flames but Bunt and her men manage to crawl clear. Tracy then drives through an exit barrier and returns, despite the efforts of the track officials, to the open road. But they haven't gone far when a sudden blizzard forces them to take shelter in a deserted barn. Here, as they settle in for the night, Bond takes the unprecedented step of popping *the* question to Tracy. She accepts, of course, and soon they are making plans on where they are going to live after they're married. If that wasn't bad enough, Bond takes this very un-Bond-like behavior a step further by making a New Year's Resolution—no more love-making until after the wedding! But thankfully his resolve soon gives way. "But it's not New Year's yet," he says and when the scene fades he's acting more like the old Bond we used to know.

It's almost a relief after all this romantic coyness when Blofeld and his men break into the barn the next morning. But they are too late.

168

After tangling with Bond, Blofeld's men finish second best.

Bond and Tracy have already left on skis. Blofeld and company immediately follow them and, as Barry's distinctive theme gathers momentum in the background, there are some beautiful shots of them skiing in single file down the brilliantly white slopes. Before long they catch up with their quarry and the chase is on again.

Again we're treated to some breathtaking skiing as Bond and Tracy try to out-distance their pursuers by skiing over the rooftops of a snow-covered village. And there's an amusing scene, taken from the book, when they ski across a road that is sunk deep in the snow and is being cleared by a snow plough. The SPECTRE skiers follow but one man doesn't make it to the other side and falls in front of the plough. With a scream he's dragged into it and as the snow emerging from the exhaust pipes turns a bright red, Bond comments, "He had plenty of guts. . . ."

It begins to look as if they will escape. But then Blofeld pulls a truly despicable trick. Coming to a halt, he orders only three of his men to carry on the chase. Then, as Bond and Tracy ski beneath a mountain slope laden with snow, he fires a grenade which sets off an avalanche. Bond, Tracy, and Blofeld's own men are all buried in the ensuing rush of snow.

The avalanche was a real one, set off by the film crew with sticks of dynamite. Every precaution was taken but, avalanches being tricky things at the best of times, the cameramen came close to being covered while filming the man-made cataclysm. Close-ups of Bond and Tracy were intercut with shots of dummies being engulfed by the snow which combined to give a very realistic effect.

When the air has cleared, Blofeld searches the area with his binoculars, and sights Tracy lying only partly buried. On his orders, Blofeld's men ski down and drag her away, while a dazed Bond digs his way free too late to save her. The next scene shows Bond back in London, re-living the memory of seeing Tracy taken away by Blofeld's thugs. Blofeld has by this time delivered his ultimatum to the United Nations; his price is a pardon for all his previous crimes and official recognition to his claim for a title. Despite Bond's urgings that an attack be launched on his mountain stronghold, the authorities intend to accede to his demands, not wanting to risk a worldwide famine. Bond has one last attempt at convincing M that Blofeld could be defeated by a direct attack, then puts a call through to Draco. "I have a demolition job for you," he tells him, while the Queen's portrait looks down in disapproval. . . .

Next, we have a beautiful shot of three helicopters, their navigation lights sparkling like jewels, flying over the Alps during sunrise. The helicopters carry the markings of the Red Cross but are filled with Draco's men, armed to the teeth. The Swiss Air Force aren't too happy though, and Draco has a hard time convincing them over the radio that his group is merely an innocent medical team on a mercy mission to aid the victims of an avalance. Things become even trickier when they are buzzed by an Air Force jet, but Draco's final bluff—that he's carrying a group of international press men— succeeds and the authorities give in.

Meanwhile, on top of Piz Gloria, Blofeld has been trying to persuade Tracy to join his side. He even wants her to share his empire

Tracy makes the most of being Blofeld's prisoner.

on a more permanent basis, as his wife! (The marriage bug seems to have bitten everyone in this film.)

"Marry me," he tells Tracy, "and I'll make you a Countess."

"But you forget," she replies, "I'm *already* a Countess."

At this point, Blofeld is interrupted by a call from his radio operator who has picked up the conversation between Draco and the Swiss Air Force. Blofeld listens for a while but decides that it has nothing to do with him and returns to Tracy. But Tracy has recognized her father's voice and realizes that help is on the way. Hoping to keep Blofeld occupied, she immediately changes her attitude towards him and suggests that they go up to the observation room together and watch the sunrise. A true egotist, Blofeld is not in the least suspicious of her sudden change. (Savalas and Rigg both seem to be greatly enjoying themselves in these scenes.) In the observation room, they celebrate with champagne and quote poetry to each other, Tracy even going so far to call Blofeld "master of the world."

It can't last, of course, and Blofeld's dreams are rudely shattered (along with his windows) when Draco's helicopters suddenly open fire, and the next moment the "master of the world" is huddled on the floor. Too late he realizes he has been fooled. Outside, Draco's men are dropping from the helicopters over the steep slopes and are fighting their way up to the Institute. Blofeld's men retaliate, but it soon becomes obvious what the outcome of the battle will be. Leaving two of his men to take care of Tracy, Blofeld retreats to his laboratory. But Tracy proves to be more difficult to "take care of" than expected. In fact, she displays more than a passing resemblance to our old friend Emma Peel. One of Blofeld's thugs is knocked unconscious with a bottle of champagne, the other one she leaves impaled on a set of ornamental spikes.

Tracy is not exactly a helpless heroine.

By this time Bond himself has arrived on the scene, machine gun blazing, and the remaining resistance soon crumbles. Bond and Tracy have another brief reunion; then he takes off after Blofeld while Draco's men complete the mopping-up operations and set the explosives. Bond discovers a map of the world in Blofeld's quarters that shows where each of the girls carrying the virus has gone and he starts to photograph every location. But as he completes his task, Blofeld appears on a balcony behind him and levels a gun at his back. There's a shot, but it misses Bond who whirls round and returns the fire. He misses too (perhaps the cold is affecting their trigger fingers) and Blofeld runs for cover.

By this time, Draco and company are pulling out as the explosives are almost due to go off. Tracy refuses to leave, however, until Bond has arrived and Draco is forced to take drastic action—in the form of a quick clip to her jaw. As she slumps unconscious he picks her up and flings her over his shoulder, muttering, "Spare the rod and spoil the child."

Seconds before everything explodes, Blofeld, closely followed by Bond, jumps to safety out of a small door at the rear. Then the whole headquarters goes up in smoke in a violent series of explosions and one just has to feel sorry for Blofeld when he looks back and gives a strangled sob at the sight. Once again his plans have come to naught and no doubt he'll have a lot of explaining to do to his creditors. But he's got no time to think about that at the moment for Bond is close on his heels.

We see Blofeld run into a shed, then re-appear pushing a bob sled. He hurls himself on it and the next moment is hurtling away down the slide. Seeing this, Bond grabs a sled of his own and follows Blofeld down the run . . . and during the next few minutes we are treated to a sequence which rivals the ski chase in excitement. As Bond and Blofeld zoom down the slide at dizzying speed a gun fight develops, then Blofeld produces a hand grenade which, after withdrawing the pin, he drops inside his own sled, recalling the similar scene in *From Russia with Love*. But, in this case, he manages to retrieve it in time and tosses it so that it lands directly in Bond's path. It explodes and Bond, and his sled, go hurtling over the wall of the run in spectacular fashion. But Bond is unhurt and manages to dash across to where the run curves in time to catch up with Blofeld's sled. He flings himself at Blofeld as he whizzes by and manages to grasp the rear of his sled. He's dragged behind for some distance before he succeeds in hauling himself up into the sled, despite Blofeld's various nasty attempts to dislodge him.

There's a furious struggle then, during which Bond is pushed out by Blofeld and for a few incredible moments travels parallel to the hurtling sled on his back. But he again manages to get back in, though Blofeld maintains the upper hand. At one point, Blofeld thrusts Bond's head out over the side of the sled so that it grinds against the icy wall of the run. The hideous crunching sound his helmet makes as it rubs along the wall is guaranteed to send cold shivers up and down anyone's spine.

The end finally comes when Blofeld, who is at that particular moment on top of Bond and busily trying to smash him to pulp, is caught round the neck by a low hanging branch and torn out of the sled. We get a final view of him hanging limply from the branch as the sled continues on its way. Finding himself suddenly alone, Bond attempts to slow the sled down but the controls come apart in his hands and the sled finishes up by crashing. Once again Bond is sent sprawling into the snow but this time help is at hand—in the form of a St. Bernard dog carrying a barrel of brandy.

The filming of the above sequence was as exciting as what appeared on the screen. The same team who handled the ski chases were again responsible, including Willy Bogner, Jr., who equalled his previous feats by this time skiing with a camera down the actual bob sled run! Praise must also go to the late John Jordan, the aerial cameraman, not only on this sequence but on others throughout the film. He hung suspended eighteen feet below a helicopter in his specially-designed harness to obtain the shots he wanted. And of course the stunt men earned their wages, especially Heinz Leu and Robert Zimmerman who doubled as Bond and Blofeld, respectively. The scene during the chase when Bond fell out of the sled and travelled down the run on his back was not in the script and quite accidental. Leu was unhurt but Zimmerman, who remained on the sled, got his face caught in the machinery, which resulted in some nasty injuries.

Blofeld's incident with the tree branch was also a difficult scene to film. At first they attempted to shoot it directly with the stuntman supported by a safety harness, but during the first take the harness broke and he collided into the tree with great force. After that it was decided to stage the stunt in the studio using reverse action and front projection (front projection, which gives a much more realistic effect than back projection, was often used in *OHMSS*).

After the snow, it's a relief to return to the warmer setting of Draco's ranch in Portugal where an historic event is about to take place: James Bond's wedding. Everyone is there—M, Miss Moneypenny, Major Boothroyd, Draco, his men, even the famous Aston Martin which has been decked out in flowers for the occasion. After the reception, Bond and Tracy make their farewells. Bond tosses his hat to a tearful Miss Moneypenny who catches it in a convulsive grip. "Careful, Miss Moneypenny. That's government property," says Major Boothroyd in pained tones as he removes the hat from her grasp and returns it to Bond. "If there's anything I can ever do to be of help, 007. . . ."

"Thanks, Q," replies Bond, "but this time *I've* got the gadgets and I know how to use them." Then he says goodbye to Draco who tries to slip him a cheque for £1 million, but Bond gives it back to him. "I told you. I don't need it."

As the crowd waves and cheers, the Aston Martin makes its way slowly through the groups of singing and dancing children, taking its occupants, apparently, towards a rosy future. At this point, one could be forgiven for assuming that the film was over but those who have read the book know that there is a sting in the tale yet to come. Actually one doubted very much if the book's ending would be included in the film, knowing the producers' preference for avoiding anything downbeat. But again it was due to the director's insistence that the ending remained the same.

So, when Bond stops on the side of a mountain road to remove the flowers that are still draped around the car, we know what to expect. No sooner has he said to Tracy that, "There's no hurry, we have all the time in the world," than a car comes roaring round the bend. There's a crackle of gunfire and we receive a quick glimpse of Blofeld, his neck in a brace, behind the driving wheel, and Bunt holding a machine gun.

"That was Blofeld!" exclaims Bond as he leaps back into the car to give chase. But there's no reply from Tracy, and the camera slowly pans across to show the shattered windshield and the hole in the center of her forehead. Moist-eyed, Bond cradles the dead Tracy on his lap. "It's all right," he tells a motorcycle patrolman who has just arrived on the scene. "There's nothing wrong. We're on our honeymoon, you see, and we have all the time in the world...."

This sequence, coming after the light-hearted action of the rest of the film, has great impact and Hunt was justified in wanting it included, though some critics considered it to be totally incongruous. One only regrets that it wasn't Connery who had the opportunity to do some real acting as Bond. (Apparently Hunt kept Lazenby confined in his trailer for most of the day when these scenes were shot in order to make him lose his temper and thus produce some sort of emotional display for the camera. Not a happy picture to have worked on from all accounts.)

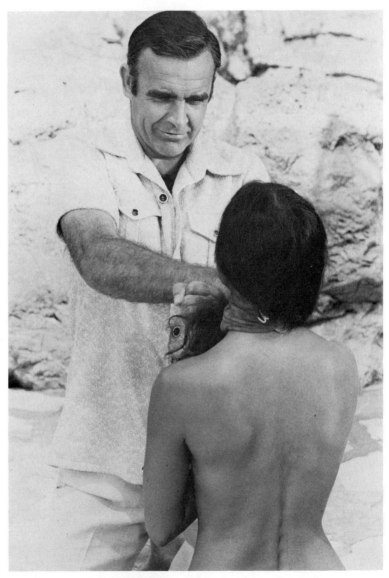

Bond helps a young lady (Denise Perrier)
get something off her chest.

9

Diamonds Are Forever

On Her Majesty's Secret Service was the first Bond film not to be a runaway financial success. Two years after its initial release it was only just beginning to break even at the box office. This was in contrast to the other films which by that time had earned almost two hundred million dollars! But OHMSS certainly wasn't a failure. For a relatively big budget film to break even in those days of economic troubles within the film industry was no mean feat. There are several possible reasons why OHMSS did not succeed as well as the earlier films, but the obvious one is that people were not prepared to accept Lazenby's version of Bond. Another reason might be that audiences didn't respond to Hunt's laudable attempts to put more emphasis on the plot, and the characters, than had been the custom in the Bond films since Goldfinger, but one hopes not.

Getting Connery back into his shoulder holster wasn't easy but both the producers and the United Artists executives thought it was worth the effort and expense.

Mr. Connery demanded, and received, a lot for his appearance in Diamonds Are Forever. It included a one-million-dollar straight fee, which he donated to the Scottish International Education Trust, a charity which he himself founded. But it also included a guarantee that he would be paid ten thousand dollars a week if the film over-ran its allotted filming schedule and, most important of all, a promise from United Artists that they would finance the production of two films of his own choice. (So far only one of these films has been made and that was *The Offence* in 1972. A psychological drama, it was a critical success but not a financial one. It was directed by Connery's friend Sidney Lumet.)

As noted earlier, *Diamonds Are Forever* reverts completely back to the old pre-*OHMSS* formula. As a result, it is no surprise to see that Peter Hunt, director of *OHMSS* and part of the Bond team from the very beginning, is not associated with this new film. Syd Cain, production designer of *OHMSS* and another one who dates back to *Dr. No*, is also missing. In his place is Ken Adam and once again his futuristic designs dominate the film. Another old team member who doesn't appear on the cast list (the result of some confusin over his availability to work on the film) is special effects man John Stears. Otherwise, most of the old familiar names are still there—including Ted Moore as director of photography, Bob Simmons as one of the stunt arrangers, and Richard Maibaum who shares the screenplay credits this time with Tom Mankiewicz. There are several new names, too, and this is a result of so much location work being necessary in the U.S.A. Working regulations being what they are in the States, it wasn't possible for a fully English production crew to film there for any long period of time. So it became necessary for the producers to hire a duplicate American film crew for the six weeks of filming there. Then it was back to Pinewood Studios in England and an English film crew for the studio shooting which took ten weeks.

The plot of the film differs greatly from that of the book. In fact it would be more accurate to say that the two have little in common. Fleming's novel concerned a diamond smuggling racket controlled by the Spang brothers, two American gangsters. The book was relatively unspectacular with regard to plot. James Bond infiltrates the smuggling pipeline and ends up in America where he has a confrontation with Seraffimo Spang, one of the two brothers. This takes place on Spang's private railway and is the only really far-fetched section of the book. Spang has built himself a replica of an entire Western town, complete with antique steam engine, and dresses in full cowboy rig, spurs and all. Bond kills Spang and returns to England with Tiffany Case, a reformed female member of the gang. During the trip back on the *Queen Elizabeth,* they are almost killed by Wint and Kidd, Spang's killers, but Bond manages to overcome them. The book ends with Bond in South Africa where he kills the other brother, Jack Spang, while he is trying to escape in a helicopter (he shoots him down with a Bofors gun).

The plot of the film is rather different. There are certain similarities during the first half but then it switches to the reliable old storyline used in *Dr. No* and *You Only Live Twice*—the space hardware takes over, Bond then infiltrates the villain's headquarters (though "infiltrate" is rather the wrong word on this occasion) and everything ends in a series of explosions.

The pre-credits sequence is, as usual, a lot of fun. We see Bond beating up various people, including a girl whom he throttles with the top of her own bikini, in an effort to find out where Blofeld is. Though it isn't mentioned in the film he is presumably seeking Blofeld to obtain revenge for the murder of his wife. Then we see Blofeld himself, this time played by Charles Gray, in conference with a group of plastic surgeons. He is demanding that a proposed operation be carried out as soon as possible. There's a jump then and we see a body being packed into a mud bath for recuperative purposes. As the medical staff leave the building they are passed by someone, also dressed in gown and mask, going in. Inside, the mask and gown are discarded to reveal a familiar face, and James Bond advances towards the mud-caked figure whom he believes to be Blofeld. As he does so a gun barrel rises slowly out of the ooze. (This scene was repeated almost shot for shot in John Boorman's *Zardoz*, which also starred Connery.) Bond spots it and dives forward, grabbing hold of a rope that releases more mud fron a container overhead. The man in the bath is completely buried under the slimy deluge and disappears from sight. When Bond is sure that he is finished he reaches into the mud and pulls the man's head up. He washes the mud off the face but discovers that it isn't Blofeld.

"Making mud pies, double-O seven?"

Bond turns and finds himself face to face with Blofeld who is accompanied by two armed guards. "Get his gun," orders Blofeld. One of the men goes to Bond and feels inside his jacket for a gun. Suddenly he screams and withdraws his hand quickly, his fingers caught in an ingenious clamp. Bond then disposes of the other guard by flinging a series of surgical scalpels into various parts of his anatomy. Blofeld attempts to stab him but Bond grabs his wrist,

The end for Blofeld—or is it?

drags him across an operating table and bashes him on the head with a lamp. Then he straps him face down on the table and sends it hurtling towards an odious looking pool of mud. Blofeld slides head-first into the pool and sinks. Grinning, Bond pulls a switch on a nearby control board which causes the mud to boil. "Welcome to hell, Blofeld," he says. But as Bond watches the bubbles rising out of the mud there is a meowing sound behind him. He turns and we see Blofeld's famous white cat spitting. The camera zooms in one of the cat's baleful eyes, freezes it . . . and the credits begin to roll.

Shirley Bassey is back singing the theme song and John Barry once again provides the theme itself, although this time it rather lacks punch. The main theme certainly doesn't compare to the one he composed for *OHMSS*. But Maurice Binder's title design is as impressive as ever, his nudes even more so.

The film proper begins with M (Bernard Lee) showing Bond a diamond collection in the London headquarters of a diamond syndicate. A meeting with the syndicate head, Sir Donald Munger (Laurence Naismith) follows and Bond is briefed on the situation over a glass of sherry. This gives him the opportunity to once again show off his expertise as regards wines.

"A Solero," he says as he sniffs the glass, "'51, I believe."

"Sherries don't have years, double-0-seven," says M testily. "Even I know that."

"I was referring to the date of the original vintage on which this sherry was based," replies Bond. He sniffs again. "*1851.*"

The film-Bond certainly doesn't seem to have the same high regard for his boss as Bond did in the books. In fact their relationship in the film seems to be one of mutual dislike.

Sir Donald describes to Bond their mining operation in South Africa. As he tells of the efficient security organization, we see on the screen how the diamonds are being stolen. Workers in the mine hide the diamonds they steal in their mouths. They are later removed by a corrupt dentist who pays each patient. The scene then changes to one of a scorpion attacking some smaller insect. (This, as Fleming fans will remember, was described in the book, as was the mud bath setting, if used in an entirely different context.) "One of nature's finest experts, Mr. Kidd," we hear a voice say as a black-gloved hand scoops up the scorpion. "One is never too old to learn from a true professional, Mr. Wint." And we have our first glimpse of Wint and Kidd, the murder team. They too featured in the book but did not appear until much later. Kidd is played by Putter Smith, Wint by Bruce Glover. As far as appearances go, they are a very bizarre couple; unfortunately, thanks to the prevailing mood of this film, they are too exaggerated to be really sinister.

They meet the dentist whom we saw collecting the diamonds from the workers. He arrives on a motorbike, hands over the diamonds, and they kill him by dropping the scorpion down the back of his shirt. Soon afterwards, a helicopter touches down and Wint and Kidd hand over a box which supposedly contains the diamonds. The machine takes off but doesn't get very far before it blows up. Mr. Wint and Mr. Kidd walk off into the desert, hand in hand. (Their homosexuality was the only thing about them that made the transfer from the novel successfully.)

Back in London, Sir Donald is still explaining the problem to Bond. It seems that the smuggling pipeline is being closed down, the various members being killed, and the diamonds being stockpiled somewhere instead of eventually turning up on the market elsewhere as they usually do. M tells Bond that they know the identity of one of the smugglers in the pipeline, a professional smuggler by the name of Peter Franks. In Amsterdam, Bond, disguised as Franks, makes contact with the member of the pipeline who is supposed to pass on the diamonds to Franks . . . a Miss T. Case. When he enters her apartment, he finds her dressed in nothing but a bra and panties . . . another one of the all too few carryovers from the book. But here the resemblance to Fleming's Miss Case ends. Jill St. John is very decorative but acting is not her chief asset. From Fleming's description of Tiffany Case she should have been played by someone similar to the young Lauren Bacall; instead she comes across like Lucille Ball.

M gives Bond a lecture on diamonds; opposite: Lois Maxwell as Miss Moneypenny

Tiffany (Jill St. John) pleads her case to Bond

"What's the T stand for?" asks Bond while she prepares him a drink. "Tiffany," she replies. "I was born there. On the first floor while my mother was looking for a wedding ring." On the pretext of getting him some ice, she takes Bond's glass into the next room and swiftly dusts it for fingerprints. These she photographs and compares to those belonging to the real Peter Franks. We are surprised to see that they match. Later, while Bond is back in his hotel room, we see why. He was wearing false fingerprints. As he peels them off he gives Q a ring in London to congratulate him on the success of his latest invention. While Q (Desmond Llewelyn again) is talking on the telephone we see in the background one of the best jokes in the film—a cluster of rockets being lowered into the front of the famous Aston Martin. But Bond receives some bad news from Q; the real Mr. Franks has escaped after killing a guard and is believed to be heading for Amsterdam. Bond immediately rushes back to Tiffany's apartment house where he intercepts Franks at the front door. Pretending to be a local, he rides with Franks in the lift. On the way up, Bond attempts to deliver an unexpected haymaker but as he draws his arm back he accidentally breaks a glass panel with his elbow which warns Franks. It would seem very difficult to stage a fight in as narrow and confining a space as that of a lift and still make it look exciting, but stunt arranger Bob Simmons succeeds in doing just that. (He did it too well—this sequence was almost completely cut out when the film was shown on British TV.) The fight ends with Franks being thrown down the stairwell, after being sprayed with a fire extinguisher. "Is he dead?" asks a shocked Tiffany. "I should certainly hope so," replies Bond as he switches wallets with Franks. Bond drags the body into her apartment where Tiffany checks his identification. On finding a Playboy Club membership card made out to James Bond she exclaims, "My God, you've killed James Bond!"

Q and a new modifier for Bond's Aston Martin

"Just goes to show that no one is indestructible," replies Bond blandly, seemingly unperturbed to learn that his fame as a secret agent has spread.

From this point on, the plot tends to become rather confusing. In fact, one of the main criticisms I have of the film is that it is needlessly complicated. Using the dead body as a means to carry the diamonds, Bond and Tiffany fly to Los Angeles accompanied (although they do not realize the fact) on the same plane by Wint and Kidd. At Los Angeles, Bond takes the coffin through customs and is met by Felix Leiter, Bond's old CIA friend. This time Leiter is played by Norman Burton, another unsatisfactory piece of casting. The coffin, supposedly containing Bond's brother, is handed over to three Mafia types who work for a mortuary called Slumber, Inc. Bond travels with them to the mortuary and watches with the owner, Morton Slumber, as the coffin slides into the oven. Soon afterwards he is given an urn full of diamonds which he is told to place in a certain niche outside. In the niche he finds an envelope containing a wad of money, but then he is struck over the head by Wint and Kidd. They load him into a coffin and send it into the oven. But Bond is freed by Mr. Slumber and a Mr. Shady Tree—who is the next link in the pipeline. They have discovered that the diamonds are fakes and demand to know where the real ones are (if they were fakes, how come they didn't burn with Franks's body when it was cremated?). Bond replies that the money they gave him is also fake and he won't divulge the diamonds' whereabouts until they pay him in real money. He leaves the mortuary, telling them that he'll be staying at the Whyte House, a combined casino and hotel owned by the mysterious millionaire Willard Whyte (any similarity between Willard Whyte and Howard Hughes is purely coincidental).

At the Whyte House Bond runs into Shady Tree, who has a regular comedy act there. As he is a pipeline member, he is next on the list to be killed but Burt Saxby, the casino manager (Bruce Cabot—who died shortly after the film was completed), receives an order over the phone that as the real diamonds haven't been received yet, Tree mustn't be killed. But it is too late. By the time Saxby reaches Tree's changing room Wint and Kidd have already paid him a visit.

188

Bond narrowly avoids cremation.

Bond gambles with his counterfeit money, after Saxby gives the okay to his staff, and soon wins fifty thousand dollars, the price agreed upon. During the game he picks up a camp follower, Plenty O'Toole ("Named after your father, no doubt," says Bond) played by Lana Wood, sister of Natalie. He takes her back to his room but before they can get down to business they are interrupted by Mr. Slumber's three hoods. One of them picks up Miss O'Toole, by this time dressed only in panties, and tosses her out the window. As the room is ten stories up, things look grim for a moment or two but fortunately Plenty lands in a swimming pool. "Exceptionally fine shot," says Bond. "I didn't know there was a pool down there," replies the hood. They retreat then, leaving Bond mystified for awhile until he discovers the cool Miss Case in his bed. Bond agrees with her to double-cross the smugglers and to split the money. He arranges for Leiter to have the diamonds presented to her in a toy dog that she wins at one of the casinos after some devious playing around (don't ask me how the CIA got hold of the real diamonds).

The plan is for the CIA to follow her and see where she goes with the gems; but Tiffany gives them the slip. So Bond returns to where she is staying and surprises her on her return. She also discovers what she thinks is her black wig floating in the swimming pool, but it turns out to be Plenty O'Toole. (Just why *she* was killed I cannot grasp; apparently there *was* a scene that explained her presence but it was cut, along with several others.) Bond learns that she has placed the toy dog in an airport locker and they return there together to watch Burt Saxby collect it. He hands it over to a Dr. Metz at a nearby service station. While Tiffany causes a diversion, Bond sneaks into the back of the Doctor's minibus and rides with him out to Whyte's Techtronics factory. Posing as a radiation checker, Bond infiltrates into Metz's laboratory where he sees a satellite encrusted with diamonds. He also spots a cassette of military music. At this point, his ruse is discovered and he is forced to make a quick getaway.

190

As I said, the plot is complicated. The main purpose of these central sequences is to show off the sights of Las Vegas and to pad out the film. But from here on, the diamond smuggling is ignored and the film's main plot begins. Bond escapes from Whyte's guards by commandeering a so-called "moon buggy." He accomplishes this in an amusing scene which shows him running through an astronauts' training ground where they are busy simulating a lunar landing. He leaps into the buggy and sends it crashing through one of the walls, then out of the factory's front gate and into the desert. He is chased by a squad of cars driven by the factory personnel but, as they are not built to bounce across the sand dunes as efficiently as the "moon buggy," they very quickly come to grief. Three guards, however, give chase on specially adapted dune buggies and Bond is forced to abandon the moon vehicle. (A shoddy piece of continuity here—we see one of the moon buggy's wheels bounce loose from the vehicle but in the next shot all four wheels are attached again.) While the other two pursue the empty vehicle, Bond kicks the third guard off his buggy and speeds away to where Tiffany is waiting by the road with a car.

By nightfall, they have arrived back in Las Vegas, unaware that the guards at the factory have radioed ahead to the Las Vegas

Bond hijacks a moon buggy.

police. Bond's car is soon spotted and the police intervene. The ensuing car chase is really the highpoint of the film . . . . Squads of police cars careen all over the streets of Las Vegas as Bond weaves in and out of the traffic, leading them a merry chase. He literally drives circles around them, and when they corner him in a parking area, causes them to collide with one another as they attempt to cut him off. He escapes by sending his vehicle, after launching it off a trailer, over the top of a row of parked cars. The police car that tries to follow ends up by landing right in their midst. But while the audience is still laughing at this, the *coup de grâce* is delivered. Chased down a dead-end alley by another police car, Bond escapes by tipping his car up so that it is riding only on two wheels. In this way, the car is able to plunge through the narrow exit at the end of the alley. The police car tries to follow suit but merely tips over. (Fifty-three cars were purchased for the filming of the chase and twenty-four were totally destroyed.)

Bond's next impressive feat is to ride on the top of an outside elevator up the side of the Whyte House to just below Willard Whyte's penthouse. Here he is left suspended when the elevator descends beneath him. Hanging on to a girder he climbs over to a ledge and then fires two bolts, with attached cords, from a special gun, into the underneath of the overhanging penthouse. A rather stomach-churning moment follows when Bond swings himself out into space, supported only by these two somewhat frail cords. Then he hauls himself up and onto the roof itself. After gaining entry through a skylight, he lowers himself in relief only to find that he is seated on a rather elaborate toilet. An amplified Texas drawl from a hidden speaker reveals to Bond that his arrival has been detected. He is asked to step through a nearby door ("Provided you haven't any unfinished personal business to attend to first, Mr. Bond"), and he does so. He enters a huge luxurious room, the centerpiece of which is a circular table set into the floor. Expecting to meet Willard Whyte, Bond is surprised when the chair on the dais at one end of the room swivels round to reveal—Ernst Stavro Blofeld. And Bond is even more perplexed when another Blofeld walks down the stairs toward him. Two Blofelds . . . but one of them is a fake, as was the one whom Bond had killed in the mud pool. Yes, Blofeld has kidnapped the real Willard Whyte and is using his vast financial empire

Charles Gray as Blofeld

for his own evil purposes (as Whyte hasn't been seen for five years he proved to be the perfect kidnap victim for Blofeld). Blofeld has been imitating Willard's voice by means of a special electronic device.

Bond is in a real quandary with the two Blofelds, until he spots the white cat walking by. Immediately, he sends the cat flying with his foot. Though he had surrendered his automatic earlier he still has possession of the bolt firing gun. When the cat leaps into the arms of one of the Blofeld's, Bond fires, sending a bolt into the forehead of the Blofeld with the cat. But no sooner has the body fallen than another cat enters the room, this one with a diamond necklace around its neck. "Right idea," says the remaining Blofeld as he draws a gun and aims it at Bond. "But wrong pussy," says Bond.

194

His double falls victim to Bond's bolt gun.

The real Blofeld forces Bond to enter a lift where he is gassed, then collected by Wint and Kidd. They take the unconscious Bond out into the desert and leave him in a length of pipe which is buried the next morning to form part of an oil pipeline. Bond wakes up to find himself buried alive and smelling of Wint's potent after-shave lotion. But he manages to attract a rescue party by sabotaging the automatic welding machine that soon comes zooming along the pipe.

Then, with the help of Q, Bond disguises his voice and makes a phone call to Blofeld pretending to be Saxby. In this fashion, he discovers where the real Willard Whyte is being imprisoned. With Leiter's men close behind, Bond travels alone to Whyte's summer house out in the desert. There he is met by Bambi and Thumper (Donna Garratt and Trina Parks), two agile young ladies who give him a very rough time indeed. In fact, it looks as if Bond has met his match when they toss him in the swimming pool, but there he manages to get the better of them and, when Leiter arrives, he has the situation well in hand.

Meanwhile Blofeld himself has escaped (wearing woman's clothing!) and has taken Tiffany with him. By the time Bond releases the real Willard Whyte, it is too late to prevent Blofeld's satellite from being launched into space. Once in orbit it refuses to obey the directions of Whyte's technicians and it soon becomes obvious that Blofeld is controlling it himself. Whyte tells Bond that the diamonds have been incorporated into the satellite to form a super laser. First Blofeld blows up a U.S. missile, a submarine, and a Russian missile base then demands a ransom or he will wipe out a U.S. city (just what the ransom could be isn't specified—what can you give the man who has everything, including a satellite full of diamonds?).

With Whyte's help, Bond deduces that Blofeld must be operating from an oil rig off the coast of California. He flies out to it alone and allows himself to be captured by Blofeld's men. "Good afternoon gentlemen," he greets them. "I represent the Acme Pollution Company. We're cleaning up the world and thought this place would be as good as any to start." Blofeld has him searched and they find a tape cassette hidden in his coat which he presumably intended to switch with the tape in the computer that is controlling the satellite.

Bond is attacked by Bambi (Donna Garratt, pouncing) and Thumper (Trina Parks).

Blofeld obligingly gives Bond the usual tour of his installation which affords our hero the opportunity to exchange the dummy tape for the real one (Tiffany had slipped him the cassette). Tiffany doesn't see him do this, however, and inadvertently puts the real one back in the computer. Bond is understandably annoyed when he finds out ("You stupid twit!" he calls her) for he has given the signal to a waiting force of helicopters which immediately sweep in and open fire on the rig.

Blofeld has set the target city to be Washington and the laser beam is only minutes away. He then seals himself in his mini-sub and orders it lowered into the sea by crane. But Bond overpowers the crane operator and uses the sub as a battering ram to break down the side of the control room and smash the computer in the nick of time. (This wasn't the ending in the original script— apparently Blofeld made it to shore but was followed by Bond and they had a final show-down—but it all had to be changed for reasons not unconnected with the budget. In the version that reached the screen, we never do learn what happened to Blofeld.) Bond then dives into the sea as the oil rig is overwhelmed by a series of explosions. Tiffany is already in the water, having fallen off the rig earlier while trying to fire a machine gun.

Kidd (Putter Smith) and Wint (Bruce Glover) enjoy their work.

The film ends with a sequence on an ocean liner (as in the book) with Wint and Kidd having one last attempt to kill Bond. They must be doing this job out of pure generosity, as there is surely no one left alive to pay their wages. As Bond and Tiffany enjoy the moonlight, their cabin is invaded by the campy twosome who wheel in two tables, one laden with drinks, the other containing a vast quantity of food including a bomb hidden in the dessert. But Bond remembers the smell of Wint's after-shave lotion and becomes immediately suspicious, and when Wint displays his ignorance of the wine he is serving their cover is truly blown.

Forced to take direct action, Kidd advances on Bond with two blazing Shish-kebabs while Wint wraps the chain attached to his wine tasting cup around Bond's neck. For a moment, things look bad for our hero but Bond coolly breaks a bottle of brandy and splashes its contents over Kidd. The flames from the Shish-kebabs spread up his arms and rapidly envelop his whole torso, forcing the unfortunate Mr. Kidd to jump over the railing.

While Wint tries to strangle Bond.

Kidd finds his shish kebabs enflamed by a shower of brandy.

Enraged, Wint tries to throttle Bond, but Tiffany lends a hand by throwing the dessert at him and inadvertently reveals its explosive content. Bond then breaks free, tangles the chain between Wint's legs (which causes Wint to squeal with delight) attaches the bomb to his coat tails and flips him neatly over the side of the ship. He explodes before he reaches the water. "He certainly left with his tail between his legs," comments Bond.

Just how does *Diamonds Are Forever* compare with the other Bond films? Well, I don't consider it to be in the same class as the first three, but I daresay that it is no better or worse than any of the films since *Goldfinger*. *OHMSS* would have been the best of these without a doubt if it had featured Connery. Guy Hamilton's direction adds a polish to the proceedings in *Diamonds Are Forever* that has been missing since *Goldfinger,* and Richard Maibaum's and Tom Mankiewicz's screenplay contains some very good dialogue. But the main flaw in the production, apart from the over complicated plot, is that everything is played more for laughs instead of thrills and suspense. This has been a growing tendency in the films of late. Instead of the clever balance between humor and excitement that the early films achieved, *Diamonds Are Forever* often lapses into sheer slapstick. As Kingsley Amis noted when commenting on *Thunderball,* it is much easier for the makers to say, "Look at this, isn't it all terribly amusing?" than it is for them genuinely to thrill their audiences. (This was to be the dominant trend in the Bond films throughout the Seventies.)

Also, there is no real sense of menace in the film. Wint and Kidd look an evil-enough pair, but they act more like a comedy team than a murder squad. Their predecessors, such as "Red" Grant and Oddjob, were just as grotesque but much more frightening. Even the grand finale on board the ship is more like something from the Marx Brothers than Ian Fleming.

200 Even Blofeld himself is not what he used to be. Charles Gray's portrayal might have been one of the best—if the script hadn't turned him into a figure of fun. In *You Only Live Twice,* Donald Pleasence played him as a "scarred, asexual monster." But in *Diamonds,* Blofeld is no longer scarred, much too charming to be a monster (one can't really take his threat to obliterate Washington, D.C. seriously) and, judging by his obvious appreciation of Miss Case, no longer asexual. Even his apparent destruction at the hands of Bond is treated as a comedy routine—bounced up and down on the end of a crane like a yo yo. I don't think Fleming would have approved.

Diamonds Are Forever does have its memorable moments, such as the car chase in Las Vegas, Bond's dizzying ascent to Whyte's lofty penthouse, and the subsequent confrontation with the two Blofelds, but overall it's a disappointment. Part of the problem lies with its ramshackle construction: not only are there too many extraneous scenes, but the grafting on of the whole laser satellite section to the original diamond smuggling plot is both perfunctory and clumsy—the join is too obvious. Just as perfunctory is the climax on Blofeld's oil rig headquarters. It's an exceedingly lame affair, as if everyone concerned was simply going through the motions. Bond, for instance, is able to fool Blofeld much too easily and the sequence where he and Tiffany overcome the guards and release the weather balloon as a signal to Leiter's men is embarrass-

Director Guy Hamilton (right) tells Putter Smith how to serve the final meal in **Diamonds are Forever.**

ingly inept. The actual helicopter assault is also as unexciting as it is predictable. There are some spectacular explosions on the rig, but as it was a real rig and had to be returned to the owners intact after the shooting it obviously couldn't be destroyed (and for some reason a miniature wasn't employed for these shots). Even the stuntmen don't fall over with the panache that is customary in a Bond film . . . all in all, it's very much a damp squib of an ending when compared to those in previous Bonds.

The film's main asset was having Connery back as Bond, even though he had appeared to age considerably since his last appearance as Bond four years previously and was distinctly overweight (he has looked much fitter, and even younger, in subsequent films). But as far as he was concerned, it was definitely the last time he would play James Bond no matter what the inducements. This time the producers believed he might be serious, though not for a moment did they entertain the idea of bringing the series to an end. Broccoli announced: "I'll make one a year 'til the end of eternity, or for as long as there are people who want to see them. . . ." But at the beginning of 1972, the big question was—*did* people still want to see James Bond?

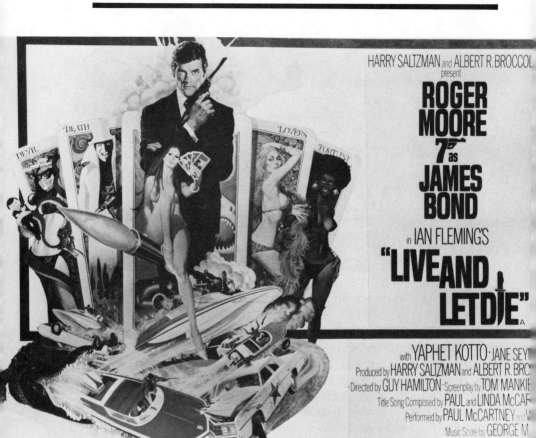

A new Bond: billboard poster for **Live and Let Die**

10

Live and Let Die

Any doubts one may have had about the Bond films continuing their success into the Seventies were quickly dispelled after the release of *Diamonds Are Forever* at the beginning of 1972. In its first week at London's Odeon Leicester Square cinema, it took £35,000, some £13,200 more than the theatre's previous record. One morning the cleaning staff arrived at 10 a.m. to find a queue of 700 people waiting for the first show. This success in London was repeated in other capital cities—in one week alone, the New York theaters showing *Diamonds* took almost as much as all the other theaters on Broadway put together, and in just twelve days a total of $24,568,915 flowed into the box-offices of the one thousand cinemas showing the film across the world. Obviously, there was still a lot of life left in James Bond. This discovery was reassuring for not only Broccoli and Saltzman, but also for United Artists who gave the go-ahead for the next Bond film in the series, *Live and Let Die,* to begin production. The only problem was—*who* was going to play James Bond?

One thing was certain—it was *not* going to be Sean Connery. As far as he was concerned, *Diamonds Are Forever* was definitely the last time he would portray Bond, no matter what financial inducements were laid before him (he has since changed his mind and has announced he will play Bond in *Warhead,* the planned sequel to

Thunderball which Kevin McClory intends to produce—see Appendix 1). So once again, the hunt was on for a new James Bond and once again opinions varied on who should play him, United Artists opting for a big American name such as Clint Eastwood, Steve McQueen, or John Gavin while the producers maintained that Bond should be portrayed by a British actor. The victor turned out to be Roger Moore who had been shortlisted to play Bond at the very beginning, but was beaten by Connery for the role in *Dr. No* back in 1962. He represented a compromise between the two camps—he was British but he was also very familiar to American audiences via the various TV series he has appeared in over the years.

Considering that some critics had mentioned that perhaps Connery was getting a little too old to play Bond, it seems odd that an even older actor was chosen as his replacement. Though Moore, born in 1927, is three years older than Connery, he has retained his boyish good looks to such a degree that one suspects he has a painting stored away somewhere that is aging in his place. His career in films began back in 1945 when he was an extra in *Caesar and Cleopatra;* during the making of the film he was spotted by the Irish director Brian Desmond Hurst who arranged for him to enter RADA. His first big break came when he understudied David Tomlinson in the London stage production of *The Little Hut,* which led to an offer from Hollywood and a part in *The Last Time I Saw Paris* (1954) with Van Johnson and Elizabeth Taylor. He had supporting roles in two other films, *Interrupted Melody* and *The King's Thief* (both 1955), and then received his first starring role in *Diane* (1955), a ludicrous historical epic co-starring Lana Turner. It was less than a resounding success, but perhaps it was the way that Moore wore his suit of armor in the film that led to him being offered the lead role in the British TV series *Ivanhoe,* which *was* a success. He returned to Hollywood in 1959 and starred in both films and TV series, the latter including *The Alaskans* and *Maverick.* It was in television that he was to achieve his biggest success before Bond, playing Simon Templar in the popular and long-running *Saint* series.

Moore is, suspiciously, the first to admit his range as an actor has its limitations. He *can* act, unlike the unfortunate George Lazenby at the time of *On Her Majesty's Secret Service,* but his specialty is undoubtedly light comedy and not melodrama. One can argue that the Bonds today *are* light comedy but, while this may be so, the character of James Bond still needs to retain some elements of his original toughness to provide the films with a central core. Moore doesn't fulfill this need and now the Bond films are a hurricane of spectacular action revolving around what amounts to a blank spot on the screen. To put it bluntly, Moore simply lacks the *presence* of Sean Connery. It's not just a case of different acting techniques.

However, once it was decided to make Roger Moore the new James Bond, the publicity machine swung into action to establish his new image and to try and eradicate the public's automatic association of Connery with the role. During the making of *Live and Let Die,* Harry Saltzman told an interviewer that Ian Fleming himself was "appalled" at the thought of Connery playing Bond. "Fleming," said Saltzman, "saw Bond as a kind of disenfranchised member of the Establishment, Eton, Harrow, and Cambridge. And Sean was none of those. Fleming would have been delighted with Roger. He is the classic Englishman. He looks good and moves good." (Connery's reaction to this was to say: "Harry's right about Fleming. But you can tell the whole thing is beginning to turn around . . . I haven't got any regrets. I'll go and see the film and then I'll go and see Roger and Guy. I may get a walk-on part in the next one. . . .")

Actually, Fleming *didn't* visualize Bond as the classic Englishman. In *Moonraker,* he has Bond reflect that he ". . . knew there was something alien and un-English about himself," and in *Live and Let Die,* when Bond is looking at himself in a mirror he observes ". . . there was the mixed blood of America in the black hair and high cheek bones. . . ." Also, Fleming often described Bond as being of a "saturnine" appearance, a description that better suits Connery than the cheery, fresh-faced Roger Moore.

Not everyone on the Bond production team automatically recanted his previous opinion about Connery. Richard Maibaum, the scriptwriter, told an interviewer in 1977 that: "I thought Sean Connery was absolutely perfect. Apart from being physically a great specimen and good-looking, he had a basic irony about him. Also, he was a much better actor that most people thought. You *believed*

Producers Albert R. Broccoli and Harry Saltzman on
location with the new James Bond

all the physical stuff that Connery did. That's not true about Roger
Moore and Roger, sensing this, plays Bond in a different key. He
makes Bond a more sophisticated character; he doesn't project the
innate toughness that Sean had, or his irony, which sets him apart
from Roger's cynicism. There's a difference between irony and
cynicism. Therefore, we had to be more extreme with Roger and
find places for him to knock girls around and that sort of thing. We
had to toughen him up."

Characteristically, Roger Moore found the process to transform
him into Bond a source of amusement: "I'm going around with a
mean look—I'm sure a lot of people feel I'm going to punch them in
the mouth. One of the first things I had to learn is that Bondian walk.
You have to move like a cat . . . and once you move it's got to look
like you'll walk through a brick wall if necessary. The trouble is, I still

see Sean Connery hovering in my mind. Last night, I was mentally vocalizing the script (of *Live and Let Die*) and the words came out with a Scottish accent. . . ."

In the book he wrote about the making of *Live and Let Die,* Moore recounted the following anecdote involving his young son: "Can you beat anyone, including a robber?" his son asked him. "Oh, yes," replied Moore. "Supposing James Bond came in," said the son. "Daddy is going to play James Bond," Moore explained. "I mean the *real* James Bond, Sean Connery," said his son.

It's ironic that Roger Moore's first appearance as Bond was in *Live and Let Die,* the most violent and sadistic of all the Bond novels when Bond himself was at his toughest, running up his highest body count and actually killing someone in cold blood, an action he disapproved of as a rule (unlike the early screen Bond). It's in this novel that Bond's CIA friend Felix Leiter turns up as a bloody bundle of bandages in a motel room with his arm and leg missing and a note in his mouth reading: "He disagreed with something that ate him."

Live and Let Die was Fleming's second novel and written at a time when he was at the peak of his enthusiasm for both Bond as a character and the whole enterprise of being a thriller writer (later it would become a chore), and as a result it has a pace and zest that none of the other books can match. The plot involved Bond being sent to investigate the source of a large number of gold coins being sold illegally in America in order to finance a Russian spy ring headed by a black criminal mastermind called Mr. Big. Not only is Mr. Big a member of SMERSH but, by exploiting a voodoo cult based around the supernatural figure of Baron Samedi, he also controls a vast network of black criminals.

Read today, Fleming's treatment of the blacks in the novel is embarrassingly patronizing. For example, when Bond first learns about Mr. Big, he is surprised because he doesn't think he's ever heard of a "great Negro criminal before." This is because: "Negroes don't seem to take to big business. Pretty law-abiding chaps I should have thought except when they've drunk too much." But then Mr. Big has a strong dose of French blood in his veins which, Fleming suggested, explained the anomaly.

Actually Fleming was quite proud of his description of Harlem and its inhabitants, even when it later came in for some criticism, particularly from his American associates. Writing to Naomi Burton at the Curtis Brown literary agency in New York in May 1955, Fleming said: "By the way and sucks to you, I had a drink with Raymond Chandler last night and he said the best bit of *Live and Let Die* was the conversation between the two Negroes in Harlem which he said was dead accurate. Perhaps you remember that you nearly sneered me into cutting it out on the grounds that 'Negroes don't talk like that.'"

They certainly don't talk like that in the film version of *Live and Let Die* which went out of its way to reflect the changes that have occurred in American Black consciousness during the years since the novel was written. The criminals are still black but they're *proud* blacks and there's not a hint of patronization in the way they're presented. In fact, if anyone is patronized it's Bond himself who acts like a typical "silly-ass Englishman" in the way that he blithely tries to infiltrate Harlem while looking more than a little conspicuous with his white face and Saville Row overcoat. Nor does he come off very well in his first confrontation with Mr. Big and his henchmen, all of whom are built like wrestlers and tower over Bond, making him look like a harmless schoolboy by comparison.

Inevitably, the film's plot is more complicated than the novel's—Mr. Big is no longer in the gold coin smuggling racket but in the heroin smuggling trade, and he is no longer just Mr. Big but also Dr. Kananga, the ruler of a Haiti-like island called San Monique, who is trying to wreck the American economy for reasons that remain vague. Mr. Big/Dr. Kananga is played by Yaphet Kotto, a powerful character actor (since seen in such films as *Blue Collar* and *Alien*) who stands six foot four inches tall but who doesn't quite measure up to Fleming's description of Big. But then, who could? Because in the book, Big is not only six-and-a-half feet tall, weighs two hundred and eighty pounds, but also has a great football of a head, twice normal size, and a complexion that shines like the face of a week-old corpse in a river.

At first, an attempt is made to suggest that Big and Kananga are two separate people but this doesn't work because Mr. Big is too

Mr. Big (Yaphet Kotto) and friend

obviously Kotto in bizarre make-up. Rick Baker, a makeup expert (*King Kong, Star Wars*) who worked on the film, suggests that Kotto himself must take the responsibility for the less-than-satisfactory makeup job. "I was supposed to do the disguise make-up on Yaphet Kotto in that film," said Baker, "but I got into a big fight with him about the concept. And it wound up with me getting fired because I wasn't black and knew nothing about black people! I wanted to send Yaphet a letter when I won an Emmy for *The Autobiography of Miss Jane Pittman* to ask him if I still didn't know anything about black people . . ."

Kotto's assertions of Black Pride caused other difficulties—such as when he made a visit to the Florida locations to be photographed with Moore and other cast members and he gave a Black Power salute just as the flash bulbs were popping. He was reprimanded by the picture's publicity director, Derek Coyte, who told him: "We're not making a political picture." The result was that Coyte became ostracized by black members of the cast, and further black/white friction developed a few days later when black stuntmen protested about some of the white stuntmen "blacking up" for one particular stunt sequence.

As with any Bond movie, the plot of *Live and Let Die* has to twist, turn, and generally contort itself into knots in order to accommodate the set-pieces and therefore isn't very logical in terms of narrative development (scriptwriter Richard Maibaum is absent from the credits on this one—for the first time since *You Only Live Twice*—and Tom Mankiewica, who collaborated with Maibaum on *Diamonds Are Forever,* gets the sole screenplay credit). The film begins with three short pre-credits sequences showing the murder of three men: one during a United Nations meeting; one during a funeral in the French Quarter of New Orleans; and the other at a voodoo ceremony complete with writhing dancers and pounding drums. As far as Bond pre-credit sequences go, these aren't exceptional though the funeral one is an amusing fragment of black comedy—the intended victim watching the approaching procession without realizing that the coffin the mourners are carrying is for him. And, after he has been knifed and swiftly concealed in the coffin, the mourners then break out into an up-tempo jazz number. . . .

The credits are, as usual, executed by Maurice Binder and feature his familiar surreal nudes. This time, however, Binder's images aren't accompanied by a John Barry title song but one by Paul and Linda McCartney, performed by the group Wings (the other music on the soundtrack was composed and arranged by George Martin, the Beatles' former musical director). The McCartneys' theme for *Live and Let Die* has an energy and excitement long missing from the Bonds and it's a pity they couldn't have been prevailed upon to compose the title songs for subsequent Bond films.

After the credits, we have our first introduction to Roger Moore as James Bond. This takes place in Bond's apartment where he is, of course, in bed with a girl (Madeline Smith). The last time we saw Bond's home (a different one) was in *Dr. No* and it's obvious that his taste in interior decoration has deteriorated over the years because there is some rather appalling wall paper in evidence (Ken Adam didn't work on this one, or the next). *Coitus interruptus* occurs when M and Miss Moneypenny, played by regulars Bernard Lee and Lois Maxwell (who, coincidentally, was at RADA with Moore), arrive to inform him of his new and urgent assignment. Miss Moneypenny also delivers the latest gadget from Q Branch, a wristwatch that can be transformed into a powerful magnet at the touch of a button. Bond is soon testing out the device by using it to unzip the girl's dress when M and Moneypenny leave. Amusingly, this scene required the services of an assistant director who, on his hands and knees out of camera range, had to pull on a wire inside Ms. Smith's dress, and the costume designer, also on her hands and knees, who had to help pull the dress down. Nothing is ever easy as it looks in a Bond film.

As Bond's jet takes off for the U.S.A., the scene is superimposed with shots of tarot cards being placed on a glass table while a girl's voice intones that a man is coming across the water who will bring death and destruction with him. The voice belongs to Solitaire, Kananga's young white clairvoyant who acts as his mystical watchdog and human lie detector (for a time it was planned to have her played by a black actress but this idea was reluctantly abandoned for various reasons). In the novel, Solitaire had persuaded Mr. Big that she wasn't interested in men but he tells Bond that he intends to marry her anyway—"She is too valuable to remain at liberty, and it will be interesting to see our children." However, her psychic powers are linked in the film to her virginity and therefore Mr. Big has a vested interest in keeping her "pure" and untouched. Solitaire is played by young English actress Jane Seymour who is attractive but a little *too* virginal in appearance. In fact, compared to the Solitaire of the book whom Fleming describes as having "high cheekbones and a wide, sensual mouth which held a hint of cruelty," with a jawline that showed "decision and an iron will," all of which adds up to a "face born to command," Ms. Seymour's Solitaire comes across as being rather insipid. More successful is the tarot card motif that the character introduces which, along with the voodoo imagery, provides the movie with an effective visual cohesion.

No sooner has Bond landed at New York than his chauffeur is shot in the head with a dart fired from the wing mirror of a passing car (surely there *had* to be an easier way) and Bond finds himself entering the city in an out-of-control limousine. He survives, of course, and is then reunited with his old friend Felix Leiter of the C.I.A. This time Leiter is played by David Hedison, an actor whose career seems never to have recovered from his appearance in *The Fly* back in 1958, surely one of the most ludicrous science fiction films ever made (he is probably best known for his role in the long-running TV series *Voyage to the Bottom of the Sea*).

Hot on the trail of Dr. Kananga, Bond foolishly allows himself to be captured in a Harlem night club when the booth he is sitting in suddenly swivels round into the wall, depositing Bond on the other side where Mr. Big's men are waiting for him. Bond not only meets Mr. Big (Kananga in disguise) but also Solitaire and Big's giant henchman, Tee Hee (Julius W. Harris), who wears an artificial arm complete with metal pincer.

Mr. Big, understandably, isn't very impressed by Bond though Solitaire is, mainly because her tarot cards have revealed that she and Bond are destined to be lovers. Big dismissively orders a couple of his men to take Bond outside and "waste him" but on their way to carry out his orders, they are both overpowered by Bond after he surprises them by bringing down a fire escape on their heads. As Moore's first fight scene playing Bond, it is more than a little disappointing and in fact must rank as one of the most weakly chore-ographed fight sequences in any of the Bond films. The second black stuntman, for instance, collapses *before* Bond actually makes contact with him. If this was any indication of how the new James Bond was going to handle his fight scenes, then dedicated Bond fans could only shudder with dismay. . . .

The action then moves to Jamaica where Bond makes contact, in more ways than one, with CIA agent Rosie Carver, played by black actress Gloria Hendry who gives a much more spirited per-formance than the leading lady. Bond and Rosie travel by launch to Kananga's island of San Monique where Bond discovers the source of Big's heroin supply—a vast crop of poppies growing beneath camouflaged netting. Rosie, however, turns out to be a double-agent but is accidentally shot by one of Kananga's remote-controlled guns hidden in a voodoo figure.

Bond later makes a night assault on Kananga's hill-top house by means of a hang glider, breaks into Solitaire's room and convinces her with a fixed deck of tarot cards that he definitely is the man who will take her away from all this, pausing only to bed her in typical Bond fashion and unwittingly destroying her psychic powers at the same time.

The next day Bond and Solitaire escape from Kananga's men by commandeering a double-decker bus; a chase sequence that repre-sents the film's first major action set-piece. The bus was shipped from London, as was the driver Maurice Patchett, a London Trans-port Driving Instructor. Not only did the bus have to perform a sudden 360-degree spin while skidding, but the climax of the chase involved the entire top deck being lopped off by a low bridge and sent hurtling on top of one of the pursuing cars, completely covering it (the upper deck was cut away and placed on rollers so that it would move easily on impact, then temporarily rebolted back onto the lower deck).

The film's second major set-piece takes place in a small Florida airport where Bond escapes Kananga's men by leaping into a two-seater Cessna plane in which a startled woman is just about to receive a flying lesson. The resulting chase around the airport, dur-ing which the pursuing cars collide with and wreck a large number of stationary planes and Bond's Cessna loses both its wings while going through a narrow hangar exit, is a satisfying blend of thrills and visual jokes.

Bond is then captured again, this time when he foolishly visits a New Orleans night club with the same name, Fillet of Soul, as the one where he was captured in New York. The difference is that on this occasion, the table sinks into the floor (one of the film's few sequences directly inspired by the novel). Bond is then faced with an interrogation by Mr. Big who tears off his unconvincing makeup to reveal that he is—surprise—really Dr. Kananga. To assist him in telling the truth, Kananga orders Tee Hee to snip off one of Bond's fingers with his mechanical pincer if he gives a wrong answer, but aided by Solitaire he survives the questioning intact (in one of Fleming's more overtly sadistic passages, the book version had Bond's little finger slowly bent back until it broke).

Instead of then simply shooting Bond as any rational villain would, Kananga has him taken out to his alligator farm which in reality is a front for a laboratory that is processing the poppies into pure heroin. Bond is left alone on a rock in a swamp surrounded by alligators but, in a moment of cinematic audacity that the Bond films can still deliver on occasion, he reaches safety by running across the *backs* of several of the reptiles, using them as stepping stones (the alligators were tied down by ropes hidden under the water and the stunt itself was performed by the owner of the farm).

This leads to the film's main set-piece—a lengthy and spectacular speedboat chase through various Florida bayous that has the jet-powered boats performing all manner of unlikely aerobatics, including hurtling over roadways, colliding with police cars, skimming across land into trees and swimming pools, and even, in one sequence, right through an outdoor wedding ceremony. Extra comedy is provided in the form of Clifton James' portrayal of a local redneck sheriff who gets involved in the chase and becomes increasingly indignant as Bond continues to elude capture (this character is a repeat of the frustrated law officer in *Diamonds Are Forever,* whose men are outwitted by Bond during the car chase through Las Vegas).

The speedboat chase through Florida's bayous

Bond then returns to San Monique, sows Kananga's poppy crop with explosives and then interrupts a voodoo ceremony where poor Solitaire, strung between two poles, is about to get it in the neck, literally, from a venomous snake wielded by a witch doctor. Bond promptly shoots the witch doctor but, before he can get Solitaire to safety, Baron Samedi himself rises out of the ground among the tombstones. Samedi is played by a lithe giant called Geoffrey Holder (a mere six-feet-six-inches tall) who also choreographed the film's dance sequences. Holder had made several short appearances prior to this sequence, successfully suggesting a malign but jovial supernatural presence.

Bond quite wisely shoots him but is surprised to see that this Samedi is merely a dummy. Then another Samedi rises from the ground, this one made of flesh and blood, but Bond disposes of him by hurling him into a coffin full of poisonous snakes. Exit Baron Samedi.

Descending via the same concealed elevator that Samedi rode up on, Bond and Solitaire enter Kananga's underground headquarters (which looks very much like Ken Adam's work even though it was designed by Syd Cain). After a short fight, they are both captured, not surprisingly, and Kananga prepares to give them a suitable send-off into the next world. In the novel, Bond is tied to a naked Solitaire and they are then both towed behind Mr. Big's yacht, his idea being to first flay them alive by dragging them over the razor-sharp coral and then let the sharks, attracted by the blood, have what's left. But Bond has planted a mine on the hull of Mr. Big's boat and it blows up just before Bond and the girl reach the coral, with the result that it is Big himself who ends up feeding the fishes: "The body in the water jerked sideways. Half of the Big Man's left arm came out of the water. It had no hand, no wrist, no wrist watch. But the great turnip head, the drawn-back mouth full of white teeth almost splitting it in half, was still alive. And now it was screaming, a long gurgling scream that only broke each time a barracuda hit into the dangling body." And after the barracuda come the sharks. ..."

Not surprisingly, events are handled rather more decorously in the film. Bond and Solitaire, both fully clothed, are tied together on some sort of metal hoist and then winched above Kananga's indoor shark pool (why on earth does he keep a shark in his basement?) but not before Kananga has slashed Bond's arm with a knife to produce a few drops of blood. Bond, however, uses his magic watch first to attract a small compressed air capsule (from Bond's anti-shark gun) which he hides in his mouth, then turns the watch into a miniature buzz saw that cuts through the ropes (this isn't fair, as the audience had no idea that the watch possessed this particular gimmick). With one bound, Bond is free and facing a knife-wielding and very annoyed Kananga. The stylish knife fight that follows was choreographed by Geoffrey "Samedi" Holder and could have gone on longer than it did; instead the fight continues in the water where it gets very silly indeed. Conveniently finding a use for that compressed air capsule, Bond jams it into Kananga's mouth and then forces him to clench down on it, causing it to explode. Kananga then expands into a very unconvincing rubber dummy that hurtles out of the water and hits the ceiling where it bursts with a wet bang,

Bond and Kananga fight it out in the latter's
underground headquarters.

distributing bits of black rubber around the set—a sequence that
Mack Sennett might have been proud of, but would have dismayed
Fleming. Mr. Big, and even Yaphet Kotto, deserved a more dig-
nified exit.

The film ends with a traditional Bondian "sting in the tale"
climax, though this one is not so much a sting as a weak nudge in
the ribs. Bond and Solitaire are seen boarding a train while Leiter
waves them goodbye. Why they're going anywhere on a train isn't
clear but of course it's really just an excuse to stage a repeat of the
famous fight in *From Russia with Love,* except this time Bond's
opponent isn't Red Grant but Tee Hee. Comparing this sequence
with the one in *From Russia with Love,* one can see just how much
the Bond films had changed in the intervening years; whereas the
earlier fight was presented seriously, being convincingly violent, and
filmed in a sombre half-light that added to the atmosphere of
menace, this one takes place in a brightly lit set and is obviously

aiming for laughs. Typical is the climax of the fight—where Bond disabled Grant by stabbing him in the arm before strangling him with his own garrotting device; in this fight, Bond disables Tee Hee by cutting through a wire in his artificial arm with a pair of nail scissors.

But there *is* one original touch before the film ends—after leaving the triumphant Bond in the carriage with Solitaire, the camera makes a sudden cut to reveal, sitting on the front of the engine, none other than a laughing Baron Samedi, thus suggesting that Bond's victory is purely illusory. Presumably, this closing shot was inserted to keep the black members of the audience happy, or perhaps it was merely intended to placate Mr. Yaphet Kotto; but, whatever the reason, it's an effective image.

Roger Moore's impersonation of James Bond aside, how does *Live and Let Die* measure up to the previous Bonds? Well, it's obviously not as good as the first three or four but, as has been noted elsewhere in this volume, they were really completely different *types* of movies from the ones that have come after *Thunderball.* Comparing *Live and Let Die* to the three Bonds that came after *Thunderball,* one must admit that it has more pace and excitement than the elephantine *You Only Live Twice* though it's not as interesting as *On Her Majesty's Secret Service* which, flawed as it was due to Lazenby's presence, remains the best Bond since *Goldfinger.* But it's certainly superior to *Diamonds Are Forever,* a rambling, badly-paced jumble of a film, because the previously mentioned tarot and voodoo motifs provide it with a stylistic consistency and enough of a plot remains to give it a semblance of cohesion, unlike some of the Bonds that have followed (such as *Moonraker*).

To determine how much of *Live and Let Die* is the work of script writer Tom Mankiewicz (whose last Bond film this was to date) is difficult, as the Bond films demonstrate better than any others that the cinema is "art by committee" and the scripts undoubtedly contain the fingerprints of many others apart from the actual script-writer. Or, as one United Artists' writer described the creation of a Bond script: "Saltzman and Broccoli worked closely together on it, then it's like a 24th of December Christmas tree with the whole family coming in to decorate it, in Bondian style." *Live and Let Die* was as expensively decorated as all the other Bondian Christmas trees but the question remained: Would there be another one? Or would Roger Moore be rejected as the new James Bond and thus bring the series to a premature end? It was up to the audiences once again.

Christopher Lee as Scaramanga

11

The Man with the Golden Gun

The audience reaction to *Live and Let Die* was a favorable one and sealed Roger Moore's fate as the new James Bond, for the next few films at least. It seemed that the public was willing to accept anyone in the Bond role providing the formula of spectacular action and special effects remained the same, which suggested that the relative hiccup in the series' fortunes created by *On Her Majesty's Secret Service* was not so much the fault of Lazenby's Australian version of Bond but because the film departed too far from the then established formula.

The flow of box office proceeds into United Artists' coffers meant that the next Bond could go ahead as planned. Roger Moore, it was announced, would return as James Bond in *The Man with the Golden Gun*.

From Fleming's second novel, the filmmakers had now jumped to his very last—the one written when he was a dying man and, in fact, published after his death. Critics have said that it's the weakest in the series (surely that ranking must go to *The Spy Who Loved Me*) but after the self-indulgence of *You Only Live Twice* with its travel book digressions and underlying obsession with old age and death, *The Man with the Golden Gun* seemed to be a genuine attempt by Fleming to return to his old form. It even began with Bond returning from the dead and turning up at his old Secret Service headquarters, much to the surprise of his former colleagues who were under the impression he had been killed in Japan (M had even written his obituary for the *London Times*). They receive an even bigger shock when Bond attempts to assassinate M with a cyanide gas pistol. But the attempt fails and Bond, who has been brainwashed by the Russians after losing his memory in Japan, is restored to something like his old self by M's personal physician Sir James Molony. He is then sent by M to prove that he is still entitled to carry the 007 prefix by dealing with Enrico Scaramanga, a psychopathic killer who works for the Russians and is in the process of organizing a SPECTRE-like organization in Jamaica.

Bond, back in his old stamping grounds, successfully infiltrates Scaramanga's group and in a final showdown in a Jamaican swamp after he, with Felix Leiter's help, has wiped out most of Scaramanga's men, succeeds in killing him, though not without being severely wounded himself.

222

The main trouble with the novel is its lack of any real originality apart from the bizarre opening chapter. By the time Fleming had come to write it, he had obviously run out of ideas and the book is a paste-up job of scenes from the previous novels—the gangster convention, for instance, is straight out of *Goldfinger,* and Scaramanga's steam train is from *Diamonds Are Forever.* Scaramanga himself may be a brave attempt on Fleming's part to get away from the Blofeld type of super-criminal, but the result is a villain who simply lacks the stature to be a worthwhile opponent of James Bond. Besides, as he's basically just a freelance assassin, it seems unlikely that he would have the inclination or ability to form his own organization. What the novel needed was another villain behind Scaramanga—someone pulling the strings.

The film of *The Man with the Golden Gun* overcomes this flaw by making Scaramanga a more up-market villain complete with his own island headquarters à la Dr. No. Scaramanga is played by Christopher Lee who was, coincidentally, originally considered for the part of Dr. No twelve years previously. "I'm distantly related to Ian Fleming," said Lee. "We used to play a lot of golf together and from time to time to tease he'd say 'Why don't you appear in a Bond movie?' and I'd reply, 'Why don't you suggest me?' When eventually the offer did come, there was no refusing it. When I first read the script, I visualized Scaramanga as a straight-down-the-middle heavy, but I must agree that he is not one of Fleming's most impressive murderers, so Guy Hamilton and I, after a lot of talk, decided to make Scaramanga a little like Bond himself. A counter-Bond, if you like, instead of the murderous, unappetizing thug of the novel. When we were out filming in Thailand down on the Andaman Sea, Guy kept on saying to Roger Moore and myself, 'Enjoy it, enjoy it! Lightly! Lightly! Lightly!' And enjoy it we did."

Perhaps they enjoyed themselves too much because there's little real tension in their scenes together. On the contrary, Lee's powerful screen presence seems very much diluted throughout this picture. Guy Hamilton—by entreating Lee to be light and to laugh a lot ("I don't laugh very easily as an actor," Lee admitted)—ended up by turning him into a counter-Roger Moore instead of a counter-Bond. If you hire an actor who possesses particular qualities, as Christopher Lee does (though admittedly not much of a range), it seems strange not to exploit them.

As expected, little remains of the original plot, though compared to subsequent Bonds, it seems a hundred percent faithful. The pre-credits sequence shows Scaramanga on his island hide-out with a female companion, Andrea (Maud Adams), and his midget man-servant, Nick Nack (Herve Villechaize). A gangster then arrives to provide Scaramanga with some live target practice in his surreal shooting gallery consisting of a mock-up Western saloon, a Prohibition-era garage, fun house mirrors, and full-size moving dummies, all accompanied by weird sound effects and flashing lights (designed by Peter Murton, this set was constructed on four tiers and stretched to the roof of the seventy-foot-high sound stage at Pinewood). After a rather unexciting game of cat and mouse, Scaramanga shoots the gangster dead, then suddenly turns and blasts the fingers off a wax dummy of none other than James Bond (Roger Moore is one of the few actors who looks as lifelike as a wax dummy as he does in reality . . .).

John Barry is back doing the music on this one, but he might as well have stayed away as his theme song for *The Man with the Golden Gun,* performed by pop singer Lulu, is singularly uninspiring. After the credits, the story proper begins with M informing Bond that a golden bullet has arrived with his number on it. Only one man uses golden bullets and that's Scaramanga (who is not to be confused with the man who uses silver bullets), and the bullet addressed to Bond means that someone has paid Scaramanga's fee of a million dollars to have him killed. Bond is doomed unless he can get to Scaramanga first. While Bond is hunting Scaramanga, M suggests that it would be very helpful if he could keep an eye out for a missing Solex Agitator—a vital piece of equipment intended for use in the first completely efficient solar energy generator. The Agitator has been stolen by a scientist working on the project who now intends selling it to the highest bidder.

After Bond locates the man who makes Scaramanga's golden ammunition, a search which involved Bond having to swallow a golden bullet that he had removed from a belly dancer's navel, he is able to track him to Hong Kong where he makes contact with Scaramanga's girlfriend, Andrea. Bond tries to find out who wants him dead so badly but she can't tell him; then, when Bond is about to collect the Solex Agitator—the British government having agreed to pay the ransom—Scaramanga strikes. However, he doesn't shoot Bond but the man with the Agitator and in the confusion that follows Nick Nack scoops up the device and disappears. It turns out that Scaramanga had no intention of assassinating Bond—the golden bullet hadn't been sent by him but by Andrea who hoped that Bond would come and kill Scaramanga on her behalf (but if Bond wasn't Scaramanga's target, why did he keep a wax dummy of him in his shooting gallery?).

Bond reports to M, now based in the capsized hull of the old Queen Elizabeth liner in Hong Kong harbor, and learns that Scaramanga is employed by a rich Chinese merchant called Hai Fat who hopes to corner the market in solar energy. Bond pays a visit to Hai Fat by pretending to be Scaramanga, disguising himself simply by gluing on a third nipple (one should explain that, like the character in the novel, Scaramanga has three nipples—a physical oddity considered by the superstitious to be a sign of invulnerability and great sexual prowess). But shortly after Bond leaves, the real Scaramanga arrives and kills Hai Fat with his golden gun, a special weapon that he constructs out of such innocent-looking items as a cigarette case, pen, lighter, etc.

Bond takes on kung fu experts.

That night Bond is captured by Scaramanga's men and wakes the following morning to find himself about to be used as a live practice dummy at a martial arts academy. In an amusing fight that both exploits and sends up the then-current Kung Fu movie craze, Bond, with the aid of two innocent-looking schoolgirls who turn out to be experts in the martial arts as well, defeats his opponents and escapes in a high-powered longboat. But during the chase that follows, which involves powerboats hurtling through Thailand's famous Floating Market, the film takes a nose dive in credibility when it reintroduces the character of Sheriff J.W. Pepper (Clifton James) from *Live and Let Die* who just happens to be vacationing in the area with his wife. . . . James is a clever performer and the character was used to good effect in the previous film, but his appearance here is a serious misjudgment, as is the scene where an elephant pushes him into the river. Having to depend on people falling into water in order to get laughs is a sure sign that the Bondian well of invention is beginning to go dry (the same gag, which was old when Mack Sennett was starting up, is used again in *Moonraker*).

Sheriff Pepper (Clifton James) gets more than he bargained for in offering to help Bond.

In Bangkok (a name that might have been invented by Fleming himself), Bond has made contact with Mary Goodnight, a British agent stationed in Thailand (Goodnight was Bond's secretary in several of the novels). Goodnight is played by Britt Eklund in a manner that makes one wonder how she ever managed to pass her Secret Service entrance exam. Still, she makes an attractive and amusing ally for Bond and confirms one's suspicion that comedy is Ms. Eklund's forte, something that seems to have escaped most filmmakers (though Richard Lester made amusing use of her in *Royal Flash*).

After learning of Andrea's treachery, Scaramanga murders her in the middle of Bangkok's largest Thai boxing stadium shortly before she is due to meet Bond. When Bond arrives and sits beside her he doesn't at first notice she's dead, a comment on either his powers of observation or Maud Adam's acting ability. Bond is then joined by Scaramanga who tells him something of his background, which is fairly close to the one described in the novel. We learn that Scaramanga spent his youth with a travelling circus, performing a trick shot act and doting on an elephant by the name of Max. One day Max went berserk due to ill-treatment by his trainer and trampled on a few people—which led, not unreasonably, to his being shot by the local police. Whereupon Scaramanga immediately reacted by shooting both police and trainer, and has been continuing this anti-social mode of life ever since—the moral of the story being that if you shoot a man's favorite elephant, you're likely to turn him into a ruthless international assassin. But at least Scaramanga is given *some* motivation for his actions, which is a good deal more than most Bond villains get.

Through sheer idiocy, Mary Goodnight ends up locked in the trunk of Scaramanga's car. Bond follows them by commandeering a car in a sales showroom, a car that just happens to contain Sheriff J.W. Pepper (why would a tourist in Thailand be looking over a new car?), a situation that leads to various comedy routines as Bond chases Scaramanga's vehicle through the streets of Bangkok and then out into the countryside. It's here that the film's most spectacular stunt takes place when Bond's car hurtles off the broken end of a twisted bridge, rotates a full 360° around its own axis as it flies through the air and then lands on the other section of bridge on the opposite shore. The sequence looks as if it could have been a very clever model shot but it was actually done using a full-sized car driven by a stuntman. Every detail had been worked out in advance on a computer, including the speed at which the vehicle should leave the end of the twisted bridge and the correct angle of the ramp. Even so, it remained an exceedingly dangerous stunt and frogmen stood ready in case the car crashed into the water.

A sequence that *was* done using a model was the one shortly afterwards where Scaramanga's car turns into an airplane and takes off into the air. A full-sized version of the winged car existed, but when it speeds off down the road and actually lifts off, there is a switch to a radio-controlled model.

Scaramanga, still with Goodnight hidden in his car, flies off towards his private island, situated off the coast of mainland China and guarded by the Red Chinese, which suggests that Scaramanga is really a communist agent. (The island is actually a one-acre outcrop of picturesque rock and sand called *Kao Ping-Kan* located near

Bond's car negotiates a demolished bridge.

the Thai resort island of Phuket, another name of which Fleming would have been proud.) Bond follows quite openly in a seaplane which he lands in the bay of Scaramanga's little island, presumably so confident of his ability to defeat the villain that he feels subterfuge to be unnecessary.

Bond is met by Nick Nack carrying a bottle of champagne and then invited by Scaramanga to look over his huge Solar Energy Plant which, thanks to the arrival of the Solex Agitator, is now fully operational, a fact that Scaramanga demonstrates quite graphically by destroying Bond's plane with a heat beam. "Now I really am the man with the golden gun," says Scaramanga happily. The problem is that it's never made clear what he is doing with this vast complex or what he intends to do with it. While a solar power generator of that size would be a valuable asset if you owned a small town or a large factory, it seems a bit of a white elephant on a small island in the middle of the sea. After you've boiled the water for your coffee

Scaramanga's solex device destroys an airplane.

and produced enough electricity for the lights, what do you do with all that excess energy, apart from blow up the transportation of the occasional visiting secret agent?

After giving Bond the guided tour and a quick lunch in his luxurious dining room, Scaramanga gets down to business and challenges Bond to a duel down on the beach. This soon leads to another game of cat and mouse in the Fun Room (the confrontation on the beach originally lasted longer but was cut in the final release version) which should be exciting but, like the similar one in the pre-credits sequence, isn't. It ends with Scaramanga simply being shot by Bond who has disguised himself as his own target dummy in the shooting gallery. It's a disappointing and rather perfunctory finish—one would have expected Scaramanga's exit to have been a little more ingenious, though at least his death wasn't as undignified as Kananga's in *Live and Let Die*.

Meanwhile, Mary Goodnight has brained Scaramanga's lone technician with a spanner and his body has fallen into one of the cooling vats, an action which sets the solar complex on the inevitable path of self-destruction. But, before they can escape, Bond must extract the vital Solex Agitator and is almost fried to death while doing so, thanks to another boob on Ms. Goodnight's part (she accidentally bumps a switch that activates the solar collector while Bond is in the path of the beam). They finally escape in Scaramanga's motorized junk just as the solar plant explodes, completely destroying the island.

Mary Goodnight (Britt Ekland) brains an enemy.

There's a small (very small) sting in the tale in the form of Nick Nack who tries to stab Bond while he's in bed with Goodnight and when that fails is reduced to biting him in the leg. Bond doesn't dispose of him in the usual Bondian manner but, instead, seals him in a suitcase and hauls him up the mainmast—an ignominious fate that all midgets who saw the film must have found rather patronizing.

For all the exotic locations and expensive sets, there seems to be something vaguely "cheap" about *The Man with the Golden Gun* compared to the other Bonds. This no doubt erroneous impression is probably caused by the fact that there is no major set-piece in this film, like the boat chase in *Live and Let Die* or the helicopter attack in *Diamonds Are Forever*. *The Man with the Golden Gun* is alone among the later Bonds in that it doesn't have a specific sequence that people tend to remember when asked about it. They may recall the stunt with the car going over the river but it happens too quickly to make a really lasting impression—and, while Scaramanga's solar complex looks impressive, it isn't utilized in any interesting way (and the fact that Scaramanga only has *one* technician to operate the whole thing adds to the suggestion of cheapness).

In one area, however, *The Man with the Golden Gun* was an improvement on many of the previous Bonds, and that was its special effects, particularly the model effects. These were handled by Derek Meddings, who is now supervisor of effects on the Bond films, and who developed his expertise with miniatures while working on such television series as *Thunderbirds* and *UFO* for the Gerry Anderson company. "I did all the model effects on *Golden Gun* except for the car that turned into a 'plane,' " said Meddings. "That was a radio-controlled disaster, though it looks alright in the finished film. There were actually a lot of model shots in that film that people don't realize were there. For instance, the long shots of the Queen Elizabeth lying on its side in Hong Kong harbor—that was *all* a model, even the whole of Hong Kong harbor in the background.

"The island where the villain had his headquarters was also a model, though based on a real island that also appeared in the film. The art department took photographs of it and we had to match them perfectly with our model because, as shots of the real island were used in the film, both islands had to look exactly the same, otherwise audiences wouldn't have been fooled. We used all kinds of tricks to get things right. Reproducing the foliage in miniature was probably the most difficult thing—we would uproot an entire garden or area just to find the right little plants, all of which have to be attached to the model in the right scale and perspective. You can't just grab a handful of foliage and glue it on the model anywhere you like—it's got to be done with a great deal of care. And color is always a problem, trying to match the various colors with the real thing.

"Then, of course, we had the problem of blowing the place up. It couldn't be a solid island, it was supposed to be hollow, so we were virtually building the explosives into it as we were building the island. It was a big model, about twelve feet high. We also had to blow up a model of the interior of the solar complex. The full size set was about 180 feet long and 90 feet high and, again, our model had to match with it in every detail."

As a look at *The Man with the Golden Gun* will confirm, it's impossible to spot the switch between reality and models in either of the above sequences and this work helped establish Meddings as one of the top model specialists in the British film industry, a position he has since consolidated with his effects in *The Spy Who Loved Me* and *Moonraker*.

With hindsight, when one compares *The Man with the Golden Gun* with the other Bond films made before and after it during the Seventies, it seems somewhat out-of-step. Admittedly, it continues the increasing emphasis on humor in the series but it represents a small diversion from the established formula with its relatively small-scale story and its treatment of the villain. However, with the next film the old formula would be back—and back with a vengeance.

Barbara Bach and Roger Moore in a publicity shot for
The Spy Who Loved Me

12

The Spy Who Loved Me

On November 11, 1975, Harry Saltzman announced that he was selling his share of Bond. After being in partnership with Albert "Cubby" Broccoli for nearly fifteen years, he was getting out and leaving Bond to Broccoli, along with United Artists and all the others who own a share of the Bond action (such as Booker Brothers who own 50 percent of Fleming's old company, Glidrose).

Saltzman had been threatening to dissolve the partnership for three years, saying that he was getting tired of the whole Bond business. In 1972, he told a reporter: "When I sell out I shan't care who it is who produces Bond. I do not kid myself that Bond is deathless prose." At the age of 57, Saltzman was becoming increasingly dissatisfied with the business of creating pure escapism and yearned to devote his energies to the field of education, a cause close to his heart. He now regretted his return to show business after his three years with UNESCO in the late Forties and announced a proposed communications university for developing countries as well as a plan to make anthropological films of all the sixty-seven tribes in black Africa.

Such schemes would, of course, cost a lot of money and this was perhaps another reason why Saltzman was realizing his investment in Bond. Over the years he, unlike Broccoli, had been involved in a variety of other projects apart from the Bond films and many of these had not been exactly profitable. One such abortive scheme concerned audio-visual cassettes which lost him millions of pounds, and since the late Sixties his independently produced films have been dogged with ill fortune—the science-fiction musical *Toomorrow* ran for only a week at a London cinema before legal difficulties prevented it from being shown again; and the planned multimillion dollar science-fiction epic *The Micronauts* was abandoned in 1975 after much time and money had been invested.

With the departure of Saltzman from the Bond scene, one was naturally curious to see how the series would develop with only one of the original producers still at the creative helm. Would the absence of Saltzman's influence make the next Bond film totally different from the others? And would it be an improvement or what? No doubt Broccoli himself was well aware that his first solo Bond production would be under close scrutiny not only from the fans but also from the various people who had a financial interest in the series. So, not surprisingly, he decided to play it safe and make *The Spy Who Loved Me* bigger and more spectacular than any of the previous Bonds, returning to the larger-than-life sets and big-scale set-pieces that had been missing from *Live and Let Die* and *The Man With the Golden Gun*. In effect, what he did was to remake *You Only Live Twice* . . ..

Part of the blame for the lack of an original plot in the film version of *The Spy Who Loved Me* lies with Ian Fleming. The author had insisted when he sold the film rights of the Bond novels to Broccoli and Saltzman that they could use the title of *The Spy Who Loved Me* but *not* the actual story. One can only presume he was either embarrassed by the work or felt that filmmakers wouldn't treat the subject matter in a suitable manner. Actually, it's very unlikely that anyone would *want* to make a film of the novel because it's something of an aberration among the Bond adventures. While one appreciates that Fleming was weary of the whole Bond business by that time and wanted to prove that his literary talents were wider than he was given credit for, it's difficult to understand what he thought he was up to with *The Spy Who Loved Me*. Basically, it's about a girl called Vivienne Michel who narrates, with the assistance of her friend Mr. Fleming, the story of her life and how she has been exploited and hurt by a series of callous men until she finally met up with a *real* man and learns that the male sex isn't completely worthless.

The real man is none other than James Bond whom she meets while on a motorcycle tour of North America. Bond, on his way back from some minor mission in Canada, saves her from a few second-rate thugs in a Vermont motel and then "semi-rapes" her in a shower stall (according to Vivienne, all women want to be semi-raped, which may come as news to a lot of them), an event that suggests that the rest of her life is going to be a sexual anti-climax. By writing this book, Fleming may have been trying to prove to his critics that he could create a believable female character—but unfortunately he didn't succeed and Vivienne remains two-dimensional and unconvincing. She exists purely to act as a one-woman appreciation society for James Bond—as a means for Fleming to present his alter-ego from a new angle—and in fact her whole life is nothing but an extended build-up for the star of the show's big entrance. Judged as either a novel or a James Bond thriller, *The Spy Who Loved Me* is a definite failure.

Faced with the opportunity of being able to create a whole new story for the film version, one might have expected that Broccoli and his writers would perhaps try and produce something out of the ordinary. In fact, Richard Maibaum did at first put forward a rather radical story idea that involved the SPECTRE hierarchy being massacred by a group of young terrorists representing the new generation and consisting of members of the P.L.O., the I.R.A., the Japanese Red Army, etc. The terrorists then take over SPECTRE's latest scheme to hijack atomic weapons and subsequently hold the world to ransom, threatening to start World War Three unless their demands are met. Not surprisingly, this scenario was rejected as being a little too political for comfort and once again it was going to good old, uncontroversial Ernst Stavro Blofeld, who would hold the world to ransom (Blofeld, despite his curious taste for Chairman Mao type clothes, is definitely apolitical. However, in the final version, Bloefeld and SPECTRE had to be dropped due to the continuing legal wrangles between the Broccoli/United Artists camp and Kevin McClory. As both that character and the SPECTRE organization first appeared in *Thunderball,* which McClory plans to remake as *Warhead,* there is some confusion as to who actually owns the right to them (and at the time of writing it still hasn't been clarified). So instead, the villain became a multimillionaire ship-owner called Stromberg.

With *The Spy Who Loved Me,* a new name appeared in the credits—that of Christopher Wood, who collaborated on the screenplay with Bond-veteran Richard Maibaum. Wood, a Cambridge graduate in economics and law, was working in an advertising agency when he started writing in his spare time. His first big success came with the *Confessions of a Window Cleaner* series of books that can best be described as humorous erotica (if one wants to be overly kind). He wrote these books under the name of "Timothy Lea" then, as "Rosie Dixon" and "Penny Sutton," followed up the success with similar sex-and-slapstick series about a nurse and an airline stewardess. His entry into the film industry came when he wrote the script of the film version of *Confessions of a Window Cleaner* with director Val Guest in 1976. This led to him writing the screenplay of *Seven Nights in Japan,* the director of which was Lewis Gilbert. Wood and Gilbert got along well together and, when Gilbert was asked by Broccoli to direct *The Spy Who Loved Me,* he brought Wood into the project with him. Broccoli approved of both Wood and his work; suddenly, the former writer of tawdry sex comedies was involved with the most successful film series of all time (he also got the choice assignment of stepping into Fleming's shoes and writing the novelizations of both *The Spy Who Loved Me* and *Moonraker*).

One is tempted to blame Wood for the increase in schoolboy humor and increasing emphasis on slapstick comedy in the Bond series—but, to be fair, both these trends were apparent before he became involved and, of course, Broccoli himself remains in overall creative control. "I sit down with the writer, director, and executive producer," said Broccoli recently, "and we decide what we want in the script. We have discussions, we have ideas. The final decision is made by me."

It seems entirely appropriate that, having decided to remake *You Only Live Twice,* if unintentionally, Broccoli chose the director of that film, Lewis Gilbert, to direct *The Spy Who Loved Me,* presumably because Gilbert had proven with the former film that he could cope with the logistics of shooting in giant sets swarming with hordes of extras. The plot of *The Spy Who Loved Me* is remarkably similar to that of *You Only Live Twice* which, in turn, was an exaggerated version of *Dr. No,* the film that became the template for so many of the subsequent Bonds. The formula is simple: mysterious incidents involving American or N.A.T.O. military hardware occur (missiles in *Dr. No,* space vehicles in *You Only Live Twice*, submarines in *Spy*); James Bond is sent to investigate and, after a series of adventures, finds himself in the villain's larger-than-life headquarters full of fairyland technology (Dr. No's underground reactor room, Blofeld's hollow volcano, and Stromberg's super tanker) which he then blows up. Simple, perhaps, but a formula that audiences never tire of.

The Spy Who Loves Me begins with a bravura pre-credits sequence that tops anything that has come before (with the exception, perhaps, of the one in *Goldfinger*). After a British nuclear submarine is overwhelmed by some unseen force, we cut to Switzerland where Bond is enjoying himself in a log cabin with a young lady. No sooner has Bond received an electronic summons from M, donned skis, and zoomed off than the girl sends a message to a group of waiting Russians (the leader of whom looks remarkably like George Lazenby but one presumes this is unintentional). Bond is soon being pursued by the machine gun-firing Russians across the snow in a sequence reminiscent of ones in *On Her Majesty's Secret Service.*

After disposing of their leader with an explosive ski stick, Bond then skis off the edge of a sheer precipice to his apparent doom. There is a nerve-racking wait as we watch his diminishing figure hurtle downwards and then suddenly a parachute blossoms out of his back-pack, a parachute defiantly emblazoned with a Union Jack. It's a good joke (the best in the picture) and one wonders whether the audiences are laughing at its sheer audacity or at the idea of anyone today wanting to flaunt the British flag.

This amazing stunt was performed by Rick Sylvester, after waiting several days for the right weather conditions. It had to be performed at a precise time in the early morning before the shadow from the cliff obscured the action, and naturally the less wind the safer the jump would be. The whole skiing sequence was supervised and filmed by Willy Bogner who had handled similar functions during the shooting of *On Her Majesty's Secret Service.*

The familiar Maurice Binder titles follow, this time accompanied by Marvin Hamlisch's theme song "Nobody Does It Better" with lyrics by Carole Bayer Sager and sung by Carly Simon. It's an adequate piece, though lacking the excitement of the McCartneys' theme for *Live and Let Die.* It is, however, an improvement on Barry's theme for *The Man with the Golden Gun* and one must admit also that Hamlisch's arrangements for the various segments of background music in the remainder of the film are more interesting than Barry's last efforts in that direction.

After learning from the naval authorities that persons unknown have found a way to track and predict the movements of NATO submarines, Bond goes to Egypt to contact an Egyptian double agent called Fekkish who is offering to sell the secret to the highest bidder. Also sent to Egypt is Russian agent Major Anya Amasova, played by Barbara Bach. Possibly smarting under the frequent accusations of male chauvinist piggery in the Bond films, Broccoli had decided to make the leading lady in this film the *equal* of Bond—in other words, a female James Bond. At least that was the idea, but it didn't work out that way. Major Amasova may have been Bond's equal on paper but in the finished film you feel that underneath her Russian uniform beats the heart of a pure sex object. In fact, even though she remains fully dressed throughout the picture, she gives the impression of being more of a sex object than the very first Bond girl, Honey Wilder (Ursula Andress). Honey, despite her bikini, came across as a genuinely independent character who treated men on her own terms. And it was Honey, remember, who placed the black widow spider in the bed of the man who raped her.

Speaking of spiders, Atlantis—the villain's headquarters— resembles a giant, black tarantula when it is first seen rising slowly out of the water. Designed by Ken Adam, back on his first Bond film since *Diamonds Are Forever,* it was the work of Derek Meddings, supervisor of effects: "The long shots were of a large model, almost twelve feet across, and the close shots were a combination of full-scale sections filmed in Sardinia, models, and matte paintings. There were a lot of very good matte shots in that picture which were done by Alan Mayley, one of the best matte painters in the business. He managed to have people walking about in his matte shots of Atlantis which added to the realism, and when we shot our model sections, we also had miniature people that gave the impression that they were walking—we moved them around mechanically. And to really confuse everybody we had a radio-controlled helicopter, a model, which flew about in the background. If people see a helicopter flying around a model they tend to say to themselves, perhaps unconsciously, 'Oh, it can't be a fake because I saw a helicopter fly through it.' "

Looking like a giant tarantula, the Atlantis rises from the sea.

Lurking within Atlantis is the villain Stromberg (or, if you prefer it, Blofeld in disguise) whom we first see sitting in his luxurious dining room surrounded by large aquariums and television monitors (that are revealed behind sliding tapestries) and listening to classical music. Stromberg is played in a somnambulistic fashion by aging German actor Curt Jurgens who doesn't look as if he has the energy to cross the room, much less conquer the world. Not that the script gives him much to do—as he complained during the making of the film: "All I get to do in this picture is push buttons." Apart from the miscasting, the main problem with Stromberg is the lack of motivation for his actions. He tells Bond later in the film that he wants to wipe out all life on land so that he can establish a new world of his own under the water, but surely with Atlantis he has done that already. He doesn't *need* to start World War Three to achieve his aims.

242

After sending a treacherous female employee down the tube (literally) into a shark tank, Stromberg then sends two of his men to Egypt to recover the secrets of the submarine-tracking device. One of the henchmen, Sandor, is played by bald muscleman Milton Reid who has made a career out of playing bald musclemen (he even appears in the first Bond film playing one of Dr. No's henchmen). Stromberg's other henchman is Jaws, played by another actor whose career has been shaped by his unusual physical characteristics—in this case, a physique measuring seven feet two inches in height and a face that resembles the carvings on Easter Island. Born in 1939, he had almost reached his present height by the age of twelve and, not unexpectedly, it has caused him problems ever since, not least in the acting profession where he has been typecast as a dumb brute. It is, however a part he plays very well, particularly in *The Spy Who Loved Me,* but the subsequent attempt to humanize the Jaws character in *Moonraker* proved to be one of the most damaging of recent developments in the Bond series. More on that later.

In Egypt, Bond clashes not only with Stromberg's two henchmen, Sandor and Jaws, but also with Major Amasova. Bond disposes of Sandor quite quickly—pushing him off a rooftop with all the callous disregard of the old James Bond—but Jaws is another matter entirely. With his set of steel teeth, he kills the double agent, Fekkesh,

Bond suspects that he may be next on the menu for
Jaws (Richard Kiel).

and almost succeeds in killing both Bond and Amasova. One of
their encounters takes place at a remote ruin in the desert where
Jaws gains the upper hand for a time until Bond causes a large
section of the structure to fall on the giant's head. But already
displaying the indestructibility that would become his trademark,
Jaws emerges unscathed from the wreckage and, as Bond and the
girl try and escape in a van, he begins to demolish the vehicle piece
by piece. They finally *do* escape, leaving Jaws holding a huge chunk
of stone which he then drops in disgust, right on his foot. It's a good
joke—one of the better ones involving Jaws.

After their bout of rivalry, Bond and Amasova are ordered by
their respective superiors to join forces—which they do, albeit un-
willingly. Their superiors, incidentally, turn up inside one of Egypt's

ancient monuments which has been converted into a Secret Service base complete with a weapons testing range. Sharing office space with M and Miss Moneypenny is General Gogol, Amasova's Russian boss. Gogol is played by Walter Gotell, who last turned up in a Bond film in 1963 when he played the SPECTRE killer with the lethal shoes in *From Russia with Love* (he was the one who delivered the poisonous kick to Vladek Sheybal as Kronsteen).

A clue on a photograph links the recent events to Stromberg's shipping line so Bond and Amasova head for Sardinia where Stromberg has his "marine laboratory" based off the coast. For some reason, they travel part of the way by train, which provides Jaws with the opportunity to launch another attack. This train fight is much better staged than the similar one in *Live and Let Die* (Richard Kiel looks even bigger than usual within the confines of a train carriage) and ends with Jaws' spectacular exit through the window and his plunge down an embankment amid a blaze of electrical sparks.

After that narrow escape, the relationship between Bond and Amasova thaws briefly but heats up again when she learns that it was Bond who killed her boyfriend—the Russian agent Bond had shot during the pre-credits sequence. Amasova vows to kill Bond when their mission is over but you know her heart isn't really in it (this attempt to inject some genuine tension into their relationship falls ludicrously flat, partly because of Ms. Bach who, though beautiful, gives a performance entirely lacking in any excitement. One feels that, if she did attempt to convey any real emotion, her rather too-perfect exterior would crack. Her scenes with Moore are very much a case of Plastic Woman versus Plastic Man . . .).

In Sardinia, Bond and Amasova, impersonating man and wife, are met by one of Stromberg's employees, the shapely Naomi played by Caroline Munro (whose film career has mainly consisted of parts in fantasy films such as *At the Earth's Core* and *Starcrash*). Pretending to be a marine biologist, Bond is taken to meet Stromberg on Atlantis and is suitably impressed by the aquariums though he does notice a girl's hand lying at the bottom of one of the tanks (careless of Stromberg not to clean up afterwards). Apart from refusing to shake hands (Stromberg is supposed to have webbed fingers but not much is made of this in the film, presumably because the makeup didn't bear up to close scrutiny), Stromberg seems fairly genial and is happy to show Bond the model of his planned underwater city. Meanwhile, as Bond's wife, Amasova is being entertained by Naomi and notices something odd about the bows on the model of Stromberg's supertanker, the *Liparus*.

Despite Bond's ability to identify rare tropical fish, Stromberg hasn't been fooled by his impersonation and orders his death as soon as they are ashore. Bond, however, is by then driving a special Lotus car that has been delivered by Q (Desmond Llewelyn as ever). The first attack occurs on a high mountain road when a motorcyclist roars up behind Bond's car and unleashes a rocket-powered sidecar. Bond outmaneuvers the mobile bomb and instead it plunges into the rear of a large truck filled with feather mattresses. The subsequent explosion sends a cloud of feathers over the motorcyclist and he hurtles out of control over the side of the cliff.

The man responsible for these spectacular scenes was again Derek Meddings: "It was all done for real on a mountain road in Sardinia. Our sidecar, which we built specially because you can't buy sidecars these days except from one remaining company, had to be bigger than normal because we had to have a stuntman inside it—a *small* stuntman—as well as an engine, steering mechanisms and rockets. The rockets actually had enough power to move the sidecar though they weren't powerful enough to maintain the necessary speed, but they certainly launched him out of the cradle we'd built on the side of the motorbike, a big 900cc Japanese machine. Part of the sidecar had to be built out of black perspex so that the man inside could see where he was going. We didn't want him going over the cliff . . . .

"Then we had to blow the truck's trailer to pieces and produce a cloud of feathers. It was a terrible drama trying to control those feathers. We had tons of them and I should think a large part of Sardinia is still covered with them. It was alright actually blowing up the trailer and producing the feathers, but then you had to do the cutting shots showing the motorcyclist going through the feathers and getting covered in them and that was difficult. We used a dummy for the shots where he goes over the cliff because we couldn't find a stuntman who was willing to jump 500 feet. We jokingly told one stuntman it was to be his next job and that was the end of that.

"The bike was fired over the edge of the cliff from a special ramp with an air ram—a long telescopic arm that shot out with a terrible noise at the push of a button. We had five cameras on that scene. The dummy had to separate from the bike as soon as possible—the director didn't want it sitting calmly on the bike for the whole drop—so we had to make a quick-release mechanism for it. Our dummy looked convincing because he was built so he wouldn't bend in any unnatural way."

After escaping from the motorbike assassin, Bond and Amasova then find themselves being pursued by a carload of gunmen including Jaws himself, but the special devices built into the Lotus soon take care of that minor problem. After the pursuing car's windshield has been covered with a layer of black paint sprayed from the rear of Bond's Lotus, it crashes off the road and hurtles straight through the roof of a farmer's hut. Once again Jaws demonstrates his invulnerability by walking calmly out of the front door, much to the owner's astonishment.

Meanwhile, Bond and Amasova still haven't come to the end of Stromberg's relay team of assassins (he obviously doesn't believe in taking chances, or has a low opinion of his employees' abilities) and next find themselves menaced by an armed helicopter that rises up from below the mountain road and is piloted by none other than Naomi. The ensuing duel between car and helicopter is excitingly filmed, but poor Naomi doesn't have much of a chance of scoring a hit because some fool mechanic back at headquarters has aligned the guns on her aircraft in such a way as to allow them to shoot bullets only down each *side* of the road instead of at the middle where Bond's car happens to be most of the time. The chase ends when the car hurtles off the end of a jetty and plunges into the sea. Once underwater, the Lotus transforms itself into a mini-submarine which then fires a small missile out the rear window. The missile zooms out of the water and hits the helicopter which promptly explodes, bringing Ms. Munro's role in the film to a sudden, regretful end.

Bond's Lotus escapes Stromberg's helicopter
attack . . .

. . . and converts itself into a submarine (studio
model).

"We had quite a big underwater operation at Nassau for those scenes," explained Meddings. "We built a special rig in Sardinia to fire the car down the jetty and it was travelling at 50 mph when it left the rig. Then, when it reached the point where it had to sink, we immediately picked it up in Nassau with a model—a very convincing model with dummies representing Bond and the girl inside—sinking into the sea. We followed it down as it sank and changed into a submarine, a process that involved *five* underwater cars, each one representing part of the transformation; the wheels coming up, the wheel arches filling in, the fins appearing, the back bumper sliding up and the fins appearing, and the propellors coming out. We also did, in miniature, the sequence where the missile shoots out of the back window and blows up the helicopter. The helicopter in those scenes was actually a radio-controlled model. Apart from the models, there was also a full-scale car that was completely drivable underwater. It was full of engines and bouyancy compensators and took a two-man crew. You could actually drive it underwater, it was fantastic! But we had to use a model in some of the later underwater scenes because the car had to go close to the huge structure of Atlantis. We built a full-scale section of Atlantis for a shot involving the real car and then we built a whole model section and used the model car."

After seeing what appears to be some sort of war room within Atlantis, Bond and Asamova are then attacked by a number of frogmen riding motorized underwater sledges, but the Lotus is equipped with the usual supply of Bondian devices that meet each hazard as it arises and the outcome of the battle is never in doubt (there's no real excitement in this sequence, only a mild curiosity about what gadget is going to do what). Stromberg's forces are routed, leaving the Lotus to make a leisurely exit from the sea onto a beach crowded with holiday-makers.

Bond and Amasova then go on board the nuclear submarine *U.S.S. Wayne* to join the hunt for Stromberg's supertanker, the *Liparus,* which is obviously the key to whatever has been going on. However, it is the *Liparus* that finds *them,* first immobilizing the submarine with an electronic beam, and then opening its bows to swallow the submarine like a shark ingesting a salmon. Once again the task of putting this bizarre spectacle on the screen fell to Derek Meddings and his team: "I knew from the beginning of the picture that we were going to have to do the tanker as a miniature but Lewis Gilbert was a little worried that it wouldn't look right. However, when he saw our first test shots he knew it would look good and that we wouldn't have to use a full-size tanker as originally planned.

"Actually our model tanker wasn't much of a miniature—it was sixty-three feet long. We built it at Pinewood in three sections and flew it out on a cargo plane to Nassau, where we put it together. Fortunately, we had found a place during location hunting called Coral Harbor where all these canals and channels had been constructed for a planned luxury complex complete with hotel, but it was never finished. The canals proved ideal for our particular situation because we had to put this twelve-ton tanker together and then launch it, and it was a real problem to handle. Only the aft section was built like an actual boat, the rest was a catamaran built on two floats.

Model of Stromberg's supertanker, the Liparus

"Something went seriously wrong on the first day we took it out to sea. I was on a barge ahead of it and, just as it was coming out of the canal, I noticed it was getting lower in the water. There were three men inside but they weren't aware of what was happening because they had very little vision—their only field of vision was looking straight down about 50 feet of tanker deck. We were in radio contact so I shouted a warning. They flung the engine in reverse and we managed to get the tanker back into the berth just as the bows went underwater. What had happened was that one of the pontoons had started to leak and two of the six pumps had packed up at the same time. But after that we never had any trouble.

"The reason we built it so large was because we had to deal with submarines in the same shots and subs are basically just featureless tubes with conning towers stuck on top—they don't displace water realistically as models unless you build them to a reasonable size, and even then you have to have all kinds of gadgets attached to them below the water line to disturb the water in order to create a realistic bow wave and wake. Water is always a problem when you're dealing with miniatures because you can't scale water. Even though our tanker was 63 feet long, it would only create a bow wave and wash that was in scale with a 63-foot-long launch. This is, of course, nothing like what a supertanker with its vast displacement of water would create, so as with the subs we had to have water disturbers all along the hull under the water line."

When the submarine is swallowed by the *Liparus,* there is a cut from Nassau back to Pinewood where the interior of the super-tanker is revealed in all its glittering glory. The huge set, designed by Ken Adam, had been constructed on a specially built stage on the studio's back-lot. Christened the "007 Stage," it's hoped that it will be a permanent fixture at Pinewood but at the time of writing there is still some doubt about its future. Local residents, whose complaints caused the huge volcano set built for *You Only Live Twice* to be torn down, are claiming that the 007 Stage, which resembles an aircraft hangar, is a blot on the landscape and should be removed. But one hopes it will be allowed to remain, both as a functioning stage for other filmmakers as planned, and as a monument to Ken Adam's grandiose visions and the Bond phenomenon in general.

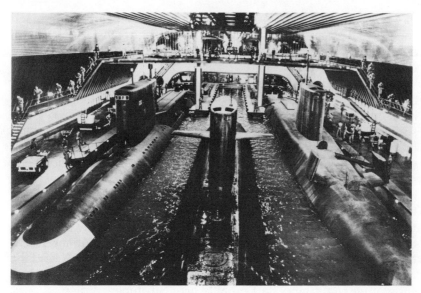
Inside the supertanker Liparus

"With the first three Bond films I worked on, *Dr. No, Goldfinger,* and *Thunderball,*" said Adam, "we had definite storylines and I knew exactly what to design and what the book demanded; whereas, on the last three Bonds I've been connected with—*You Only Live Twice, Diamonds Are Forever,* and this one—we found that we could not use the Fleming books and the producer had to come up with more or less original screenplays. But the film we have shot now has very little resemblance to the original screenplay for *The Spy Who Loved Me* because as we went along we developed certain ideas. At the beginning of this one, I knew we would require the interior and exterior of a supertanker which swallowed three nuclear submarines. I knew this much, and since it was going to be a big and difficult set to build, I decided to immediately start designing it, but I really didn't know what the exact requirements would be. I knew there was eventually going to be a big punch-up inside the set, but I didn't know the specific playing area and so on. So I had to cover myself and design it in such a way to give the director maximum opportunity for a variety of playing areas and camera angles, and almost counter-designed it against the interior of a supertanker which I believe, though I've never been on board one, isn't all that interesting."

The interior of the tanker is certainly a spectacular sight, a dazzling cavern of glittering metal dominated by the three submarines afloat in its center (the subs, made of fiberglass, were not completely full scale but appear so on the screen). It did, however, strongly remind one of Adam's volcano set, especially the box-like control room with its steel venetian blinds, and the monorail system along the set's perimeter. And, from this point on, events closely follow those in *You Only Live Twice:* Bond is spotted by Stromberg and captured, then forced to watch as the villain sets into action his scheme to start World War Three. Two of the submarines, now crewed by Stromberg's men, leave the tanker en route to predetermined locations where they will fire nuclear missiles at both the U.S.A. and the U.S.S.R. But Bond breaks free and, in turn, frees the imprisoned submarine crews who start a battle with Stromberg's men.

Stromberg, in the company of Ms. Amasova, has already left for Atlantis when this happens and so misses all the fun. Instead, it's the ship's captain (played by Sydney Tafler) who has the responsibility of trying to cope with the situation. Bond's companions make short work of Stromberg's troops but, as in *You Only Live Twice,* they find the shuttered control room seemingly impregnable. In the previous film, Bond gained entry simply by sneaking in the back way, after overpowering Blofeld's lone henchman, but this time a more complicated method is utilized. This involves dismantling one of the nuclear missiles in order to remove its high-explosive detonator, which Bond then carries to the control room's shutters by hitching a ride on a remote-controlled television camera unit. This whole sequence, though tense, is something of a misjudgment because it slows down the pace of the film too abruptly after the excitement of the battle.

After the explosion demolishes the shutters, Bond enters, snatches up a handy instruction book and swiftly reprograms the nuclear missiles about to be fired from the two submarines which have already reached their destinations (obviously jet-propelled).

When the missiles are subsequently fired, they don't head towards the U.S.A. and U.S.S.R., but pass each other in mid-air and come down on the submarines (an idea taken from Fleming's *Moonraker* novel). The tanker is now being gutted by a series of explosions and obviously near the end of its life. Bond and the surviving Navy men pile into the remaining submarine, fire a torpedo to blow open the tanker's bow and then escape into the open sea, just barely avoiding a falling gantry . . . .

"We spent days blowing up the tanker," said Meddings, "and then we had a controlled sinking showing it going under. It's still there, at the bottom of the sea in the Bahamas. We also built a model of the inside of the tanker for the final sequence where the submarine blasts its way out. Our model interior was thirty feet long with all the details of the full-size set. It even had a lot of little dead men lying around. We blew it up with a series of explosions and finally had the catwalk that spans the interior come crashing down just as the sub leaves its berth. We had to do that with a model because we couldn't bring down the catwalk in the full-size set, it would have been too dangerous. Actually, I didn't do any of the floor effects—the explosions, etc.—in the full-size set. I left that to one of my assistants, John Evans. He's very good and can be left totally alone."

253

The supertanker "blows up."

Quickly assembling a speedy waterscooter provided by Q, Bond sets off for Atlantis knowing that he has only a few minutes to rescue Amasova before the American Navy torpedoes Stromberg's establishment (time and distances are now becoming severely telescoped). After avoiding a trip down the tube into Stromberg's shark tank, Bond finds the old villain alone in his dining room and enjoying a meal (of fish, naturally), apparently unperturbed at the failure of his plans. Bond accepts his invitation to sit down at the opposite end of the long table, unaware that there is an equally long gun barrel stretching under the table and pointing right at him. But Bond leaps out of the way just as Stromberg fires and, with the words "You've shot your bolt, Stromberg, now it's my turn," fires his own gun into the long barrel. For some inexplicable reason, Bond's bullet isn't stopped by the firing mechanism at the other end and Stromberg doubles up in pain, hit in the lower regions. Bond then finishes him off with a couple more shots (unusually violent for a Bond film, this scene) and Stromberg collapses face down into his fish dinner.

After the realism of Stromberg's death, it's back to fantasy land for Bond's final encounter with Jaws, who seems to be the only employee of Stromberg's left in the giant structure. First, a bullet fired by Bond bounces off Jaws' steel teeth and then when Bond succeeds in dropping him in the shark tank, he *eats the shark*!

"We could never find decent photographs of sharks when we were making ours at Pinewood," said Meddings, "so it wasn't as marvellous as we would have liked it to be but it looks very good in the film. You see it swimming around in the tank and it looks realistic. It was very simple in comparison to the one they had in *Jaws*—it had a mouth that could be worked mechanically and moved on wires suspended from an overhead trolley. Apart from the sequence with Richard Kiel, we took it out to Nassau for the sequence where it attacks the girl at the beginning of the picture but we didn't use it as much as we intended to out there because we found that real sharks could be handled safely by the Americans working for us and could do a much more convincing job, of course. The scene with the girl was shot in a swimming pool and we did use the dummy shark for the shots where it actually got hold of her

Bond attacked by Jaws in the shark tank area.

around the waist. There was a lot of blood and shaking about—it looked very convincing."

Bond locates Amasova just as Atlantis is hit by torpedoes and the whole establishment begins to fill up with water. But they manage to get inside a luxuriously furnished escape capsule which comes complete with fur lining and a chilled bottle of champagne. After they have floated comfortably to the surface, there's a brief moment of tension when the girl remembers her vow to kill Bond and she aims her gun at him. But the only bang comes from the champagne bottle and she quickly melts under his high-powered charm, giving up all ideas of revenge. When the capsule is hauled aboard a naval rescue ship, on which M and Miss Moneypenny are waiting (just as they were on board the submarine at the end of *You Only Live Twice*), Bond and Amasova are discovered locked in a passionate but discreet embrace under a blanket. When asked by a shocked M what he is doing, Bond replies: "Just keeping my British end up, sir." Perhaps Maibaum is to blame for that line, but I suspect the heavy hand of Wood . . . .

Champagne melts Barbara Bach.

The Spy Who Loved Me is basically an anthology of all the Bond films that have gone before. It's as if Broccoli and his team deliberately set out to take a number of the more memorable set-pieces and remake them, even bigger and more spectacular. The pre-credits sequence, with its skiing scenes, for instance, comes from *On Her Majesty's Secret Service*; the fight on the train comes from *From Russia with Love* and *Live and Let Die;* the scene involving the motorcycle assassin and his rocket-powered sidecar is obviously inspired by the similar scene in *Thunderball*; the car chase with the gimmicked-up Lotus is a repeat of the one in *Goldfinger* with the Aston Martin; the underwater battles are from *Thunderball*; and the basic plot, together with the final climactic scenes in the tanker, are, as we've mentioned before, from *You Only Live Twice*.

Surprisingly, however, it all *works. The Spy Who Loved Me,* though without an original bone in its body, ends up a very entertaining movie and it works precisely because it *is* a kind of lavish *resumé* of the whole Bond series (almost a collection of edited highlights). It has style, pace, and enough of a coherent plot to provide the set-pieces with some reason for existing. And, of course, the set-pieces are excellent—a blend of fine stunt work (Bond veteran Bob Simmons was back in charge of the stunts) and brilliant special effects. Also, in this film, Bond's character is given a slightly harder edge than usual and this helps to offset the increasing jokiness and the sheer fantasy of the Jaws character (who pops up unscathed out of the sea at the end of the film). Unfortunately, this balance wasn't to be maintained in the next film, *Moonraker,* which, for all its many attractions, must rank as something of a low point in the series as a whole.

As usual, Bond gets the girl.

Special-effects supervisor Derek Meddings displays
model of **Moonraker.**

13

Moonraker

The huge box office success of *The Spy Who Loved Me* proved that Broccoli on his own was just as adept at giving the audiences what they wanted as when he was working with Saltzman. It also proved to United Artists that upping the budget on the films was a good investment, so they gave Broccoli what amounted to a financial free rein on the next one. As a result, whereas *The Spy Who Loved Me* cost in the region of $13,000,000, *Moonraker* cost nearer $30,000,000. Inflation and more elaborate special effects explain much of the increase in costs, but part of the added expense was due to the production being based in France. Broccoli, forced out of Britain because of the increasing severity of the tax laws, was unable to use Pinewood Studios, which had been the home of the Bond films since the very beginning, so instead the interiors for *Moonraker* were shot at three different studios in Paris. The only parts of *Moonraker* shot in England were the model sequences, again supervised by Derek Meddings.

After *The Spy Who Loved Me,* Broccoli had intended to film *For Your Eyes Only* (as was announced in the end credits of *Spy*), but the incredible success of another movie in 1977 led him to change his mind. The rival money-maker was *Star Wars,* so he decided that the next Bond should be one with an outer space theme and the one unfilmed Bond novel that fitted that requirement was *Moonraker.* In a way, it's ironic that Bond should have joined the ranks of the many *Star Wars* imitations when *Star Wars* itself owes so much to the Bond films. It's also rather sad when one remembers that once it was the Bond films that produced imitators and not *vice versa*.

Of course, Broccoli maintains that *Moonraker* is *not* a science fiction movie at all. "It's science fact," he said. "According to the scientists at N.A.S.A., everything that we have in our picture can actually happen in the near future, not a couple of centuries from now." Which, according to most definitions, still makes it science fiction. It doesn't matter whether you're extrapolating about events a thousand years in the future or the day after tomorrow. In fact, *Moonraker* is nearer to being classified as science fiction than *Star Wars* which, strictly speaking, is a fantasy that exploits the imagery of sci-fi.

Moonraker was the third James Bond novel, published in 1955 and, understandably, a little dated now. The plot concerned a mysterious millionaire from South Africa called Hugo Drax who is helping to finance the British space program (how times change!) out of his own pocket. He has set up a base on the south coast of England from where he is planning to launch his "Moonraker" rocket, the first step to putting an Englishman on the moon. For these patriotic services, he has become a national celebrity, despite possessing a face that has borne the brunt of shoddy plastic surgery and now has hair growing out of it in odd places, and has even been granted a knighthood. However, M becomes suspicious of him when he discovers that he cheats at cards (the cad!) and sends Bond to investigate. It turns out that Drax is really a Nazi agent planning to wreak vengeance on England for Germany's defeat by having "Moonraker," fitted with a nuclear warhead, come down in the middle of London (the sort of behavior you'd expect from a man who cheats at cards). But Bond fixes the rocket's guidance system so that it comes down on Drax's submarine instead. . . .

It goes without saying the film is a little different. Drax, for one thing, has gone up in the world—he's now a multibillionaire and he's no longer interested in just obliterating London but the whole human race.

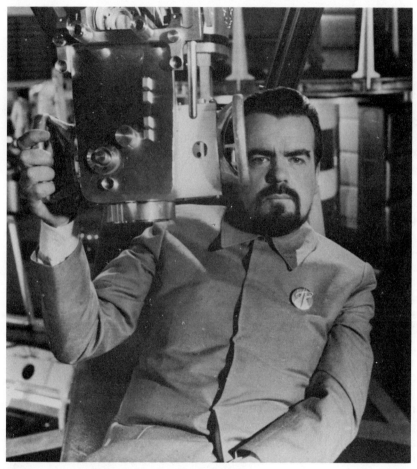

Megalomaniac millionaire Sir Hugo Drax (Michael
Lonsdale)

Moonraker begins with a pre-credits sequence that is literally breathtaking before it deteriorates into sheer absurdity—thus setting a pattern for the remainder of the film. After we see a shuttle being hijacked right off the back of a 747 (impressive model work courtesy of Meddings and crew), we cut to a small plane high over South America. Inside, Bond is in a familiar situation—in close embrace with an attractive girl, his hand stroking her thigh. "If you go any higher, Mr. Bond, my ears will pop," she tells him. Then she produces a gun and Bond finds himself about to be left behind in the sabotaged plane while both the girl and the pilot parachute to safety. But Bond attacks the pilot and after a fight, pushes him out of the plane, only to be pushed out into space himself by none other than the villain from the last film, Jaws (Richard Kiel). Bond has been in some tight places before but this has to be the ultimate one—hurtling through the air thousands of feet above the ground without a parachute.

His solution to this apparently insoluble problem is ingenious— putting his arms to his sides he skydives down at great speed (in a marvellous parody of Superman), catches up with the pilot and, after a struggle, removes his parachute and puts it on, leaving the other man to his own devices which, under the circumstances, are limited. It's an amazing sequence that is almost worth the price of admission (*almost*). Except for a few close-ups, it was all done for real with stuntmen wearing special slim-line parachutes under jackets designed to split easily up the back. Enormously complicated to film, it involved countless jumps by both stuntmen and cameramen before the necessary footage was obtained. It's also an impressive achievement in terms of editing (by Bond veteran John Glen)—the matching of Moore with the stuntman as he begins the fall is nothing short of masterful.

Unfortunately, things take a turn for the worst after Bond has grabbed the parachute—a classic case of not leaving well alone, for out of the sky comes Jaws who catches up with Bond and tries to sink his metal teeth into his leg. Bond escapes by opening his chute but, when Jaws tries to follow suit, the handle of his rip cord breaks off. Vainly flapping his arms like a giant bird, he plummets at great speed into a circus tent below, bringing the whole structure down like a punctured balloon. *Moonraker,* the most expensive slapstick movie since *It's a Mad Mad Mad Mad World,* has begun.

After the astounding visuals of the pre-credits sequence, the credits themselves come as a severe anticlimax due mainly to John Barry's unexciting and forgettable theme song. Sung by Shirley Bassey, it's hard to believe that it was composed by the same man who produced *Goldfinger* and *On Her Majesty's Secret Service.* Perhaps he sought to counterpoint the hard technological imagery of the film by having an ultra-light romantic theme but, if so, the idea didn't work. And without much in the way of musical support, Maurice Binder's usual series of surrealistic shots featuring nude women wafting through space, though cleverly executed, don't make much of an impression . . . .

The return of the indestructible Jaws

When the film proper begins, we learn that the "Moonraker" shuttle had been on loan to the British government from N.A.S.A. Bond begins his investigation by going to see the owner of the company that manufactured the shuttle under license—Hugo Drax. Arriving in Los Angeles, Bond is met at the airport by one of Drax's many female employees, Corinne Dufour (Corinne Clery, best known for her role in *The Story of O*). Corinne flies him by helicopter to Drax's huge establishment that appears to include the Palace of Versailles, complete with surrounding forests. Bond is then introduced to Drax himself in his luxurious sitting room where he is about to partake of afternoon tea, flanked by two well-trained Doberman Pinschers (so well trained are the dogs that they ignore the meat that Drax tosses to them until he gives them an almost imperceptible command with his hand).

Drax is played by the French actor Michael Lonsdale (co-star of *The Day of the Jackal*), and after Curt Jurgen's lackluster villain in *The Spy Who Loved Me,* he comes as a refreshing change (James Mason was offered the role first, but he turned it down). In fact, he is probably *too* good—his portrayal of the smoothly urbane but completely ruthless megalomaniac is so convincing that he doesn't quite fit in with the film's relentlessly light-hearted tone. Discussing his role, Lonsdale said: "Lewis asked me to be more of a *smiling* Drax. I personally would have played the character as more severe, but Lewis pointed out that Drax is a *happy* character, content with what he's doing."

Even so, Lonsdale's Drax still creates a powerful impression, and he also gets most of the film's best lines. For instance, after their first encounter he tells his Japanese servant, Chang (Toshiro Suga): "Take care of Mr. Bond. See that some harm comes to him." Or perhaps, it's just the way he says them.

After Drax, we are introduced to the film's other principal character, Holly Goodhead, whose name (nudge, nudge) follows in the tradition established by Pussy Galore and Plenty O'Toole. She is played by American actress Lois Chiles—a great improvement on Barbara Bach, being not only a better actress but also possessing a much more interesting screen presence. In fact, at times she suggests the smoldering sensuality of the young Lauren Bacall, though her performance could have been given a stronger focus by director Lewis Gilbert. Like Major Amasova in *The Spy Who Loved Me,* Holly Goodhead, despite her name, is supposed to represent the New Woman and be an equal as opposed to simply being Bond's sexual plaything. To reinforce this new image, Ms. Chiles, like Ms. Bach before her, removes a minimum of clothing during the film and certainly doesn't appear in the costume she is seen wearing in the poster illustration—which may be a blow for Women's Liberation, but a minor catastrophe for all the male chauvinist pigs in the audience.

Lois Chiles as Holly Goodhead

Ms. Goodhead is a space scientist on loan to Drax from N.A.S.A. and at first seems impervious to Bond's charms, such as they are these days. She does give him a guided tour around part of Drax's establishment—all shimmering metal walls and sloping ceilings with the name Ken Adam stamped everywhere. The tour includes a visit to the centrifuge room and Bond accepts her invitation to take a ride in the machine (why would doing that help his investigation, one wonders), but Ms. Goodhead is called away and Bond finds that Drax's henchman, Chang, has taken over in the control room and is pushing the machine's acceleration towards fatal limits. It looks bad for a moment or two, as does Roger Moore when the flesh on his face is sent rippling back towards his ears due to the incredible velocity (achieved with a high speed blower) but then he uses his special dart-firing wrist gun, given to him by Q, to blow up the control panel and the centrifuge slows to a halt (this sequence reminds one of the traction-machine one in *Thunderball*).

Goodhead might be impervious to Bond's charms but Corinne isn't, and that night, after Bond has seduced her, she reveals to him the whereabouts of Drax's safe, the contents of which provide him with a vital clue (it doesn't matter what—it's just another Bondian MacGuffin). Their actions, however, haven't gone unnoticed, for Chang, the Japanese manservant, is lurking in the shadows. The next day, Bond is invited to join Drax in an early-morning pheasant shoot, seemingly unaware that one of Drax's men is perched in a tree with a rifle aimed at him. A bird rises from the grass, Bond swivels and fires . . . and the bird flies on untouched. "You appear to have missed, Mr. Bond," says Drax. "Have I?" asks Bond innocently as the would-be killer falls dead from the tree. This is an amusing scene, but it doesn't bear examining too closely (but then *nothing* should be examined too closely in a Bond film) for what it means is that Bond now knows for certain that Drax is up to no good, and Drax knows that Bond knows, therefore there is nothing to prevent Drax from having Bond killed on the spot. Instead, Bond calmly gets into a waiting limousine and is driven to the airport by one of Drax's men.

Corinne, however, isn't so fortunate and is forced to be the film's obligatory sacrificial lamb, a fate that befalls at least one woman in every Bond film (though there wasn't one in *The Spy Who Loved Me,* unless you count Naomi). Corinne's death, though photographed with all the lush romanticism of a hair spray commercial, is an unpleasant one with Drax offering her as breakfast on the hoof to his two dogs. . . .

The clue in Drax's safe leads Bond to a certain glass factory in Venice that is manufacturing a specific type of container for Drax. Coincidentally, Ms. Goodhead also turns up there and later, in her hotel room, Bond tells her that he knows she is a CIA agent. "Very astute of you," she says, "How did you find out?" "I have friends in low places," replies Bond, which shows that the CIA's fall from public grace is now being reflected even in Bond's fantasy world.

Earlier, when Bond was pondering on Ms. Goodhead's presence in Venice while being poled down a canal in a gondola, he was suddenly attacked by a knife-throwing assassin who appeared out of a coffin in a passing hearse. After using the assassin's own knife to kill him, Bond speeds away in his motorized gondola and straight into *Moonrakers'* more embarrassing slapstick sequences. One can imagine the scene at the script conference when the sequence was being devised: "Hey, what if Bond's gondola is a high-powered, armored speedboat with a whole mess of hidden gadgets?" "Yeah, great idea! And, when it's finally cornered in a dead end on the canal, he presses another button and the gondola turns into a hovercraft!" "Marvellous!" "Yeah, and then the hovercraft goes up these steps and straight into Piazza San Marco which will be full of amazed tourists. It will be like that scene in *The Spy Who Loved Me* when Bond's car came out of the water onto the beach, only a lot funnier. We can have shots of drinkers doing double takes and looking at their wine as Bond goes by, and waiters can spill things . . . we can even cut to a dog and a pigeon doing double takes as well. It'll be real crazy. The audience will howl . . ." "Yeah, and then we can have one of Bond's pursuers act so surprised he falls off the launch into the water!" At that point, the script conference probably had to be halted for awhile so that the participants could ease their aching sides and wipe the tears of laughter from their eyes. (It brought tears to my eyes, too, when I saw it . . . but not for the same reason.)

After getting rid of his rather conspicuous means of transport, which couldn't have been easy, Bond then pays a nocturnal visit to the glass factory and discovers a secret laboratory where a deadly nerve gas is being manufactured. With a sample of the substance in a glass vial in his pocket, Bond is attacked as he leaves the laboratory by Chang dressed in full Japanese fighting costume. There's an amusing fight in the glass factory's museum full of rare and valuable pieces of glassware, during which the whole place is reduced to a shambles before Bond sends his opponent hurtling through a glass clock-face and into the square below where he lands right on top of an orchestra.

Bond makes a deadly discovery in Flax's Venetian laboratory.

The next day, Bond takes both M and the Minister of Defense (Geoffrey Keen, who played the same role in *The Spy Who Loved Me*) to the location of the secret laboratory, insisting that they wear gas masks before opening the door (the door, incidentally, opens only when the theme from *Close Encounters of the Third Kind* is played). But instead of finding the fully equipped laboratory of the night before, they discover Drax sitting in an ornate but otherwise empty office. He regards their gas masks quizzically and says: "Forgive me, gentlemen, but not being English, I don't share your unique sense of humor."

It's an observation that could be applied to the movie as a whole, particularly in connection with the treatment of the Jaws character. In *The Spy Who Loved Me,* his apparent invulnerability was an amusing innovation that was handled reasonably well but, like so much in *Moonraker,* this time it's carried to ridiculous extremes. Actually, his first appearance in the film is quite effective—it takes place during the carnival sequence in Rio de Janeiro (a repeat of the Junkanoo carnival setting in Nassau in *Thunderball*) and he appears in long shot down an alley wearing a giant clown's head. The effect, as he moves bobbingly towards the camera, is subtly menacing and stands out in a film where subtlety is a dirty word.

After that, however, it's downhill all the way as far as Jaws is concerned. Bond next encounters him on a cable car high above Rio where a spectacular fight, also involving Holly Goodhead, takes place. Bond and Goodhead escape from the car by sliding down the cable on a length of chain, leaving Jaws to crash into the cable car terminal at the base of the mountain. Emerging from the wreckage completely unscathed, like a character in a Tom and Jerry cartoon, he then meets the filmmakers' biggest error in judgement—a pneumatic little blonde woman with glasses and pigtails who looks as if she came off a calendar advertising farm machinery. She is, we soon learn, supposed to be Jaws' "love interest" and no doubt their scenes together were supposed to be amusingly touching but instead they are exercises in mawkish bathos that leave one writhing with embarrassment.

Goodhead is captured shortly after this and Bond sets off alone up the Amazon in a special speedboat fitted with the usual arsenal of

269

Bondian gadgets. Before long, he is being chased by a flotilla of mortar-firing high-speed launches in a spectacular but perfunctory reconstruction of the boat sequence in *From Russia with Love*. After blowing up two of his pursuers, he escapes from the third boat by going over a waterfall in a hang glider that has magically sprouted out of his craft. Yet, after going to all that trouble to avoid death or capture, he then simply *walks* into the villain's headquarters without any attempt at concealment whatsoever. Some secret agent—he might as well carry a neon sign around with him!

After a boring fight with a giant water snake, which he kills with a device we didn't know he had (another example of the Bondian rules being broken), Bond finally gets to find out what happened to the missing "Moonraker" shuttle. It seems that Drax himself stole the shuttle back because one of his own had developed a serious fault and couldn't be used. Used for what? Well, that remains a mystery for the time being.

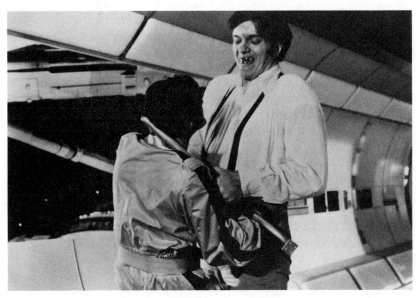

Another desperate encounter with Jaws

"Mr. Bond must be cold after his swim. Put him somewhere warm," Drax instructs Jaws, and Bond finds himself sharing space with Goodhead in a chamber directly beneath one of the rockets—a situation inspired directly by the novel.

Earlier, in Drax's pyramid-shaped control room, we have seen various "Moonrakers" take off from the secret bases around the world, all of which appear very convincing, thanks to the skills of Derek Meddings and his team. "The space shuttles we used were completely authentic," he said. "Aims, the company that has been building the real shuttle for N.A.S.A. invited us to their base in California and were most helpful. They gave us all the photographs they could lay their hands on and all the information available. There were no problems at all in getting information because it's not a secret operation or a military project, so our interiors are exact replicas of the real thing. We also saw the space shuttle itself because they were actually building two while we were there and one was nearly completed. And, from the way they described their proposed launching system, I believe ours was exactly like the launches will be. Certainly the N.A.S.A. technical adviser we had on the film, Eric Burgess, was thrilled to bits with our launching scenes. The biggest problem we had was in trying to create a realistic amount of intense heat in the models so that their exhaust will look right. It has to be powerful but not intense enough to burn the model. We used a very powerful firework, a mixture of magnesium and gunpowder, which we crammed into the tails of the shuttle boosters made out of aluminium. These 'motors' had a trick release on them and, immediately we had an ignition, a technician wearing asbestos gloves would run to the shuttle, pull a pin on the side and the motors would fall into a metal tray beneath the model, then we could use the rest of the model again. On one occasion, however, things didn't go as planned and the model caught fire. It produced a lot of smoke and the model was ruined but otherwise no harm was done . . . ." The shuttles varied in size depending on the shot they were used in. For the launch sequences, models of about five feet in length were used, and the largest was over six feet long; but some, used in long shots, were quite tiny.

Bond and Goodhead escape from the blast chamber by climbing up a ventilation shaft (exactly as in the novel) and then take the place of the two pilots in a shuttle about to blast off. Fortunately, Ms. Goodhead, being a space expert from N.A.S.A. knows how to operate the craft (if one forgets she isn't really from N.A.S.A., but the C.I.A.) and the "Moonraker" takes off successfully to rendezvous with the other shuttles in outer space. Again the special effects are immaculate, due partly to the total absence of matte lines around the models. The reason for this is that Meddings is wary of the blue screen matting process and likes to combine as many of the image components as he can of any one shot in the camera. That is, he prefers to film his models against a "real" background instead of having the background later added optically. For instance, to create the Earth's horizon seen moving in the background of many of the shots, he used a large spindle-shaped drum about fifteen feet long, painted to resemble the surface of the Earth.

"I used the method first when I did a science fiction movie called *Doppelganger* in 1968. It seemed to me, after weeks of struggling trying to think how I could show the Earth rotating, this was the only way to do it—unless you built a huge monster of a sphere. It's just like a cylinder really; the one in *Moonraker* was particularly large because we were putting models in front of it but you can make them any size you want depending on the sort of shot you want. I used this sytem on *Superman*, too.

"I shoot my space ships in a different way to John Dykstra who did *Star Wars*—his models were suspended in front of a blue screen on rods covered in the same blue material and the camera did all the moving. But blue screen worries me as I think it worries most people—you do part of the shot and then several weeks later they start putting in the background and it's not until then that you find out if there's anything wrong, such as shrinkage or an incorrect color balance. So I try to shoot my models and backgrounds at the same time if I can, though it's not always possible.

"I use all sorts of methods to animate the models—sometimes we put them on rods, sometimes we fly them on wires or we attach them to a sheet of glass. Every shot has its own set of problems. The main problem is getting them to move really smoothly so that we

Bond and Holly Goodhead experience zero gravity aboard Moonraker.

can shoot sixteen frames a second—we need to get the depth of focus and the right amount of light so we can run at high speeds. The difference between *Moonraker* and our work in the previous Bond is that a supertanker is something that everyone in the audience has had the opportunity to see, either in real life or on documentaries. Now when it comes to space, people have seen documentary footage of American spacecraft but it's always a bit confusing because you never see the vehicles cruising past the camera as you do in *Star Wars,* instead you see close-up of *parts* of them because usually the footage is being taken by the man who's *in the* thing. But what you invariably see in this type of footage are shots of the Earth, and that's what we tried to simulate in *Moonraker*—we tried to get the Earth to look real. If you can get the audience to accept the real Earth on the screen, then you can hang anything in front of it and they will accept that too . . . hopefully."

One certainly accepts the model of Drax's orbiting space station which first appears as a row of jewelled lights in the darkness of space and then comes into full spectacular view as it moves out of the Earth's shadow (the sharp contrast between shadow and light in outer space is skillfully simulated in all of *Moonraker's* space sequences). Designed by Ken Adam, it's an ingenious collection of tubes and spheres that dazzle the eye like a drawing by M.C. Escher. As usual, Adam eschewed naturalism and let his imagination run loose: "At N.A.S.A., they showed me lots of artists' concepts of future space colonies. They were exciting in terms of reality but they weren't exciting in terms of filmmaking," he said. "By that, I mean I could have used the traditional space-wheel concept that Kubrick used in *2001* and that would have been valid scientifically. However, when you get inside it, it's like filming inside a large bicycle tire. Another type of space station that I saw was a series of cylinders. That sent me going. Using that principle, I started off deisgning a *mobile,* a hanging structure. I used cylinders of varying lengths and angles and combined them with various spheres. Whenever it moved or rotated, the camera got a different angle on it."

The space station was a large "miniature," over sixteen feet across and too big to be hung directly in front of Meddings' revolving Earth simulator. "We did have to 'matte' that against the Earth," said Meddings, "but not with a blue screen. We did it with front projection. We hung the model before a front projection screen that projected a plate of the revolving drum that we'd already shot. I don't mind those type of matting shots because you can see the results the following day. I had to shoot the station model and the various sections of it, some of which were full scale, in the giant 007 Stage because I needed enough room to be able to get the station and the other models together in one shot and be able to wander around them with the camera."

When the shuttle containing Bond and Goodhead docks with the station, we then get the opportunity to see the interior and it proves just as interesting as the exterior. "To keep the interior from getting dull," said Adam, "I decided to treat all my circular planes in a non-concentric way. The central lift shaft was, therefore, not the center of the set. The sides of the set sloped down in a 'forced perspective.' I made the giant telescope as a compositional feature. Then I broke the whole space of the set-up with a series of horizontal tubes and one big vertical tube."

Impressive it may be, but it's here that the much-vaunted "scientific accuracy" goes out the window, particularly in connection with the artificial gravity that is seen to exist within the station. It's true that once the station started to rotate, the centrifugal force would simulate gravity to some extent but only at the *outer edges* of the structure, yet gravity is seen in operation within the station's central sphere. What's more, it appears to be a uniform effect; in other words, "down" is all in the same direction, whereas in reality, "down" would be in the direction of the station's outer edges, while "up" would be towards its center. Obviously the N.A.S.A. adviser failed to win the argument on this point, as he also lost the argument about hearing sounds in space (with the exception of Kubrick, no filmmaker has been able to resist adding sound effects to space sequences).

Bond and Goodhead, still in disguise, are present when Drax gives his followers a morale-boosting talk about their mission. Like Stromberg, he isn't doing it for the money (which would be unlikely seeing as he's the richest man in the world), but because he wants to become nothing less than a god. His plan is to destroy all human life on Earth with a special nerve gas distilled from a rare South American orchid, and then repopulate the planet with a race of perfect people, all pre-selected by him. They will go forth and multiply, obeying his every command while he orbits above them in his man-made celestial throne. With Drax, the Bond series has taken megalomania about as far as it can go. . . .

Our two heroes sabotage the mechanism that creates a radar barrier around the station, thus enabling it to be detected on Earth (another quibble about the so-called scientific accuracy—an object that large would be plainly visible from Earth), but are then captured by Jaws who takes them before Drax. "Mr. Bond, you reappear with the inevitability of an unloved season," says Drax and we understand just how he feels. He orders Jaws to shove them out of an airlock, saying to Goodhead: "You wanted to be the first American woman in outer space, you are about to get your wish." But events take an unexpected, and an unlikely, turn when Bond convinces Jaws that neither he nor his beloved Dolly (Blanche Ravaloc) are going to fit into Drax's vision of perfection and are therefore both expendable. So Jaws turns on his master and has to be overpowered by Drax's men wielding modified cattle prods. . . .

Things are looking grim when the cavalry arrives on the scene in the form of a N.A.S.A. shuttle launched to investigate Drax's station. Drax orders it to be destroyed with a laser cannon, but Bond saves the day by getting to the control panel, just as the shuttle is moving into the laser's line of fire, and activating the station's retro-rockets. This has the effect of halting the station's rotation and sending everyone inside it into free fall, foiling the proposed laser blast (one wonders how the stationary laser was able to draw a bead on the approaching shuttle while the station was rotating).

Drax's men then don space suits to attack the American shuttle directly, and we see them moving down one of the transparent tubes and launching themselves into space—a clever shot achieved with a split screen, producing a cut from real men to puppets at the actual point of exit. An even more impressive special effects shot

Holly Goodhead swings a haymaker aboard the space station.

Drax's space station is destroyed.

follows, when we see the shuttle open like a giant flower to reveal a squad of "space marines" rising up to meet Drax's force. The space battle that follows is visually exciting despite the fact that movements in space, like ones made underwater, tend to be slowed down and there was a danger that the action would drag as it did during the underwater fight at the climax of *Thunderball,* but this was overcome by some fast editing and dazzling optical effects involving the blue-colored laser flashes. The battle itself was achieved by Meddings using a blend of close shots of live actors—supported by wires and manipulated by technicians above them—and long shots of mechanically operated puppets.

The fight moves into the space station and, with the assistance of Bond, Goodhead, and Jaws, the space marines gain entrance to the control room and, for a few moments, the interior is full of brilliant laser blasts and falling bodies (if anything, this particular fight is over *too* quickly). Drax, no fool, realizes the game is up and retreats into one of the exit tubes, but is followed by Bond who confronts him near the airlock. Drax quickly snatches up a laser from a fallen marine and purrs, "Allow me to put you out of *my* misery." But Bond shoots him in the heart with one of the darts fired from his wrist gun, then pushes him into the airlock, saying, "Take a few giant steps for mankind, Drax." He then opens the outer door and the surprised-looking Drax is sent hurtling backwards into the void, a journey from which it is unlikely he will return—a pity seeing that Lonsdale made Drax one of the best Bond villains we've seen in a long time.

Severely damaged by the shooting, the space station station starts to break up. While the space marines return to their shuttle, Bond and Goodhead commandeer Drax's "Moonraker" with the aim of catching up with and destroying the three spheres containing the nerve gas that he has already fired towards Earth. Meanwhile, Jaws has located his Dolly and they run towards each other in romantic slow motion through the wreckage of the disintegrating station . . . a sequence that rates very highly on one's scale of Most Embarrassing Moments in the Movies.

Afterwards, while drinking champagne and saying his first words—"Here's to us"—Jaws and friend notice that Bond's shuttle is having trouble separating from the doomed station. Jaws, obviously reformed by love, uses his brute strength to overcome the mechanical fault and the shuttle floats free. The following sequences involving Bond and Goodhead tracking down the deadly spheres and destroying them with the laser in the "Moonraker's" nose are excellent on a technical level but rather anticlimactic in dramatic terms. After all the comic-book antics that have gone before, it's hard to accept for a moment that the spheres represent any *real* threat to life on Earth and, therefore, it all falls a bit flat (it is also too obviously an imitation of the climax of *Star Wars* where the hero has to fire a torpedo down a small vent in the Death Star in order to save the day).

The film ends with the obligatory "embarrassment scene" with Bond and Goodhead being discovered in a passionate embrace by their respective superiors. Not only is their bout of lovemaking in freefall (despite the lack of gravity, their bodies are coyly concealed within a draped blanket—another example of scientific inaccuracy) witnessed by M and company, but the scene is also transmitted to both the White House and Buckingham Palace. "What does Bond think he's up to?" splutters M. "I think he's about to attempt re-entry, sir," says Q innocently. Christopher Wood has to take the blame for *that* one because his is the only name on the screenplay credits this time, Richard Maibaum having presumably retired.

Holly Goodhead, unperturbed at being observed by so many dignitaries, says to Bond: "Take me one more time around the world, James," and, as the "Moonraker" recedes into the distance, the end credits begin to roll, promising that James Bond will return in *For Your Eyes Only.*

Comparing *Moonraker* to *Dr. No,* one might find it hard to believe at first, that they belong in the same series of films. There *are* similarities, of course, apart from the central character having the same name—the basic plots are roughly the same and there is the same ambiguous emphasis on technology; the sensual presentation of its stylized, glittering surface, while simultaneously exploiting it as a threat. But the differences between the two films are more marked: the changes in the character of Bond, the sheer *scale* of *Moonraker* compared to *Dr. No.* (*Dr. No* cost about $900,000—less than a *thirtieth* of the budget of *Moonraker*), and the corresponding increase in the fantasy element. But the biggest difference between the two films is in their approach to humor—there *is* humor in *Dr. No* but it is mainly black and conveyed via Bond's laconic asides, whereas in *Moonraker* the humor is predominantly visual and on a crude slapstick level. Even more damaging is the jokey treatment of the Jaws character, an innovation that must be regarded as an unfortunate error in judgment on the makers' part. With Jaws, the Bond series now has *two* unkillable characters, the other one being Bond himself. We always know that James Bond is going to survive and, as Broccoli has pointed out, the entertainment comes not from wondering *if* he will survive each new predicament but *how.* But, in theory at least, he's still supposed to be a flesh-and-blood human being. Jaws, however, isn't; he's a cartoon character. No matter what happens to him, he's going to pop up undamaged in the next scene like the cat or the mouse in a Tom and Jerry cartoon. A good vehicle for easy laughs, perhaps, but when you put such a character in a film, it means that you can't take *any* of it seriously and any attempt to create tension or excitement is a waste of time. Instead of being comedy-thrillers, the Bonds are becoming simply comedies.

But, of course, the big question is: Will the audiences mind? Apparently not, is the answer, for *Moonraker,* at the time of writing, seems set to become the biggest Bond money-maker of all. It's only the hardline Bond fans who bemoan the increasing jokiness of the series and they're very much in the minority. Also in the minority are the people who know Bond via the novels—the books still sell relatively well but on nothing like the scale they did in the sixties—and one can imagine someone familiar only with the screen-Bond finding the novels rather quaint and dull today (which is why Christopher Wood was assigned to write novelizations of both *The Spy Who Loved Me* and *Moonraker*).

As far as Broccoli is concerned, he's giving the audiences what they want—the more farfetched the Bonds get, the better they like it—and who can say he's wrong? After all, he can produce the ultimate argument to prove his point—success. It's a success that has lasted nearly two decades and shows no sign of slowing down. James Bond, it seems, will be returning for a long time to come.

POSTSCRIPT: Since writing the above, the author has heard rumors that producer Broccoli has taken the adverse criticism (particularly in America) that *Moonraker* received to heart and is intending that the next Bond film will be nearer the earlier ones in style with a much "tougher" James Bond. It will be interesting to see the result.

Appendix 1:

The Other Bonds

When Broccoli and Saltzman bought the film rights to the Bond
novels in 1961, they managed to secure the rights on all but two of
the books. One of these was *Casino Royale* which Fleming had sold
to Gregory Ratoff in 1955; the other was *Thunderball* which, by
then, was the subject of a court case initiated by Kevin McClory who
was claiming that Fleming had based the book on ideas he'd devised jointly with McClory and Jack Whittingham.

Casino Royale

In 1960, Ratoff's widow had sold the rights to *Casino* to Charles
K. Feldman, a former lawyer and talent agent who'd become a very
successful Hollywood producer (his films include *To Have and
Have Not, The Big Sleep, Red River, A Streetcar Named Desire,
The Seven Year Itch,* and *A Walk on the Wild Side*). With the
success of the Saltzman/Broccoli Bonds, Feldman naturally decided
the time was ripe to launch his own Bond, though he was rather
unsure about how to approach it. After going to Saltzman and
Broccoli with the suggestion of a joint production and being turned
down, he decided that there was nothing in *Casino Royale* that
hadn't already been exploited in the other Bond films so he would
have to turn it into something completely different. And, having just
had a success with a zany sex comedy starring Peter Sellers and
Woody Allen, *What's New Pussycat?,* he decided to make *Casino*

Royale into a comedy—and not just an ordinary comedy but one that would be wilder and bigger than anything seen on the screen before.

Everything about *Casino Royale* is larger than life—it boasts *five* directors: Joe McGrath, Robert Parrish, John Huston, Ken Hughes, and Val Guest; and at least five scriptwriters (though some are uncredited): Wolf Mankowitz, Michael Sayers, Ben Hecht, Terry Southern, and Billy Wilder. The lineup of stars is also impressive: Peter Sellers, Woody Allen, Ursula Andress, David Niven, William Holden, Deborah Kerr, Charles Boyer, Daliah Lavi, John Huston, George Raft, Joanna Pettet, Orson Welles, Peter O'Toole, and Jean-Paul Belmondo. It also featured not one but *several* James Bonds played by such diverse people as Niven, Sellers, Allen (as little Jimmy Bond), and even Ursula Andress.

284 Not surprisingly, the film turned out to be an over-blown mish-mash of contrasting comedy styles and forced zaniness. With all those different creative influences, it was more like a collection of separate comedy routines than a single picture, though there was a vague plot line running through it. The man who had the unenviable task of trying to pull all the disparate pieces together was writer/director Val Guest:

"Charlie Feldman called me in right at the beginning and said, 'Look, I'm going to give you six scripts of *Casino Royale* and I want you to try and get *one* out of them all.' And they were as widely varied as you could possibly get; there was one by Ben Hecht, one by Terry Southern, one by Dore Schary, and so on, all top writers. And eventually we didn't use any of them at all, it just became a sort of psychedelic nightmare because Charlie would call me up in the middle of the night and say: 'Look, I can get Bardot next Wednesday, what set are we on? Well, write her in.' And that was the way we got those eighteen or so international stars. He started off conning Sellers into doing it by saying that Niven was going to do it, then he called Niven and said Sellers is going to do it, so then he got Niven. I used to sit in Charlie Feldman's place while he conned people on the telephone. He got Bill Holden because he used to be his agent at one time, and I remember we had a terrible time telling Ursula Andress: 'You've got to get Jean-Paul Belmondo to come in this film!' And she said: 'He doesn't want to know!' But we pinned her down in Charlie's flat one day and said, 'Now call him . . . .'

And finally Belmondo gave in and said: 'Okay, I'll do anything. Just get her out of my hair!'

"When I came into the film Charlie had nothing, no script, but he did have a start date with Sellers. I really had to go on the start date because he didn't want to lose Sellers. Then Charlie flew Woody Allen over and I worked with Woody for a long time, which was great because I think he's marvelous and it was fun to work with him, but Charlie would go through the stuff we'd beaten out, and cut out all the gags! He'd just leave the build-ups to the gags! You had no idea at times with him . . . .

"Originally I was supposed to be on the picture for seven weeks and I ended up being on it for nine months. They made me what was laughingly called the 'coordinating director.' I did the last third of the film because no one knew how to finish it. They went on the floor without a script and Charlie said to me, 'You've got to write some links,' so I did all the links and I pulled back Ursula and David Niven to go through it even though they had officially finished, and I wrote the last third to tie everything up with everybody, including Woody Allen. I took over for John Huston when he said, 'I've had enough of this!' and went off to play poker in Dublin or something. So I took over and shot extra bits for John, I shot extra bits for Bob Parrish. Then Sellers got fired from the picture and, before he fired him, Charlie said to me, 'Look through everything we've got and see if we've got enough of him on film to make sense of his part.'

"One of the main problems was that we were shooting in three different studios and we used to commute from MGM at Elstree to Pinewood to Shepperton. We had standing sets in each studio. It was a madhouse. However, it made money. It made a lot of money."

Despite being one of the most expensive (it cost over £4,000,000) cinematic in-jokes ever made, there *are* parts of *Casino Royale* that are quite funny. The opening sequence with Sir James Bond (David Niven) being urged out of retirement by M (John Huston in a red wig) is amusing, as is the following sequence with Deborah Kerr playing a mad Scotswoman. The Berlin Wall episode with its Caligari-type sets and a deranged Ronnie Corbett with faulty pacemaker is memorable, and the wild climax involving Woody Allen as the spoof-Blofeld—head of F.A.N.G.—and the big fight in the casino, is suitably loony. There are other moments scattered throughout the film that one remembers with some fondness—Sellers' goonish piece of business with the racing car, Vladek Sheybal shooting at a car and then turning to a nearby watching policeman and giving a casual shrug, Orson Welles as Le Chiffre complete with his conjuring act, the flying saucer landing in Trafalgar Square, and many others. But, amusing as it occasionally was, it was certainly nothing to do with James Bond. . . .

Warhead

One film that *will* have plenty to do with Bond, even to the extent of featuring Sean Connery in his old role again, is McClory's proposed production of *Warhead*. The court case over *Thunderball* ended in 1963 with McClory being assigned all the film and television rights to the novel. McClory subsequently made the film in association with Broccoli and Saltzman and, according to McClory, part of their agreement stated that the film rights would revert back to McClory after a period of ten years. As far as McClory is concerned, this now gives him the right to remake *Thunderball* using all the characters who originally appeared in the film, including Ernst Stavro Blofeld, Felix Leiter, M, Miss Moneypenny, and (of course) James Bond himself.

McClory announced the project in 1976 and started work on a screenplay with the thriller writer and historian Len Deighton. At first, the film was going to be called *James Bond of the Secret Service,* the title of one of the original scripts that he wrote with Fleming and Whittingham, but later he changed it to *Warhead.* He approached Connery and asked him to play Bond again, but Connery refused; however, he did accept an offer to work on the script with McClory and Deighton. Then he changed his mind about playing Bond and told McClory that he *would* return to the role (for a time there was also talk about Connery directing the film as well).

Not surprisingly, however, both Broccoli and United Artists were less than enthusiastic about McClory's proposed Bond film, with the result that a legal wrangle over the project quickly developed. At the time of this writing, the outcome is still not clear—McClory is still optimistic about making the film and is currently trying to arrange financial backing and a distribution deal, but one suspects that it's going to be a long time, if ever, before we see *Warhead* on the screen.

Appendix 2:

Credits

Joseph Wiseman as Dr. No

Opposite: Bond and Honey are captured by Dr. No's guards.

DR. NO *(1962)*. Produced by: Harry Saltzman and Albert R. Broccoli (Eon Productions). Directed by: Terence Young. Screenplay by: Richard Maibaum, Johanna Harwood, and Berkely Mather. From the Novel by: Ian Fleming. Music Composed by: Monty Norman. Orchestrated by: Burt Rhodes. Conducted by: Eric Rodgers. James Bond Theme played by: The John Barry Orchestra. Director of Photography: Ted Moore, B.S.C. *(Technicolor)*. Production Designer: Ken Adam. Production Manager: L. C. Rudkin. Editor: Peter Hunt. Main Titles Designed by: Maurice Binder. Animation: Trevor Bond, Robert Ellis. Art Director: Syd Cain. Assistant Director: Clive Reed. Camera Operator: John Winbolt. Continuity: Helen Whitson. Make-up: John O'Gorman. Hair Stylist: Eileen Warwick. Sound Recordists: Wally Milner, John Dennis. Special Effects: Frank George. Distributed by: United Artists. 105 mins. *CAST:* Sean Connery *(James Bond)*, Ursula Andress *(Honey)*, Joseph Wiseman *(Dr. No)*, Jack Lord *(Felix Leiter)*, Bernard Lee *(M)*, Anthony Dawson *(Prof. Dent)*, John Kitzmiller *(Quarrel)*, Zena Marshall *(Miss Taro)*, Eunice Gayson *(Sylvia)*, Lois Maxwell *(Miss Moneypenny)*, Lester Prendergast *(Puss-Feller)*, Tim Moxon *(Strangways)*, Margaret LeWars *(Girl Photographer)*, Reggie Carter *(Jones)*, Peter Burton *(Major Boothroyd)*, William Foster-Davis *(Duff)*, Louis Blaazer *(Playdell-Smith)*, Michele Mok *(Sister Rose)*, Dolores Keator *(Mary)*, Yvonne Shima *(Sister Lily)*.

 289

Daniela Bianchi as Tatiana and Lotte Lenya in **From Russia with Love**

FROM RUSSIA WITH LOVE *(1963)*. Produced by: Harry Saltzman and Albert R. Broccoli (Eon Productions). Directed by: Terence Young. Screenplay by: Richard Maibaum, Joanna Harwood. From the Novel by: Ian Fleming. Director of Photography: Ted Moore, B.S.C. *(Technicolor)*. Editor: Peter Hunt. Production Manager: Bill Hill. Art Director: Syd Cain. Title song written by: Lionel Bart. "From Russia with Love" sung by Matt Munro. "James Bond Theme" written by Monty Norman. Orchestral Music Composed and Conducted by: John Barry. Assistant Director: David Anderson. Second Unit Cameraman: Robert Kindred. Camera Operator: Johnny Winbolt. Continuity: Kay Mander. Make-up: Basil Newall and Paul Rabiger. Hairdresser:; Eileen Warwick. Location Manager: Frank Ernst. Istanbul Production Assistant: Ilham Filmer. Special Effects: John Stears, assisted by Frank George. Stunt Work arranged by: Peter Perkins. Sound Recordists: John W. Mitchell and C. Le Mesurier. Assembly Editor: Ben Rayner. Dubbing Editors: Norman Wanstall and Harry Miller. Costume Designer: Jocelyn Rickards. Wardrobe Mistress: Eileen Sullivan. Wardrobe Master: Ernie Farrer. Assistant Art Director: Michael White. Set Dresser: Freda Pearson. Titles designed by: Robert Brownjohn, assisted by Trevor Bond. Distributed by: United Artists. 116 mins. *CAST:* Sean Connery *(James Bond)*, Daniela Bianchi *(Tatiana Romanova)*, Pedro Armendariz *(Kerim Bey)*, Lotte Lenya *(Rosa Klebb)*, Robert Shaw *(Red Grant)*, Bernard Lee *(M)*, Eunice Gayson *(Sylvia)*, Walter Gotell *(Morzeny)*, Francis de Wolff *(Vavra)*, George Pastell *(Train Conductor)*, Nadja Regin *(Kerim's Girl)*, Lois Maxwell *(Miss Moneypenny)*, Aliza Gur *(Vida)*, Martine Beswick *(Zora)*, Vladek Sheybal *(Kronsteen)*, Leila *(Belly Dancer)*, Hasan Ceylan *(Foreign Agent)*, Fred Haggerty *(Krilencu)*, Neville Jason *(Rolls Chauffeur)*, Peter Bayliss *(Benz)*, Mushet Auaer *(Mehmet)*, Peter Brayham *(Rhoda)*, Desmond Llewelyn *(Boothroyd)*, Jan Williams *(Masseuse)*, Peter Madden *(McAdams)*.

291

"I don't think much of his tailor." Bond and Kerim aboard the Orient Express

Honor Blackman as Pussy Galore

GOLDFINGER *(1964)*. Produced by: Harry Saltzman and Albert R. Broccoli (Eon Productions). Directed by: Guy Hamilton. Screenplay by: Richard Maibaum and Paul Dehn. From the Novel by: Ian Fleming. Production Designed by: Ken Adam. Director of Photography: Ted Moore, B.S.C. *(Technicolor)*. Editor: Peter Hunt. Production Manager: I. C. Rudkin. Art Director: Peter Murton. Goldfinger Title Song sung by: Shirley Bassey. Title Song lyrics by: Leslie Bricusse and Anthony Newley. Music Composed and Conducted by: John Barry. Assistant Director: Frank Ernst. Camera Operator: John Winbolt. Continuity: Constance Willis. Make-up: Paul Rabiger and Basil Newall. Action Sequences by: Bob Simmons. Special Effects: John Stears, assisted by Frank George. Assembly Editor: Ben Rayner. Dubbing Editors: Norman Wanstall and Harry Miller. Sound Recordists: Dudley Messenger and Gordon McCullum. Hairdresser: Eileen Warwick. Wardrobe Supervisor: Elsa Fennell. Wardrobe Mistress: Eileen Sullivan. Wardrobe Master: John Hilling. Assistant Art Directors: Michael White and Maurice Pelling. Set Dresser: Freda Pearson. Titles Designed by: Robert Bornjohn. Distributed by: United Artists. 109 mins. *CAST:* Sean Connery *(James Bond)*, Honor Blackman *(Pussy Galore)*, Gert Frobe *(Goldfinger)*, Shirley Eaton *(Jill Masterson)*, Tania Mallet *(Tilly Masterson)*, Harold Sakata *(Oddjob)*, Bernard Lee *(M)*, Martin Benson *(Solo)*, Cec Linder *(Felix Leiter)*, Austin Willis *(Simmons)*, Lois Maxwell *(Miss Moneypenny)*, Bill Nagy *(Midnight)*, Alf Joint *(Capungo)*, Varley Thomas *(Old Lady)*, Nadja Regin *(Bonita)*, Raymond Young *(Sierra)*, Richard Vernon *(Smithers)*, Denis Cowels *(Brunskill)*, Michael Mellinger *(Kisch)*, Bert Kwouk *(Mr. Ling)*, Hal Galili *(Strap)*, Lenny Rabin *(Henchman)*.

293

Q shows Bond his ejector-seated Aston Martin in **Goldfinger.**

Largo bids for freedom in his converted hydrofoil in
Thunderball.

THUNDERBALL *(1965)*. Produced by: Kevin McClory. Directed by: Terence Young. Screenplay by: Richard Maibaum and John Hopkins. Based on an Original Screenplay by: Jack Whittingham, Kevin McClory, and Ian Fleming. Production Designed by: Ken Adam. Director of Photography: Ted Moore, B.S.C. *(Panavision, Technicolor)*. Supervising Editor: Peter Hunt. Production Supervisor: David Middlemas. Music Composed and Conducted by: John Barry. "Thunderball" Lyrics by: Don Black. Sung by: Tom Jones. Art Director: Peter Murton. Assistant Director: Gus Agosti. Camera Operator: John Winbolt. Continuity: Joan Davis. Make-up: Paul Rabiger and Basil Newall. Action Sequences by: Bob Simmons. Assembly Editor: Ben Rayner. Special Effects: John Stears. Dubbing Editors: Norman Wanstall and Harry Miller. Sound Recordists: Bert Ross and Maurice Askey. Hairdresser: Eileen Warwick. Costumes Designed by: Anthony Medelson. Wardrobe Mistress: Eileen Sullivan. Wardrobe Master: John Brady. Assistant Art Director: Michael White. Set Dresser: Freda Pearson. Main Title Designed by: Maurice Binder. Underwater Sequences: Ivan Tors Underwater Studios Ltd. Underwater Director: Ricou Browning. Underwater Cameraman: Lamar Boren. Underwater Engineer: Jordan Klein. Distributed by: United Artists. 125 mins. *CAST:* Sean Connery *(James Bond)*, Claudine Auger *(Domino)*, Adolfo Celi *(Largo)*, Luciana Paluzzi *(Fiona)*, Rik Van Nutter *(Felix Leiter)*, Bernard Lee *(M)*, Martine Beswick *(Paula)*, Guy Doleman *(Count Lippe)*, Molly Peters *(Patricia)*, Desmond Llewelyn *(Q)*, Lois Maxwell *(Miss Moneypenny)*, Roland Culver *(Foreign Secretary)*, Earl Cameron *(Pinder)*, Paul Stassino *(Palazzi)*, Rose Alba *(Madame Boiter)*, Philip Locke *(Vargas)*, George Pravda *(Kutee)*, Michael Brennan *(Janni)*, Leonard Sachs *(Group Captain)*, Edward Underdown *(Air Vice Marshal)*, Reginald Beckwith *(Kenniston)*.

Poison dripping down a string kills Aki in **You Only Live Twice.**

YOU ONLY LIVE TWICE *(1967)*. Produced by: Harry Saltzman and Albert R. Broccoli (Eon-Danjaq). Directed by: Lewis Gilbert. Screenplay by: Roald Dahl. Director of Photography: Freddie Young, B.S.C. *(Panavision, Technicolor)*. Second Unit Director: Peter Hunt. Editor: Thelma Connell. Production Designed by: Ken Adam. Art Director: Harry Pottle. Production Supervisor: David Middlemas. Special Effects: John Stears. Action Sequences: Bob Simmons. Main Title Designed by: Maurice Binder. Music Composed, Conducted, and Arranged by: John Barry. Title Song Lyrics by: Leslie Bricusse. Sung by: Nancy Sinatra. Technical Advisor: Kikumaru Okuda. Second Unit Cameraman: Bob Huke. Aerial Unit Cameraman: John Jordan. Underwater Cameraman: Lamar Boren. Assistant Director: William P. Cartlidge. Location Manager: Robert Watts. Camera Operator: Ernie Day. Continuity: Angela Martelli. Make-up: Basil Newall and Paul Rabiger. Dubbing Editors: Norman Wanstall and Harry Miller. Sound Recordist: John Mitchell. Wardrobe Mistress: Eileen Sullivan. Hairdresser: Eileen Warwick. Set Dresser: David Ffolkes. Distributed by: United Artists. 116 mins. *CAST:* Sean Connery *(James Bond)*, Akiko Wakabayashi *(Aki)*, Tetsuro Tamba *(Tiger Tanaka)*, Mie Hama *(Kissy Suzuki)*, Teru Shimada *(Osato)*, Karin Dor *(Helga Brandt)*, Lois Maxwell *(Miss Moneypenny)*, Desmond Llewelyn *(Q)*, Charles Gray *(Henderson)*, Tsai Chin *(Chinese Girl)*, Bernard Lee *(M)*, Donald Pleasence *(Blofeld)*, Alexander Knox *(American President)*, Robert Hutton *(President's Aide)*, Burt Kwouk *(SPECTRE 3)*, Michael Chow *(SPECTRE 4)*.

The wedding reception—a prelude to tragedy

ON HER MAJESTY'S SECRET SERVICE *(1969).* Produced by: Harry Saltzman and Albert R. Broccoli (Eon-Danilaq). Directed by: Peter Hunt. Screenplay by: Richard Maibaum. Associate Producer: Stanley Sopel. Production Supervisor: David Middlemas. Director of Photography: Michael Reed *(Panavision, Technicolor).* Production Designer: Syd Cain. Editor and Second Unit Director: John Glen. Special Effects: John Stears. Assistant Director: Frank Ernst. Continuity: Joan Davis. Camera Operator: Alex Mills. Stunt Arranger: George Leech. Second Unit Cameramen: Egil Woxholt, Roy Ford. Aerial Cameraman: John Jordan. Ski Cameramen: Willy Bogner Jr., Alex Barbey. Art Director: Bob Laing. Wardrobe Designer: Marjory Cornelius. Set Decorator: Peter Lamont. Hairdresser: Eileen Warwick. Wardrobe Supervisor: Jackie Cummins. Make-up: Paul Rabiger, Basil Newall. Dubbing Editors: Nicholas Stevenson, Harry Miller. Sound Recordists: John Mitchell, Gordon McCallum. Stock Car Sequence Director: Anthony Squire. Additional Dialogue: Simon Raven. Music by: John Barry. Lyrics by: Hal David. Main Title Design by: Maurice Binder. Distributed by: United Artists. 140 min. *CAST:* George Lazenby *(James Bond),* Diana Rigg *(Tracy),* Telly Savalas *(Ernst Stavro Blofeld),* Ilse Steppat *(Irma Bunt),* Gabriele Ferzetti *(Marc Ange Draco),* Yuri Borienko *(Grunther),* Bernard Horsfall *(Campbell),* George Baker *(Sir Hilary Bray),* Bernard Lee *(M),* Lois Maxwell *(Miss Moneypenny),* Desmond Llewelyn *(Q),* Angela Scoular *(Ruby),* Catherine Von Schell *(Nancy),* Dani Sheridan *(American Girl),* Julie Ege *(Scandinavian Girl),* Joanna Lumley *(English Girl),* Mona Chong *(Chinese Girl),* Anoushka Hempel *(Australian Girl),* Ingrid Black *(German Girl),* Jenny Hanley *(Italian Girl),* Zara *(Indian Girl),* Sylvana Henriques *(Jamaican Girl),* Helena Ronee *(Israeli Girl),* Geoffrey Cheshire *(Tousaint),* Irvin Allen *(Che Che),* Terry Mountain *(Raphael),* James Bree *(Gumpold),* Virgina North *(Olympe),* Brian Worth *(Manuel),* Norman McGlen *(Janitor),* Dudley Jones *(Hall Porter),* John Crewdson *(Draco's Helicopter Pilot),* Josef Vasa *(Piz Gloria Receptionist),* Les Crawford *(Felsen),* George Cooper *(Braun),* Reg Harding *(Blofeld's Driver),* Richard Graydon *(Draco's Driver),* Bill Morgan *(Klett),* Bessie Love *(American Guest),* Steve Plytas *(Greek Tycoon),* Robert Rietty *(Chef de Jeu),* Elliott Sullivan *(American Guest).*

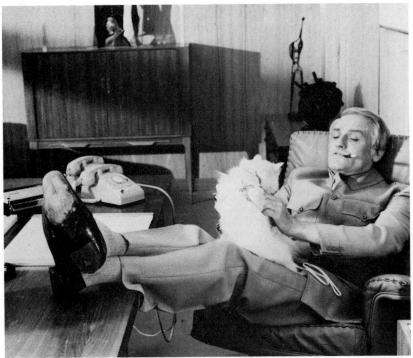

Charles Gray enjoys a moment of triumph in
Diamonds are Forever.

DIAMONDS ARE FOREVER *(1971)*. Produced by: Harry Saltzman and Albert R. Broccoli (Eon Productions). Directed by: Guy Hamilton. Screenplay by: Richard Maibaum and Tom Mankiewicz. Associate Producer: Stanley Sopel. Music by: John Barry. Lyrics by: Don Black. Title Song Sung by: Shirley Bassey. Director of Photography: Ted Moore, B.S.C. *(Panavision, Technicolor)*. Production Designer: Ken Adam. Editors: Bert Bates and John W. Holmes. A.C.E. Production Managers: Claude Hudson and Milton Feldman. Main Title Designed by: Maurice Binder. Wardrobe Supervisors: Elsa Fennell and Ted Tetrick. Assistant Directors: Derek Cracknell and Jerome M. Siegel. Sound Recordists: John Mitchell and Al Overton. Dubbing Editors: Teddy Mason, Jimmy Shields, and Gordon McCallum. Location Managers: Bernard Hanson and Eddie Saeta. Visual Effects: Albert Whitlock and Wally Veevers. Stunt Arrangers: Bob Simmons and Paul Baxley. Second Unit Cameraman: Harold Wellman. Miss St. John's Costumes: Donfeld. Production Buyer: Ronnie Quelch. Special Effects: Leslie Hillman and Whitey McMahon. Set Decorators: Peter Lamont and John Austin. Art Directors: Jack Maxsted and Bill Kenney. Camera Operators: Bob Kindred and Bill Johnson. Continuity: Elaine Schreyeck and Del Ross. Distributed by: United Artists. *CAST:* Sean Connery *(James Bond)*, Jill St. John *(Tiffany Case)*, Charles Gray *(Blofeld)*, Lana Wood   301 *(Plenty O'Toole)*, Jimmy Dean *(Willard Whyte)*, Bruce Cabot *(Saxby)*, Putter Smith *(Mr. Kidd)*, Bruce Glover *(Mr. Wint)*, Norman Burton *(Leiter)*, Joseph Furst *(Dr. Metz)*, David Bauer *(Mr. Slumber)*, Bernard Lee *(M)*, Desmond Llewelyn *(Q)*, Leonard Barr *(Shady Tree)*, Lois Maxwell *(Miss Moneypenny)*, Margaret Lacey *(Mrs. Whistler)*, Joe Robinson *(Peter Franks)*, Donna Garratt *(Bambi)* Trina Parks *(Thumper)*, David de Keyser *(Doctor)*, Laurence Naismith *(Sir Donald Munger)*.

Bond's artillery menaces the enemy in **Live and Let Die.**

LIVE AND LET DIE *(1973).* Produced by: Harry Saltzman and Albert R. Broccoli (Eon Productions). Directed by: Guy Hamilton. Screenplay by: Tom Mankiewicz. Photography: Ted Moore *(Eastman Color).* Second Unit Photography: John Harris. Production Supervisor: Claude Hudson. Production Managers: Stephen F. Keston, (USA) Steven P. Skloot. Shark Scenes Directed by: William Grefé. Assistant Directors: Derek Cracknell, (USA) Alan Hopkins. Special Photographic Effects: Charles Staffell. Editors: Bert Bates, Raymond Poulton, and John Shirley. Supervising Art Director: Syd Cain. Art Directors: (USA) Stephen Hendrickson, Bob Laing, Peter Lamont. Special Effects: Derek Meddings. Music: George Martin. Title Song: Paul McCartney and Linda McCartney. Sung by Paul McCartney, Linda McCartney, and Wings. Costumes by Julie Harris. Choreography: Geoffrey Holder. Titles: Maurice Binder. Sound Recordists: John Mitchell, Ken Barker. Sound Re-recordists: Teddy Mason, Jimmy Shields, Chris Lancaster. Stunt Co-ordinators: Bob Simmons, Jerry Comeaux, Ross Kananga, Bill Bennot, Eddie Smith, Joie Chitwood. Distributed by United Artists. 121 mins. *CAST:* Roger Moore *(James Bond),* Yaphet Kotto *(Dr. Kananga),* Jane Seymour *(Solitaire),* Clifton James *(Sheriff Pepper),* Julius W. Harris *(Tee Hee),* Geoffrey Holder *(Baron Samedi),* Davidson Hedison *(Felix Leiter),* Gloria Hendry *(Rosie),* Bernard Lee *(M),* Lois Maxwell *(Moneypenny),* Tommy Lane *(Adam),* Earl Jolly Brown *(Whisper),* Roy Stewart *(Quarrel Junior),* Lon Satton *(Strutter),* Arnold Williams *(1st Cab Driver),* Ruth Kempf *(Mrs. Bell),* Joie Chitwood *(Charlie),* Madeline Smith *(Beautiful Girl),* Michael Ebbin *(Dambala),* Kubi Chaza *(Sales Girl),* Gabor Vernon *(Hungarian Delegate),* B. J. Arnau *(Singer).*

303

Bond (Roger Moore) and Mary Goodnight talk things
over in **The Man with The Golden Gun.**

THE MAN WITH THE GOLDEN GUN *(1974)*. Produced by: Harry Saltzman and Albert R. Broccoli (Eon Productions). Directed by: Guy Hamilton. Screenplay: Richard Maibaum, Tom Mankiewicz. Associate Producer: Charles Orme. Photography: Ted Moore, Ossie Morris *(Eastman Color)*. Production Supervisor: Claude Hudson. Bangkok Coordinator: Santa Pestonji. Assistant Director: Derek Cracknell. Location Manager: Frank Ernst (Thailand), Eric Rattray (Hong Kong). Second Unit Photography: John Harris. Camera Operator: Bob Kindred. Sound Mixer: Gordon Everett. Production Designer: Peter Murton. Art Directors: John Graysmark, Peter Lamont. Construction Managers: Leon Davis (Studio), Michael Redding (Location). Supervising Editor: John Shirley. Editor: Ray Poulton. Make-Up: Paul Engelen. Miniatures: Derek Meddings. Special Effects: John Stears. Music: John Barry. Title Song: John Barry, Don Black. Sung by: Lulu. Titles: Maurice Binder. Hairdressers: Mike Jones, Elaine Bowerbank. Wardrobe Supervisor: Elsa Fennell. Continuity: Elaine Schreyeck. Casting Directors: Maude Spector, Weston Drury. Props Master: Patrick Weymouth. Unit Publicist: Geoff Freeman. Sound Editors: Jimmy Shields, Chris Lancaster, Charles Crafford. Sound Recordist: Gordon Everett. Sound Re-recordist: Ken Barker. Stunt Coordinator: W. J. Milligan, Jr. Stuntman Furnished by: American Thrill Show, J.M. Productions Inc. Golden Gun Made by: Colibri Lighters. AMC Astro Spiral Jump-Mathematical and Computer Technology Furnished by Calspan Corp. Distributed by United Artists. 125 mins. *CAST:* Roger Moore *(James Bond)*, Christopher Lee *(Scaramanga)*, Britt Ekland *(Mary Goodnight)*, Maud Adams *(Andrea)*, Herve Villechaize *(Nick Nack)*, Clifton James *(Sheriff J. W. Pepper)*, Soon Taik Oh *(Hip)*, Richard Loo *(Hai Fat)*, Marc Lawrence *(Rodney)*, Bernard Lee *(M)*, Lois Maxwell *(Moneypenny)*, Marne Maitland *(Lazar)*, Desmond Llewellyn *(Q)*, James Cossins *(Colthorpe)*, Chan Yiu Lam *(Chula)* Carmen Sautoy *(Saida)*, Gerald James *(Frazier)*, Michael Osborne *(Naval Lieutenant)*, Michael Fleming *(Communications Officer)*.

Supertanker (actually a 63-foot model) in **The Spy Who Loved Me**

THE SPY WHO LOVED ME *(1977)*. Produced by: Albert R. Broccoli (Eon Productions). Directed by Lewis Gilbert. Screenplay by: Christopher Wood and Richard Maibaum. Associate Producer: William P. Cartlidge. Music: Marvin Hamlisch. Title Song ("Nobody Does It Better"); Performed by: Carly Simon; Lyrics by: Carole Bayer Sager; Composed by: Marvin Hamlisch; Produced by: Richard Perry. Production Designed by: Ken Adam. Photography: Claude Renoir. Editor: John Glen. Main Title by: Maurice Binder. Production Manager: David Middlemas. Assistant Director: Ariel Levy. Assistant Director (Second Unit): Chris Kenny. Location Managers: (Egypt) Frank Ernst, (Bahamas) Golda Offenheim. Production Coordinator: (Canada) Rene Dupont. Naval Adviser: Richard Kennan. Underwater Cameraman: Lamar Boren. Ski Sequence: Willy Bogner. Assistant to Producer: Michael Wilson. Production Controller: Reginald A. Barkshire. Art Director: Peter Lamont. Assistant Art Director: Ernie Archer. Production Accountant: Brian Bailey. Production Assistant: Marguerite Green. Casting Directors: Maude Spector, Weston Drury, Jr. Construction Manager: Michael Redding. Camera Operator: Alec Mills. Continuity: June Randall. Assembly Editor: Alan Strachan. Dubbing Editor: Alan Sones. Assistant Editor: John Grover. Sound Recordist: Gordon Everett. Dubbing Mixer: Gordon K. McCallum. Make-up: Paul Engelen. Hairdressing: Barbara Ritchie. Fashion Consultant: Ronald Paterson. Wardrobe Supervisor: Rosemary Burrows. Script Editor: Vernon Harris. Second Unit Directors: Ernest Day, John Glen. Action Arranger: Bob Simmons. Ski Jump Performed by: Rick Sylvester. Special Visual Effects: Derek Meddings. Special Optical Effects: Alan Maley. Special Effects (Studio): John Evans. Distributed by United Artists. 125 mins. *CAST:* Roger Moore *(James Bond)*, Barbara Bach *(Major Anya Amasova)*, Curt Jurgens *(Stromberg)*, Richard Kiel *(Jaws)*, Caroline Munro *(Naomi)*, Walter Gotell *(General Gogol)*, Geoffrey Keen *(Minister of Defense)*, Bernard Lee *(M)*, George Baker *(Captain Benson)*. Michael Billington *(Sergei)*, Olga Bisera *(Felicca)*, Desmond Llewelyn *(Q)*, Edward De Souza *(Sheik Hosein)*, Vernon Dobtcheff *(Max Kalba)*, Valerie Leon *(Hotel Receptionist)*, Lois Maxwell *(Miss Moneypenny)*, Sydney Tafler *(Liparus Captain)*, Nadim Sawalha *(Fekkesh)*, Sue Vanner *(Log Cabin Girl)*, Eva Rueber-Staier *(Rubelvitch)*, Robert Brown *(Admiral Hargreaves)*, Marilyn Galsworthy *(Stromberg's Assistant)*, Milton Reid *(Sandor)*, Cyril Shaps *(Bechmann)*, Milo Sperber *(Markovitz)*, Albert Moses *(Barman)*, Rafiq Anwar *(Cairo Club Waiter)*, Feliciti York, Dawn Rodrigues, Anika Pavel, Jill Goodall *(Arab Beauties)* and The Egyptian Folklore Group. Shane Rimmer, Bob Sherman, Doyle Richmond, Murray Salem, John Truscott, Peter Whitman, Ray Hassett, Vincent Marzello, Nicholas Campbell, Ray Evans, Anthony Forrest, Garrick Hagon, Ray Jewers, George Mallaby, Christopher Muncke, Anthony Pullen, Robert Sheedy, Don Staiton, Eric Stine, Stephen Temperley, Dean Warwick *(U.S.S. Wayne Crew)*. Bryan Marshall, Michael Howarth, Kim Fortune, Barry Andrews, Kevin McNally, Jeremy Bulloch, Sean Bury, John Sarbutt, David Auker, Dennis Blanch, Keith Buckley, Jonathan Bury, Nick Ellsworth, Tom Gerrard, Kazik Michalski, Keith Morris, John Salthouse *(H.M.S. Ranger Crew)*. George Roubicek, Lenny Rabin, Irvin Allen, Yasher Adem, Peter Ensor *(Stromberg Crew)*.

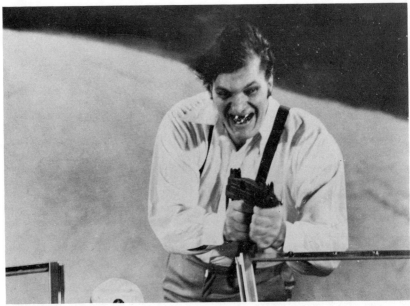

The giant Jaws aims at Bond in a watery chase scene
from **Moonraker.**

MOONRAKER *(1979)*. Produced by: Albert R. Broccoli (Eon-Les Productions Artistes Associés). Directed by: Lewis Gilbert. Screenplay by: Christopher Wood. Executive Producer: Michael G. Wilson. Associate Producer: P. William Cartlidge. Production Controller: Reginald A. Barkshire. Production Managers: (France) Jean-Pierre Spiri Mercanton, (Great Britain) Terence Churcher. Location Managers: (Brazil) Frank Ernst, (Italy) Philippe Modave, (Florida) John Comfort. Unit Managers: (France) Robert Saussier, (Great Britain) Chris Kenny. Second Unit Directors: Ernest Day, John Glen. Assistant Directors: Michael Chegco, Chris Carreras, (Second Unit) Peter Bennett, Meyer Berreby, (Models) Gareth Tandy. Photography: Jean Tournier *(Panavision, Technicolor)*. Camera Operators: Alec Mills, Michael Deloire, John Morgan, Guy Delattre, James Davis. Second Unit Photography: Jaques Renoir. Visual Effects Supervisor: Derek Meddings. Visual Effects Photography: Paul Wilson. Optical Effects Photography: Robin Browne. Optical Effects: (France) Michael Francois Films. Visual Effects: (France) Jean Berard. Process Effects: (France) Louis Lapeyre. Process Consultant: Bill Hansard. Editor: John Glen. Production Designer: Ken Adam. Art Directors: Max Douy, Charles Bishop, (Visual Effects) Peter Lamont, (Space) Harry Lange. Set Decorators: Peter Howitt, Pierre Charron, Andre Labussiere. Special Effects: John Evans, John Richardson, Rene Albouze, Serge Ponvianne. Music: John Barry. "James Bond Theme" by Monty Norman. "The Magnificent Seven Theme" by Elmer Bernstein. Title Song: John Barry, Hal David. Performed by Shirley Bassey. Costumes: Jacques Fonteray. Make-up: Monique Archambault, Paul Engelen. Titles: Maurice Binder. Sound Editors: Alan Sones, Colin Miller, Dino Di Campo. Sound Recordist: Daniel Brisseau. Sound Re-recordists: Gordon K. McCallum, Graham V. Hartstone, Nicholas Le Messurier. Sound Effects: Jean-Pierre Lelong. Space Consultant: Eric Burgess. Dolby Consultant: John Iles. Stunt Arrangers: Bob Simmons, (France) Claude Carliez. Stunts: Claude Carliez, Martin Grace, Richard Graydon, Dorothy Ford, Michael Berreur, Daniel Breton, Guy Di Rigo, Paul Weston. Distributed by: United Artists. 126 mins. *CAST:* Roger Moore *(James Bond)*, Lois Chiles *(Holly Goodhead)*, Michael Lonsdale *(Hugo Drax)*, Richard Kiel *(Jaws)*, Corinne Clery *(Corinne Dufour)*, Emily Bolton *(Manuela)*, Toshiro Suga *(Chang)*, Irka Bochenko *(Blonde Beauty)*, Geoffrey Keen *(Frederick Gray)*, Lois Maxwell *(Moneypenny)*, Nicholas Arbez *(Drax's Boy)*, Bernard Lee *(M)*, Desmond Llewelyn *(Q)*, Anne Lonnberg *(Museum Guide)*, Jeanne-Pierre Costaldi *(Pilot, Private Jet)*, Blanche Ravalec *(Dolly)*, Michael Marshall *(Colonel Scott)*, Leila Shenna *(Hostess, Private Jet)*, Walter Gotell *(General Gogol)*, Douglas Lambert *(Mission Control Directors)*, Arthur Howard *(Cavendish)*, Alfie Bass *(Consumptive Italian)*, Brian Keith *(U.S. Shuttle Captain)*, George Birt *(Captain, Boeing 747)*, Kim Fortune *(R.A.F. Officer)*, Lizzie Warville *(Russian Girl)*, Johnny Traber's Troupe *(Funambulists)*, Guy di Rigo *(Ambulanceman)*, Chris Dillinger and George Beller *(Drax's Technicians)*, Claude Carliez *(Gondolier)*, Denis Seurat *(Officer, 747)*, Chichinou Kaeppler, Christine Hui, Francoise Gayat, Nicaise Jean-Louis, Catherine Serre, and Beatrice Libert *(Drax's Girls)*.